GREAT LIVES OBSERVED

Gerald Emanuel Stearn, *General Editor*

EACH VOLUME IN THE SERIES VIEWS THE CHARACTER AND ACHIEVEMENT OF A GREAT WORLD FIGURE IN THREE PERSPECTIVES—THROUGH HIS OWN WORDS, THROUGH THE OPINIONS OF HIS CONTEMPORARIES, AND THROUGH RETROSPECTIVE JUDGMENTS—THUS COMBINING THE INTIMACY OF AUTOBIOGRAPHY, THE IMMEDIACY OF EYEWITNESS OBSERVATION, AND THE OBJECTIVITY OF MODERN SCHOLARSHIP.

MAURICE HUTT, *the editor of this volume in the Great Lives Observed series, is Chairman of the History Subject Group at the University of Sussex, England. He is the author of an original biography of Napoleon and has written numerous articles on the French Revolution.*

057881

GREAT LIVES OBSERVED

NApOLEON

Edited by **MAURICE HUTT**

He was an able chess player,
and the human race was the opponent
to whom he proposed to give checkmate.

—Madame de Staël

A SPECTRUM BOOK

PRENTICE-HALL, INC., ENGLEWOOD CLIFFS, N.J.

Library of Congress Cataloging in Publication Data
Hutt, Maurice, comp.

  Napoleon.
  (Great lives observed) (A Spectrum book)
  Bibliography: p.
  1. Napoléon I, Emperor of the French, 1769–1821.
I. Title.
DC203.H93 1972   944.05'0924 [B]   72–38815
ISBN 0–13–609248–9
ISBN 0–13–609230–6 (pbk)

PRENTICE-HALL INTERNATIONAL, INC. (*London*)
PRENTICE-HALL OF AUSTRALIA, PTY. LTD. (*Sydney*)
PRENTICE-HALL OF CANADA, LTD. (*Toronto*)
PRENTICE-HALL OF INDIA PRIVATE LIMITED (*New Delhi*)
PRENTICE-HALL OF JAPAN, INC. (*Tokyo*)

Contents

5

In the Field 57

6

He Reflects 68

PART TWO

NAPOLEON VIEWED BY HIS CONTEMPORARIES

7

His Appearance 79

15

16

Introduction

It soon became clear that the coup d'état of 18 Brumaire/November 9, 1799, was not just another of the type with which Frenchmen had become all too familiar in recent years. This time a strong man had arrived, and instead of a mere adjustment in the now much-discredited world of politicians, the coup turned out to be the beginning of a new regime which must be reckoned, in terms of its impact on the world, as one of the most remarkable in history.

There were good reasons for Frenchmen to welcome a strong man —there always are after years of turmoil, uncertainty, and fear. At the very least such a government meant an end to coups, to the warring of factions, to proscriptions and counterproscriptions. And as this man was one of the world's greatest generals, he provided another type of security too, security from defeat and invasion at the hands of France's numerous enemies. Frenchmen—citizens since 1789, and no longer mere subjects of a king—could justifiably see in him the savior of France; and as her enemies threatened to restore the deposed Bourbon kings, they could acclaim him as the defender of the Revolution. A vote (of a sort), equality before the law, an "open" society (no castes—save the "castes" of poor and well-off), a land system purged of the lingering relics of feudal dues, and seigneurial privilege and procedures—so long as France remained undefeated, these revolutionary achievements would remain undisturbed, as would the massive transfers of property carried out at the expense of the Church and the royalists.

At the very least, then, here was a defender, a shield. But behind that shield France herself was deeply divided and ill-governed; her strength and her potential for prosperity and greatness largely lay unrealized. The strong man showed he was almost as remarkable a statesman as he was a general. A careful policy of "fusion" helped to reknit a social fabric torn by ten years of revolution; and he showed the apprehensive that even the Church and the émigrés could be brought back (on politic terms) into a society that needed them and that was in any case firm enough now to constrain them should they become obstreperous. And this was not merely because French society was safeguarded, "scaffolded" and directed by a state vastly more efficient than those in other countries: it was also because that society was itself tough and fairly resilient. The legal Codes, which perhaps are the most enduring monument of that regime, "summed up," to

1

quote Villat, "the whole long tradition of the past, revitalised and renewed by the Revolution. Being national [they were] an agent of unity" [1]—and unity meant strength until, 150 years later, the scaffold of institutions came, society having changed, to seem an unduly restricting corset.

Security, unity—and glory. The Empire, in 1810, stretched from Lübeck to Bayonne, from Gaëta to the Pyrenees. Beyond that were her vassal states and an arc of allies—many of them erstwhile enemies broken in battles the names of which are carved in the stones of the Arc de Triomphe. Seemingly invincible, the French armies swept over Europe, founding states, overturning dynasties, bearing with them the "gift" of the Revolution that France had now transmuted into imitable, imposable institutions. And all this at so little cost to France herself!—if we discount, of course, the price that every dictatorship exacts: "there must," the strong man decreed, "there must not be any opposition" . . . "there is in France only one single party and one single will." [2] For the material cost of France's conquests—in terms of money and blood—was borne for the most part by the people who lived outside her frontiers. This, to put it mildly, stirred the hostility of the apathetic and turned the initial enthusiasm shown by certain sections of these communities into a mounting anti-French feeling. The Liberator became the Oppressor, the Ogre who, after his final defeat, was sent to die on a distant island thousands of miles from a Europe which, after the impact of his regime, could never be the same again.

The strong man was not a Frenchman—though he said he loved France (which is probably true: she gave him so much). Napoleone Buonaparte was born on Corsica in 1769, just after the French had taken over the island. Educated in French schools—and, even more important, reading voraciously once he had left school to join the artillery—he studied to make his career in the army. And once the Revolution had broken the hold of the privileged classes on the senior ranks, he could hope to climb high. Furthermore the Revolution, by firing volunteer soldiers with enthusiasm, had created, in potential, the sort of army that could be deployed in accordance with the latest tactics, and that in the face of mercenaries lacking zest and initiative, could be well-nigh irresistible. From 1792 to 1815 France was almost continuously at war: with his "strength of will, character, application, and daring" (his own evaluation), Captain

---

[1] Quoted in J. Chevallier, *Histoire des institutions et des régimes politiques de la France moderne* (Paris, 1967), p. 163; translated in R. Holtman, *The Napoleonic Revolution* (New York, 1967), p. 98.

[2] Quoted in G. Lefebvre, *Napoleon*, and J. C. Herold, *Mind of Napoleon: A Selection from His Written and Spoken Words* (New York, 1961), p. 85.

Bonaparte might go far—and all the farther because, as he said, he "had no definite plans, only projects," and thus could fluidly exploit whatever opportunity Fortune or circumstances offered.[3]

He first came to the notice of the government in 1793 when, at Toulon, he played a competent part in driving the English invaders out of the port; and again in 1795 when he put down a royalist rising in Paris. Then in 1796–97 he showed the people—and the troops—that they had a hero; a general, aged twenty-seven, capable of sweeping the Austrians out of northern Italy and (regardless of the government's wishes) of setting up new republics modeled on that of France. His campaigns had been astonishing, and the one in Egypt the following year added a further touch of glamor sorely needed at a time of crisis and hardship. Clearly here was the man to employ, thought the politicians who were plotting to use the army to break an unworkable constitution. But they underestimated his political skill and ambition. After the coup the First Consul, Bonaparte, not merely towered above the other two: he towered over France. And within three years he became Consul for life. Why?

On the one side, of course, there was his own ambition, an ambition "so intimately linked with my very being that it is like the blood that circulates in my veins." [4] But then on the other there was the fact that a plebiscite gave him his (semirepublican) title. It was, in a sense, a reward for his achievements and a token of the need which France felt she had of him. He had brought peace: the Austrians, defeated once more, signed the Treaty of Lunéville in 1801, accepted the Rhine as France's permanent eastern boundary, and swallowed the fact of their own expulsion from northern Italy. The British, too, isolated, made peace the next year by the Treaty of Amiens. He brought firm government back to France, and order and a "single will" in place of confusion and vacillation.[5] "Unity of command is vital in war"—and in the state as conceived by the soldier who made that remark. There were assemblies but, with strong public support, Bonaparte soon limited their independence. Executive power, not legislative, was what mattered—and it was served by the Council of State, a body of expert civil servants appointed by the First Consul. He also appointed the prefects, who in turn appointed the mayors of the smaller towns:[6] the Revolution's department and commune were thus preserved but tied to Paris just as the Bourbon kings and their Council had tied local government to the center. The judicial system created in the

---

[3] Quoted in Herold, *Mind of Napoleon*, p. 43.

[4] See below p. 139.

[5] See G. Rudé, *Robespierre*, Great Lives Observed (Englewood Cliffs, N.J.: Prentice-Hall, Inc., 1967), p. 10.

[6] He appointed the mayors of towns with over 5,000 inhabitants.

Revolution was also kept—and even the jury, though Bonaparte himself was against this. Still, he was soon able to bypass the due process of the law when "reasons of state" dictated it—and he increasingly was the judge of what the state needed.

Certainly the mass of Frenchmen seemed to agree the state needed order, discipline, and a closely regulated freedom to prevent its being abused by men on the left or right who sought to bring it down. Such opponents were treated ruthlessly. In December 1800, Bonaparte was nearly assassinated. Almost at once 130 Jacobins were deported, even though he knew the royalists had been responsible. Then the arrest of royalists began, and a hundred or more of them were put in prison. Liberal opponents like Mme. de Staël were also exiled; the number of newspapers in Paris was cut from seventy-three to thirteen and subsequently to only four, while each department was allowed only one. The newspapers, along with books and plays, were not only censored, the government also filled them with propaganda: for Bonaparte knew that mere repression could not bind a nation together nor create that positive loyalty which the new state, unlike those before the Revolution, required of its citizens. Hence this use of propaganda; hence also the importance accorded to the education of the pliable young. In 1802 primary and secondary education was restructured, while a law of 1806 regulated higher education. Staffed by teachers sound in their principles, the lycées, collèges and faculties could be expected to produce well-trained bureaucrats to man the Empire. Less attention was paid to the primary schools: but then the Church could be relied upon to diffuse among the mass of the people the morality, the sense of shared values, without which society falls apart.

French Catholics had split asunder ten years before when half the clergy had, at a time of intransigent attitudes on both sides, refused to accept reorganization at the hands of a lay assembly; and in subsequent years even the "constitutional" Church was persecuted and finally separated from the state. Bonaparte disapproved of this separation. With the mass of the population still Catholic, an institution over which the state had no control might well achieve undue authority. Besides, the Bourbons had said they would restore the Church: this furnished them with hordes of potential supporters, especially in western France—supporters Bonaparte could win if, in the teeth of Jacobin opposition, he could bring back the Church. And he did. By the Concordat of 1801 the Catholic Church was restored in France. It was no longer the privileged corporation it had been before the Revolution; its confiscated property was not returned; Protestants and Jews were afforded complete toleration; and its independence was curbed to a degree that Louis XIV himself had not been able to achieve. But it came back: that was the main thing for millions of Catholics, and Bonaparte knew that it was vital for him to "hold [his] place in the hearts of the masses"—their support was the source of his power.[7]

Glory, unity, security—but even with the Life Consulship was his regime secure? True, it was founded, in a sense, upon consent; but was this as potent a form of legitimacy as monarchy? A new hereditary monarchy would not merely gratify his ambition: it would surely put a permanent end to the war between Republic and Bourbon, a war inimical to the stability that France needed. Efficiency and effective command, glory and well-designed institutions were necessary— but not enough. In 1804 the Pope came to Paris to bless the crown Napoleon placed on his own head. He was Emperor, now, "by the Grace of God and the constitution." This was not all. "I needed an aristocracy. . . . Without it the State is a rudderless ship. . . . Democracy may establish sovereignty but only aristocracy can preserve it."[8] Soon the Legion of Honor was instituted to reward services, and (an even more direct affront to the revolutionary principle of equality) imperial dukes and counts and princes were created. He still lacked, however, a son to succeed him. As Joséphine, whom he had married a dozen years earlier, could not provide one, he divorced her in 1809 and married the daughter of the Austrian Emperor. In 1811 the son he needed, the son France needed, was born and titled the King of Rome, for now that the Papal States had been annexed by Napoleon, Rome was declared to be the second city of his enormous Empire.

Enormous, efficient, hereditary—still the Empire was not totally secure, for there yet remained enemies whom Napoleon could not defeat and whose power he was incapable of neutralizing. The Pope symbolized one type of opposition he could not break. Napoleon could seize his states, imprison him even—but still Pius VII would not do what he was told. There is a limit, as Napoleon, in reflective moments, knew quite well, to what force can achieve; belief, opinion, and loyalty cannot be brought into existence by exhortation or command. England was the symbol of another type of opposition, an opposition he could not reach out to crush because she commanded the sea as firmly as France commanded the land. On her own, England could not do much—except hold out. But even though security and permanence were in the forefront of Napoleon's mind, restlessness and voracity were also part of his makeup, and thanks to this, England could always find allies.

Napoleon pushed too hard to be acceptable as a neighbor; and

[7] Quoted in Herold, *Mind of Napoleon,* p. 164.
[8] *Ibid.,* pp. 96–97.

even he could not take over the whole of Europe, though he did try. Austria had been excluded from Italy: her centuries-old influence in Germany, too, was undermined when, after Lunéville and Auster-litz, the map of Germany was redrawn. Even Prussia, which had kept neutral for a decade, found this too much to stomach: she declared war in 1806. As for the third of the "eastern powers," Napoleon was, for a time at least, able to conjure away the enmity that time after time had brought Russia into the field against France. After defeating her yet again at Friedland in June, 1807, the Emperor deluded the Czar into thinking that henceforth their mighty empires could coexist in friendly partnership. But the shaky alliance formed at Tilsit and patched in talks at Erfurt in 1808 finally crumbled in the course of 1810. The principal reason was the so-called "Continental System."

England had to be defeated. When the Peace of Amiens collapsed in 1803, Napoleon laid successive plans to collect his scattered fleets, hold the Channel, and ship across an invading army. In August, 1805, it seemed that perhaps the scheme might come off; but his admirals did not, could not, do exactly what he wanted, and in any case he was obliged to use the army massed at Boulogne against a new threat from Austria. Thereafter invasion was out of the question, for at Trafalgar Nelson broke any lingering hope that French fleets might one day command the Channel. So the Emperor tried economic warfare. With Austria defeated at Austerlitz, Prussia at Jena, and with the Tilsit agreement in force, the continent over which he towered could, he hoped, be made to serve two complementary purposes. First, its pattern of trade and industry could be shaped to favor the growth of the French economy; and second, English exports to the continent could be blocked. Denied this apparently crucial market, her economy would collapse. All that was needed—"all"—was to seal the coastline of Europe.

Naturally there was resistance to such a policy, and any resistance had to be broken. The Pope and Napoleon's brother Louis, King of Holland, had their states annexed; part of the north German coast was taken too; and in 1807 armies were sent into Spain and Portugal, their monarchs deposed, and Joseph Bonaparte made king in Madrid. But the resistance here proved impossible to break. The British were able to land and maintain an increasingly effective army in Portugal, while the Spanish, instead of welcoming the enlightened rule of their new king, rebelled and persistently harassed French armies sent to subdue the peninsula. Had this been the only theater of war Napoleon could have dealt with the problem; but he had to cope simultaneously with Austria and Russia—and Russia meant more than a mighty army. It meant open plains on which Napoleon was repeatedly unable to trap his opponents with the tactics he had perfected in the very different terrain he had usually fought in; it meant long lines of communication stretched, as in Spain, across a countryside hostile to him; it meant a disastrously savage winter. Of the half-million men who invaded Russia perhaps 50,000 survived the horrific retreat from Moscow.

In 1813 the jaws of the vice began to close. The Duke of Wellington fought his way from the Portuguese border across northern Spain, while in the east the Prussians joined the advancing Russians. Yet even now the Emperor was not prepared to pay a generous price to keep the Austrians out of the war. At Dresden, on June 26, his belligerent obstinacy led Metternich to conclude that the Czar was right to insist that "So long as Napoleon lives there can be no security";[9] though for the moment the coalition thought less in terms of "lives" than of "reigns in France." In December their armies crossed the Rhine and the Pyrenees; and the Emperor, for all the brilliance of his maneuvering, had to give in. He lost the magnificent throne he had conquered and left Fontainebleau on April 20 to sit on the minor one which the allies decided to let him occupy. But the island of Elba was not big enough for Napoleon. Besides, the Bourbons were not popular in France; and the coalition seemed to be on the verge of breaking up. So in March, 1815, the Emperor landed with a handful of men and marched, triumphantly, on Paris. This time, he promised, he would reign in a constitutional manner—though thinking Frenchmen found that hard to believe. "My system has changed: no more war and no conquests." [10] But the allied powers did not believe him: his past gave the lie to that assurance. So the armies massed once again and this time, after Waterloo, Napoleon was sent into exile on St. Helena; and though he still lived for another six years, he could no longer directly trouble the peace of Europe.

Indirectly, of course, he did trouble that "peace" and continued to do so for generations. This was not merely because his regime, in the reaction that followed his downfall, came to seem more and more attractive to men who forgot its darker side. It was also because he had loosed on Europe precedents and conceptions which could not be dismantled in the way that his Empire was. His sovereignty, for all the flummery of the coronation, was rooted in consent; his state, the Concordat not withstanding, was a secular state. And, to quote Professor Hampson, "He took it for granted that [the] government [of the state] implied the solution of problems in terms of reason and common sense, without regard to traditional rights and the prac-

---

[9] Alexander to Lord Aberdeen, quoted in J. H. Rose, *The Life of Napoleon I*, 2 vols. (London, 1914), II, 374.

[10] Quoted in F. Markham, *Napoleon* (London, 1963), p. 214.

tices of the past—in other words it was a matter of scientific administration," carried out by professionals, by trained bureaucrats operating
in accordance with norms laid down by the government.[11] And furthermore his government took it for granted that it must, and should, take
cognizance of other fundamental changes that had been effected in
the course of the Revolution. The land had been freed from dues
and tithes and other relics of the so-called "feudal system." Equality
before the law had been proclaimed. And the Codes and institutions
that enshrined these principles and translated them into law and into
practice were not confined to France. Wherever the French were in
command, their Codes, their institutions, their methods were, to varying degrees, enforced or imitated. The "consolidation . . . of the
Revolution" may, as Robert Holtman puts it, have made Napoleon
"a conservative in France"—conservative by comparison with, say,
Robespierre and the Jacobins; "but [it made him] a revolutionary in
ancien-régime areas abroad." [12] And while, for a time, the political
revolution he effected could be reversed, the revolution on the land,
in the law, and in social organization was a one-way revolution because it coincided with the way that changes were already flowing.
Napoleon had correctly sensed that his lifetime coincided with a
watershed in human affairs, and on St. Helena his reminiscing certainly had behind it the conscious purpose of trying to ensure that
future generations would hail him as having been "on their side." [13]
And this, his last campaign, a campaign of propaganda, was remarkably (and deservedly?) successful. A "legend" was born, the "cult" of
Napoleon reinforced—with results not only in history-writing but also
in history-making too.

[11] N. Hampson, *The First European Revolution, 1776–1815* (London, 1969), p. 137.
[12] Robert Holtman, *The Napoleonic Revolution,* p. 195.
[13] H. A. L. Fisher, *Bonapartism* (Oxford, 1961), p. 115, quoting Napoleon to Las
Cases: "Our situation here [on St. Helena] may even have its attractive [aspects]:
the whole world is looking at us, we remain the martyrs of an immortal cause."

Chronology of the Life of Napoleon

1769   Born at Ajaccio, Corsica, August 15, the second surviving child of Letizia and Carlo Buonaparte.

1779–85   Educated at Brienne, in Champagne, and the Royal Military Academy, Paris.

1785–93   Regimental duties and often on leave in Corsica; deeply involved in the island's political affairs—in which he loses out.

1793   (September–December) helps as commander of the artillery to recapture Toulon.

1794   (August) arrested and "investigated" after Robespierre's fall on 9 Thermidor.

1795   October 5—"13 Vendémiaire" by the Revolutionary calendar introduced in 1793—he smashes a royalist insurrection in Paris.

1796   Given command of the Army of Italy (February 23); marries Joséphine de Beauharnais (March 9). Battles of Montenotte, Lodi, Castiglione, and Arcola (April 12, May 10, August 5, November 16).

1797   Battle of Rivoli (January 14), the Cisalpine Republic founded; truce at Leoben (April 18) and Peace of Campo-Formio (October 17).

1798–99   Campaign in Egypt and Palestine (July 1–August 22).

1799   The coup d'état (18–19 Brumaire/November 9–10) and the new constitution published (December 24).

1800   The constitution approved by plebiscite (January); revised local government and a working party on the Civil Code established; Battle of Marengo (June 14) and the "infernal machine" attempt on his life (December 24).

1801   The Concordat signed; peace with Austria (Lunéville, January 8) and Russia, and peace talks with Britain.

1802   Peace of Amiens (March 25); Legion of Honor founded, and by plebiscite he becomes Consul for Life (August 2).

1803   Germany "reorganized," and Louisiana sold to the U.S.A.

1804   Civil Code (March 27); proclaimed and crowned Emperor (December 2).

1805   Crowns himself King of Italy (May 26); Battles of Trafalgar, Ulm, and Austerlitz (October 21, October 29, December 2) and Peace of Pressburg (December 26).

1806	Joseph made King of Naples and Sicily, and Louis of Holland; the Holy Roman Empire dissolved and the Confederation of the Rhine established; Battle of Jena (October 14).
1807	Eylau (February 8) and Friedland (June 14); (June) the Tilsit talks and (July) the creation of the Kingdom of Westphalia (under Jérôme) and of the Grand Duchy of Warsaw. The invasion of Portugal (November) and occupation of northern Spain. The "continental system" launched by the Milan Decrees (December 17).
1808	Rome occupied (February) and Madrid (May); Joseph made King of Spain. (September–October) talks at Erfurt and then (November) campaign in Spain.
1809	Leaves the Iberian peninsula [where Wellington lands (May)] to fight at Aspern/Essling and Wagram (May 22 and July 6); Pope Pius VII imprisoned (July 5); Peace of Vienna (October 14); his divorce announced (December 15).
1810	Marriage with Maria-Louisa of Austria (April 2). Holland (July) and Oldenberg, Bremen, Hamburg, Lübeck annexed (December); the Czar openly breaks with him.
1811	Difficulties in Spain and with the Church. Preparations for invasion of Russia.
1812	(June) invasion of Russia; (September 7) Borodino; (September 14–October 19) in Moscow; (December 5) leaves the army for Paris.
1813	Campaign in Germany—Lützen and Bautzen (May 2 and 21); Dresden (August 26), Leipzig (October 18). France is invaded (December).
1814	Campaign of France—Brienne, Montmirail (January 29, February 11), but nevertheless Paris falls (March 13); the Senate declares him deposed (April 3) and he abdicates (April 6) and leaves for Elba (arrives May 3).
1815	(March 1–20) lands in France and returns to Paris; a new constitution is announced (April) and parliament meets (June). Waterloo (June 18) and into exile on St. Helena.
1821	(May 5) death.
1840	(December 15) his remains interred at the Invalides in Paris.

PART ONE

NAPOLEON LOOKS AT THE WORLD

There are certain difficulties here relating to evidence. Despite the colossal bulk of the material available, we lack a series of speeches or declarations of intention which are sufficiently uncalculated, for Napoleon was usually very conscious of his audience, of the effect his words might produce, and of what we would call propaganda or "salesmanship." This was especially true, of course, of the year on St. Helena—hence Creevey's comment: "I am perfectly satisfied Bonaparte said all that O'Meara puts into his mouth; whether that is all true is another thing." [1] *But it was also true, to varying degrees, throughout his career. Even his correspondence often provides only an indirect revelation, as it were, of his view of the world and of his place in it.*

Thus, it is essential, in order to detect this view, to watch him in action, to see what he did, and to remember of his successive plans, ambitions, and dreams that he is very often spelling them out with the completely conscious motive of influencing his contemporaries or posterity.

When deeply engaged in conversation, however, Napoleon sometimes, it seems, let himself talk very freely—and one rich source for observations made by the Emperor is, of course, the writings of contemporaries. And what a mass of memoirs has been written! Many of the authors, however, were out to present a particular picture of Napoleon; many wrote long after the event. And so the observations attributed to the Great Man/ Ogre may not always be very accurate—and may at times be downright apocryphal. And the repository of reflections by Napoleon is, of course, the writings of his companions in exile— when he was out not merely to justify himself, but to build a legend. What he had to say on St. Helena about himself and his career is fascinating—and revealing—even though (or because) there are many excuses, self-justifications, and plain wishful thinking, as well as pieces of what seem efforts at an honest self-appraisal.

[1] Letter of June 18, 1822, to Miss Ord. From J. Gore, ed., *The Creevey Papers* (London, 1963), p. 176. On Dr. O'Meara, see below, p. 31 n. 19.

*"He Reflects" forms the last section of this part of the book—
the last before his death. And before "He Reflects," we see him
in action "In the Field," "Governing and Commanding," the
general, and the brisk authoritarian. We also see the percipient
statesman rebuilding a nation torn apart in the Revolution, attempting to reconcile "equality" with "aristocracy," healing
wounds with a policy of "conservation and fusion." But first we
see him in the years before he came to power in France—as "The
Young Man."*

1
The Young Man, 1769–99

*Napoleon was a Corsican and it was to Corsica that,
in his youth, he felt attached. An "outsider" at school—and in a
sense throughout his life—it was only when his ambitions in
Corsica were blocked and that great prospects opened before him
in France that he, significantly, began to spell his surname in the
French way and began to attach himself to a nation which he
certainly served, and as certainly used, but with which, perhaps,
he never wholly identified. Nevertheless the cry of liberty and
equality caught at his heart in 1789—even if it is also true that the
Revolution was all the more welcome to him because his head
told him that it was likely to open great prospects to an able
young officer. For this Corsican was not only a romantic, a
dreamer even: he was also a calculator and a ruthless realist.*

TO GENERAL PAOLI, IN LONDON

Auxonne, June 12, 1789 [1]

General,
   I was born as our country was dying. Thirty thousand Frenchmen
spewed onto our coasts, drowning the throne of liberty in rivers of

[1] From *Letters and Documents of Napoleon* (London, 1961), I, 23–24; edited and
translated by John Eldred Howard. Copyright © 1961 by John Eldred Howard.
All selections from this volume reprinted by permission of Barrie and Jenkins Ltd.
and Oxford University Press, Inc.
   Paoli had led Corsican resistance to French troops occupying the island as a
result of a treaty with its "owner," Genoa; he was driven into exile just two months
before Napoleon was born at Ajaccio.

blood. . . . The cries of the dying and the groans of the oppressed
. . . surrounded my cradle.

You left the island, and the hope of happiness went with you; slavery
was the price of our submission: crushed under the triple chains of the
soldier, the lawyer and the tax collector, our compatriots live despised.
. . . Is that not the cruellest torture for a man of feeling?

To justify themselves, traitors to our country, vile souls corrupted
by love of sordid gain, have spread calumnies against the national
government and against your person in particular. Writers have accepted them as truths and are transmitting them to posterity.

Reading them my anger grew hot and I determined to sweep away
this fog born of ignorance. . . . I wish to compare your administration
with the present administration. I wish to blacken with the brush of
infamy those who have betrayed the common cause. I want to call
those who govern before the tribunal of public opinion. . . .

I am still young, and my undertaking may be rash, but love of truth,
of our country, of my compatriots, and the enthusiasm which leads me
always to hope for an improvement in our condition will support me.
If, General, you will deign to encourage the efforts of a young man
. . . whose parents were always attached to the right party, I shall
dare to look for some success.

I know that [my book] will rouse against me the French officials who
govern our island, but what does that matter if it is in the interest of
our country. . . .

Allow me, General, to offer you the homage of my family and, why
should I not say, of my compatriots. They sigh at the memory of a
time when they hoped for liberty. My mother, Madame Letizia, asks
me to remember [her] to you. . . .

TO THE ABBÉ RAYNAL

1789? [2]

A friend of free men, you are interested in the fate of Corsica, the
character of whose people destined it for liberty. . . . But some in-
explicable fate has always armed its neighbours against her. . . .

What a picture modern history presents! People killing each other
for family quarrels, or murdering one another in the name of the
Prime Mover of the Universe; greedy and dishonest priests misleading
them by the potent means of fear, imagination, and love of miracles!
What can an enlightened reader find to interest him in this confused

---

[2] Reprinted from J. M. Thompson, ed., *Napoleon's Letters* (London: J. M. Dent
& Sons, Ltd., 1954), pp. 35–37. All selections from this volume are reprinted by
permission of J. M. Dent & Sons, Ltd., and E. P. Dutton, Inc.

Raynal, having fallen foul of the censor, had had to flee France in 1781.

scene of affliction? But then a William Tell appears, and our hopes are centred in this avenger of the nations. The picture of America ravished by brigands, and by the power of the sword, inspires a detestation of the human race; but we share the labours of a Washington, we enjoy his triumphs, we follow his two thousand leagues' march; for his cause is that of the human race. . . .

TO HIS UNCLE, ARCHDEACON FESCH

Serve, Dauphiné
February 8, 1791 [3]

I am in a poor man's cabin where it is pleasant to write to you after a long conversation with these worthy souls. . . . Everywhere I find the peasants very firm in their views, especially in Dauphiné, where they are all ready to die in support of the Constitution.[4]

All the priests of Dauphiné have taken the civic oath and are laughing at the ravings of the bishops.

At Valence I found the people resolute, the soldiers patriotic and the officers aristocratic. . . .

Everywhere the women are royalist. That is not surprising; liberty is a prettier woman, who eclipses them.

TO LUCIEN (OR JOSEPH?) BONAPARTE

Paris, July 3, 1792 [5]

The men at the head of affairs are a poor lot. One must admit, upon closer acquaintance, that the people are hardly worth all the trouble that is taken to merit their support. You know the history of Ajaccio. That of Paris is exactly the same, though perhaps people here are pettier, viler, more abusive, and more censorious. You have to look closer before you realize that enthusiasm is still enthusiasm, and that the French are an ancient and independent people. . . . Every individual is out for his own interests, and will forward them, if he can, by insult and outrage: intrigue is as underhand as ever. All this discourages ambition. . . .

---

[3] J. E. Howard, ed., *Letters and Documents*, I, 25.

[4] Namely, the Constitution being evolved, piece by piece, in the Constituent Assembly and promulgated in September, 1791. The oath referred to was required of clergymen and implied acceptance of the Civil Constitution of the Clergy, an oath all but seven of the bishops refused. So did about one-half of the clergy in France: hence the schism between *constitutionnels* and *réfractaires* (or *abdicataires*).

[5] From J. M. Thompson, ed., *Napoleon's Letters*, p. 41.

A CONVERSATION WITH CAULAINCOURT

in December, 1812 [6]

This conversation led the Emperor to speak of . . . his youthful days. . . . "The reading of history," he said, "very soon made me feel that I was capable of achieving as much as the men who are placed in the highest ranks of our annals, though I had no goal before me, and though my hopes went no farther than my promotion to General. . . . But I was not long in discovering that the knowledge that I set myself out to acquire and which I had hitherto regarded as the end I needed to attain was very far short of the distance to which my abilities might carry me. So I redoubled my application; what seemed to present difficulty to others to me appeared to be simple."

TO JOSEPH BONAPARTE

Paris, July 12, 1795 [7]

. . . Here in Paris, luxury, enjoyment, and the arts are resuming their sway in surprising fashion. . . . Smart carriages and fashionably dressed people are seen about again: they have the air of waking up after a long dream. . . . The bookshops are open again. There is a succession of lectures on history, chemistry, botany, astronomy, and so forth. The place is crammed with everything that can distract, and make life agreeable. No one is given time to think. Anyhow, who could be a pessimist in this mental workshop, this whirlwind of activity? . . .

Paris, August 12, 1795 [7]

Personally, I hardly care what happens to me. I watch life almost indifferently. My permanent state of mind is that of a soldier on the eve of battle: I have come to the conclusion that, since a chance meeting with death may end it all at any minute, it is stupid to worry about anything. Everything disposes me to face my destiny without flinching. At this rate, my friend, I shall end by not stepping out of the way of a passing carriage. As a reasonable man I am sometimes astonished at

[6] From T. Hanoteau, ed., *Memoirs of General Caulaincourt, Duke of Vicenza,* trans. H. Miles, 3 vols. (London, 1950), II, 241. Reprinted by permission of Cassell & Co. and Librairie Plon.

Caulaincourt (1773–1827), France's ambassador to Russia before the invasion, accompanied Napoleon when he left the shattered Grand Army near Vilna and hurried to Paris (December 6–18, 1812).

[7] From J. M. Thompson, ed., *Napoleon's Letters,* pp. 43, 44.

"Luxury" and "fashion" had not been in favor during the democratic Republic of the year II (see G. Rudé, *Robespierre,* p. 10, and note pp. 53, 55).

this attitude; but it is a natural tendency produced in me by the moral state of the country, and by the habit of running risks. . . .

TO MADAME BEAUHARNAIS

Paris, December, 1795 [8]

On waking I find every thought going through my head is of you. Your portrait and the memory of yesterday evening cause a tumult inside me. Sweet and incomparable Joséphine, what an extraordinary effect you have on my heart! . . . If you are sad, if you are troubled . . . all peace of mind is denied me. . . .

I shall see you in three hours. Till then, *mio dolce amor,* a thousand kisses—but don't return any of them for they set my blood on fire.

TO HIS WIFE

Nice, March 31, 1796 [8]

Not one day has gone by without my loving you, not one night without my hugging you. . . . I cannot drink a cup of tea, even, without cursing the fact that glory and ambition keep me away from the light of my life. Whether I am immersed in business, leading my troops, inspecting the camps, my adorable Joséphine fills my heart and dominates my being. And yet in your letters of [March 13 and 16] you call me "vous." "Vous" to you! How can you have written such a cold, unfeeling letter, you wretch! And then, from the 13th to the 16th, four blank days—what were you doing that you didn't write to your husband? . . .

Joséphine, Joséphine, do you recall what I once said to you—that nature has made me strong and resolute, while you she has made all of lace and gauze? Have you stopped loving me? Forgive me, soul of my life [but] my heart, so full of you, knows fears which make me miserable. . . .

P.S. The war this year has changed out of all recognition. I have seen to it that meat, bread and fodder have been supplied. . . . My soldiers have incredible confidence in me. Only you cause me unhappiness—only you, the joy and torment of my life. . . .

---

[8] From L. Cerf, ed., *Lettres de Napoléon à Joséphine* (Paris, 1928), pp. 1–2, 5–7; translated by M. Hutt. Six years older than Napoleon, and of aristocratic birth, Joséphine was the widow of the Vicomte de Beauharnais, a Republican general dismissed and executed in 1794. Her son, Eugène, was fourteen; her daughter, Hortense, was in due course (1802) married to Louis Bonaparte.

TO THE ARMY OF ITALY

H. Q. Milan, May 20, 1796 [9]

Soldiers!

You have rushed like a torrent from the heights of the Apennines: you have overthrown, dispersed and scattered everything that opposed your advance.

Delivered from the Austrian tyranny, Piedmont has returned to its natural love of peace and friendship towards France.

Milan is yours, and the republican flag floats over the whole of Lombardy. . . .

Such success has brought joy to the heart of our country; there, your fathers, your mothers, your wives, your sisters, your sweethearts are rejoicing in your successes and proudly proclaim that they belong to you.

Yes, soldiers, you have done much; but is there not still much to do? Shall it be said of us that we knew how to conquer, but not how to exploit victory? . . . Well then, let us go! There are still forced marches to be made, enemies to be defeated, laurels to be won, insults to avenge. . . .

But let the Italian people have no fear; we are friends to all peoples, and particularly to the descendants of Brutus, of Scipio and the great men whom we have taken for models. To rebuild the Capitol and place in honour there the statues of the famous heroes, to awaken the Roman people benumbed by centuries of slavery, such will be the fruit of your victories. You will have the immortal glory of changing the face of the loveliest part of Europe.

The French people, free and respected throughout the world, will bring to Europe a glorious peace which will repay them for the manifold sacrifices they have made for six years. Then you will return to your homes, and your fellow citizens will point you out and say: "He was of the Army of Italy!"

PROCLAMATION TO THE INHABITANTS OF LOMBARDY

Milan, May 25, 1796 [10]

A misguided horde . . . is committing excesses in several communes in flagrant contempt of the Republic and of an army which has triumphed over several kings. This incredible delirium is worthy of

---

[9] From J. E. Howard, ed., *Letters and Documents*, I, 123–24.

[10] *Correspondance de Napoléon I, publiée par ordre de l'Empereur Napoléon III,* 32 vols. (Paris, 1858–69). The letters are arranged in chronological order; translated by M. Hutt.

pity, for these unfortunate people are simply being led astray. The general-in-chief, faithful to the principles adopted by the French nation, which does not make war on peoples, wishes to leave the way open to repentance. But those who do not, within twenty-four hours, lay down their arms and take an oath of loyalty to the Republic, will be treated as rebels and their villages burned. Let the terrible example of Binasco open their eyes. That will be the fate of all the towns and villages which remain in a state of revolt.

TO THE DIRECTORY

Milan, January 6, 1797 [10]

The more I go into the terrible defects in the administration of the army of Italy, the more I am convinced that we must remedy them at once. The army's accounts are in complete disorder; while the well-earned reputation of the Comptroller for swindling is matched by the incapacity of the other officials. . . . The army is shown to be consuming five times more than is necessary, because those in charge of the depots make out false chits and split the profits with the contractors. . . . There is only one way to sort this out. We need a court consisting of one or three people, and with . . . the power to shoot any army administrator [found guilty of corruption].

TO THE ARMY OF ITALY

H.Q. Milan, July 14, 1797 [11]

Soldiers, today is the anniversary of the 14 July. . . .

I know you are deeply concerned at the evils threatening the nation; but the country is not in real danger. The same men are there who made it triumph over united Europe. Mountains separate us from France; but, were it necessary in order to uphold the Constitution, to defend liberty, to protect the Government and the republicans, then you would cross them with the speed of the eagle.

Soldiers, the Government is watching over the body of laws entrusted to it. If the royalists show themselves they will die. Have no fear, but let us swear by the shadow of the heroes who have died at our side for liberty, let us swear on our new flags: *Implacable War to the Enemies of the Republic and of the Constitution of the Year III!*

[11] From J. E. Howard, ed., *Letters and Documents,* I, 196–97.

On July 14, 1789, the Bastille had been taken; the Constitution of the year III was that promulgated on August 22, 1795, and replaced by the (Consular) Constitution of 1799.

But was that government, in fact, capable of guarding the laws and the Republic? Was the Republic itself really sacrosanct in Bonaparte's eyes? Certainly the next letter is genuine: but if we did not know what happened two years later, would we attach any particular significance to such a letter? And how accurate were Miot de Melito's reminiscences? Surely he cannot have recalled the exact words used by the young general—though his son-in-law does say that he used to "write down every evening all that he had learned or observed during the day." Perhaps, then, he did not make it up—consider what Napoleon himself said to Las Cases.

TO TALLEYRAND, MINISTER OF FOREIGN AFFAIRS

Passariano, September 19, 1797 [12]

. . . For all our pride, our thousand-and-one pamphlets, and our blustering, airy orations, we are extremely ignorant of the science of political conduct. We have never yet defined what is meant by the executive, legislative and judicial powers. . . . Why should it be thought a function of the Legislative Power to declare war and peace, or to regulate the amount and character of the taxes? . . . Why, in a Government whose whole authority emanates from the nation, why, where the sovereign is the people, should one include among the functions of the Legislative Power things which are foreign to it? There is only one thing, so far as I can see, that we have really defined during the last fifty years, and that is the sovereignty of the people. . . . The French people are organized only in outline.

In the early summer of 1797 Bonaparte's headquarters were in the palace of Mombello, near Milan. There Bonaparte, says Miot de Melito, one day spoke with entire frankness about his projects to himself and Melzi d'Eril:

"What I have done so far," he said, "is nothing. I am only at the beginning of the course I must run. Do you imagine that I triumph in Italy in order to aggrandize the pack of lawyers who form the Directory? What an idea! A Republic of thirty million men! and with our manners, our vices! how is it possible? The Republic is a fancy of which the French are at present full, but it will pass away like all the others. What they want is Glory and gratified Vanity; but as for Liberty, they

[12] From J. M. Thompson, ed., *Napoleon's Letters*, p. 65.

do not understand what it means. . . . The nation must have a chief, and a chief rendered illustrious by glory, not by theories of government, by phrases, by theoretic speeches, which Frenchmen do not understand. Give them baubles—that suffices them; they will be amused and will let themselves be led, so long as the end towards which they are going is skilfully hidden from them." [13]

A CONVERSATION WITH LAS CASES

September 1–6, 1815 [14]

"Vendémiaire and even [the battle of] Montenotte," said the Emperor, "never induced me to look upon myself as a man of a superior [type]; it was not until after [my victory at] Lodi that I was struck with the possibility of becoming a leading actor on the scene of political events. It was then that the first spark of my ambition was kindled."

But dreams were not, in Bonaparte's case, a substitute for action; they were a prelude to it, while the decision to act and the choice and timing of the action followed a cold assessment of what was feasible in practice as well as what was desirable.

On October 26, 1799, General Thiébault breakfasted with Bonaparte and his wife:[15]

Hardly were we seated, just the three of us, when he began to talk to me about the last two campaigns. . . . Something he said made me think of speaking to him of my plan for a new campaign in Italy; but the opportunity vanished because of the sudden way in which he all at once contrasted with what we were saying about the devotion of the troops and the zeal of the commanders that which had gone on and was going on at home. He attacked the Government with a violence

[13] From Miot de Melito, *Memoirs,* ed. Fleischmann, trans. C. Hoey and J. Lillie (London, 1881), I, 188 and see I, iii.

Count Miot de Melito (1762–1841) was then a civil servant in the War Ministry; in January, 1801, he became a Counsellor of State.

[14] From Count de Las Cases, *Mémorial de Sainte Hélène: Journal of the Private Life and Conversations of the Emperor Napoleon at St. Helena,* 4 vols. (London, 1823).

Although Las Cases (1766–1842) was only on St. Helena until November 1816, his devoted journal was the most influential single work so far as the creation of "the Napoleonic Legend" is concerned.

[15] From *The Memoirs of Baron Thiébault,* translated and condensed by A. Butler (London, 1896), II, 16–17.

which amazed me. Here are a few phrases which my memory recalls: "A nation is always what you have the wit to make it. . . . The triumph of faction, parties, divisions, is the fault of those in authority only. . . . No people are bad under a good government, just as no troops are bad under good generals. But what can you expect of fellows who know neither their country nor its needs, who understand neither the age nor the men of it, and who meet only with resistance where they should find support?" Then he launched a volley of attacks on the Directory. "I left peace, and I come back to war. The influence of victory has been replaced by shameful defeats. Italy had been won; now it is invaded, and France is threatened. I left millions, and everywhere there is poverty. These men . . . are dragging France down to [their own] level . . . and she is beginning to repudiate them. . . ." [And] he went off into fresh . . . expressions of disgust at the idea of the selection of generals depending on intrigues, ignorance and the authority of "lawyers"—a word he used in such a way as to express utter contempt. . . . "What can generals expect of this government of lawyers? For lieutenants to care about their work they need a chief capable of appreciating them [and of] backing them up." From the tone in which the word "lieutenants" was spoken, I thought I was listening to Cæsar; the ground seemed uneasy beneath me, and I took my leave.

ORDER OF THE DAY

H.Q. Paris,
18 Brumaire, Year VIII (November 9, 1799)[16]
Soldiers, for two years the Republic has been misgoverned. You have hoped that my return would put an end to such ills; you have celebrated it with a unity which imposes obligations upon me and these I am fulfilling; you will fulfil yours and support your general with the energy, steadfastness and confidence that I have always found in you. . . .
Long live the Republic!

BONAPARTE

PROCLAMATION TO THE FRENCH NATION

Paris, 21 Brumaire, Year VIII (November 12, 1799)[16]
The Constitution of the Year III was dying. It was incapable of protecting your rights, even of protecting itself. Through repeated assaults it was losing beyond recall the respect of nations. Selfish factions were despoiling the Republic. France, indeed, was entering the last stage of general disorganization.

[16] From J. E. Howard, ed., *Letters and Documents*, I, 310, 314–315.

But patriots have made themselves heard. All who could harm you have been cast aside. All who can serve you, all those representatives who have remained pure, have come together under the banner of liberty.

Frenchmen, the Republic, strengthened and restored to that rank in Europe which should never have been lost, will realise all the hopes of her citizens and will accomplish her glorious destiny.

Swear with us the oath we have taken to be faithful to the Republic, one and indivisible, founded on equality, liberty and the representative system.

The Consuls of the Republic
BONAPARTE, ROGER DUCOS, SIEYÈS

Already, some of the crucial characteristics of the Consul and Emperor are apparent in the young man. There is energy, vision, hardheadedness, and ruthlessness. There is the great leader of men in the field, the astonishing general who, for all his planning and calculating, kept himself unencumbered, free, never trapped in his first conclusions, never chained down by his own procedures. There is the Jacobin who hated privilege—but also the soldier, wedded to order. There is ambition, too, but one of a vaulting, lofty kind. Bonaparte was possessed of a sense of something needing to be done—something colossal, to be made by him; a sense of destiny in accordance with which he would be carried onwards and upwards without (or so it seemed to him— those he trod on felt otherwise) his having to push and shove. And he would move onwards and upwards, not merely to power, but to power for a purpose. The commander-censor-tyrant element had appeared in the young man: but that was only one aspect of him: there was also the servant-midwife-guardian, conscious of and obedient to the fact that what had happened in the Revolution was irreversible, that a new, and better, sort of society could emerge—and would emerge all over Europe, provided the right institutions were built, the right laws passed (where "right" means "appropriate to," and "consonant with," the needs and the spirit of the age).

2
Conservation and Fusion

BONAPARTE TO THE COUNCIL OF STATE

[1801][1]

We have finished the romance of the Revolution, we must now begin its history, only seeking for what is real and practicable in the application of its principles, and not what is speculative and hypothetical. To follow any other course at the present [time] would be to philosophize and not to govern.

A CONVERSATION WITH GENERAL BERTRAND

March 15 or 16, 1821 [2]

A distinction should be drawn between Revolutionary *interests* and Revolutionary *theories*. The theories came first, while the interests only came into play on the night of 4 August 1789, after the suppression of the nobility and of the payment of tithes. I retained all the Revolutionary interests because I had no reason to destroy them. This was one of the sources of my strength. It also explains why I was able to set aside the Revolutionary theories . . . the only use [for which] is to destroy counter-revolutionary theories. . . . Everyone felt reassured, because everyone knew that the Emperor did not and could not wish for a counter-revolution. Under my rule, freedom of the press was unnecessary; added to this was the fact that everyone had had enough of the Revolution, of Assemblies, of unrest and of internal dissensions.

TO THE COUNCIL OF STATE

December 20, 1812 [3]

It is to this ideology, the . . . metaphysics which would base political legislation on subtle principles derived from first causes in-

[1] From Miot de Melito, *Memoirs*, I, 395–96.

[2] From *Napoleon at St. Helena: Memoirs of General Bertrand, Grand Marshal of the Palace, January–May, 1821*, deciphered . . . by P. Fleuriot de Langle, trans. F. Hume (London: Cassell & Co., 1953), pp. 128–29. All selections from this volume reprinted by permission of Cassell & Co.

[3] From J. C. Herold, *Mind of Napoleon: A Selection from His Written and Spoken Words* (New York, 1961), p. 69. Reprinted by permission of Columbia University Press.

stead of adapting it to our knowledge of human psychology and to
historic lessons, that every misfortune experienced by our beautiful
France must be attributed. These errors were bound to, and in fact
did, bring about the reign of terror by blood-stained men. Who proclaimed the principle that rebellion was a duty? Who fawned on the
people by proclaiming its sovereignty, which it was incapable of ex-
ercising? Who destroyed the awe and sanctity of the laws by making
them depend, not on the sacred principles of justice, not on the
natural order, not on civil law, but merely on the will of an assembly
whose members were ignorant of civil, penal, administrative, political,
and military laws?

He who has been called upon to regenerate a State must follow
absolutely opposite principles. History paints the human heart. In
history we must seek the advantages and disadvantages of the various
systems of law.

The heart of a statesman should be in his head.[4]

A CONVERSATION WITH CAULAINCOURT

December, 1812 [5]

[Napoleon's observations showed] a firm resolve to make the
utmost of all the Revolution had produced that was great and useful.

"It was," he said, "an era that gave new life to France when she
had been stricken prostrate by a succession of favourites, of kings'
mistresses and all the abuses that followed in their train. To end all
that it was necessary to pool all opinions, and to make use of men
violently opposed to one another."

A CONVERSATION WITH LAS CASES

August 24, 1816 [6]

The [great battle] of the century had been won and the Revolution accomplished; [now all that had to be done was] to reconcile
it with what it had not destroyed. That task belonged to me. . . . I
became the arch of the alliance between the old and the new, the
natural mediator between the old and the new orders. I maintained
the principles and possessed the confidence of the one; I had identified
myself with the other. I belonged to them both. . . .

[4] Quoted, with other of his sayings, in H. A. L. Fisher, *Napoleon*, 2d ed. (London,
1967), p. 147.
[5] From J. Hanoteau, ed., *Memoirs of General Caulaincourt*, II, 326–27.
[6] From Las Cases, *Mémorial de Sainte Hélène*.

A COMMENT BY MME. DE RÉMUSAT [7]

How often has he made use of these specious words, in order to allay apprehension: "The French Revolution need fear nothing, since the throne of the Bourbons is occupied by a soldier!" And at the same time he would assume towards Kings the attitude of a Protector of Thrones—"for," he would say, "I have abolished Republics."

A CONVERSATION WITH CAULAINCOURT

December, 1812 [8]

I have always considered [Louis XVI's] death a crime, and I thought so before I became a sovereign myself. Since I have worn a crown I have shown clearly enough that I mean to close the doors against revolution. The sovereigns of Europe are indebted to me for stemming the revolutionary torrent that threatened their thrones; but to prevent the evil breaking out again it is useless to rake up the memory of wrongs done at a time of general upheaval. People must be induced to forget, or remember only in order to prevent a recurrence. I am far from being an advocate of the Convention, but if anyone is to be called to account for the evils done at that time, it is not the men of the Convention, who were carried away by the frenzy of the time, but the Revolution which had been brought about by the Court itself. As a matter of strict justice the reckoning for our past misfortune should be laid to the Princes and men of the Court who caused the Revolution. . . . These men (he went on) ought to have laid down their lives on the steps of the throne instead of attacking it. Speaking generally, the nobility ought to have fought to the death instead of saving themselves by flight abroad, which was nothing but a convenient way of escaping danger by professing a false devotion. As for the others, those called revolutionaries, they belonged to a lower class which naturally wanted to raise itself. They looked after themselves, and circumstances proved stronger than they. [The émigrés] who carried on intrigues abroad did more to bring about the death of the King than the Convention. . . .

My government has always acted on the principle that what happened prior to its establishment did not take place, always making an exception of services rendered. That is the principle to adopt in

---

[7] From *Memoirs of Mme. de Rémusat*, trans. C. Hoey and J. Lillie (London, 1880), II, 50–51.

She and her husband were aristocrats of the Old Regime, and so he was useful to Napoleon as his Imperial Court Chamberlain. He also kept an eye on Paris theatres. These memoirs were written in 1818.

[8] From J. Hanoteau, ed., *Memoirs of General Caulaincourt*, II, 243–44.

order to avert reaction, to quench all hatred and stifle revenge. The greatest seigneurs of the old regime [now] dine with [former] revolutionaries. My government has brought about this fusion. . . .

TO COUNT FOUCHÉ, MINISTER OF POLICE

Benevento, December 31, 1808 [9]

I am informed that some of the émigré families are refusing to let their children enlist, and are keeping them in undesirable and culpable idleness. . . . I want you to draw up a list of ten of the leading families in each Department, and fifty in Paris. I intend to issue a decree by which all the young people belonging to these families between the ages of sixteen and eighteen shall be sent to the Military School at Saint-Cyr. If any one objects [simply state] that I wish it so. [The younger] generation must not be allowed to suffer for the petty hatreds and passions of [our own]. . . .

PROCLAMATION TO THE INHABITANTS OF THE WESTERN DEPARTMENTS OF FRANCE

Paris, December 28, 1799 [10]

Unjust laws have been passed and executed; arbitrary acts have undermined the security of the citizen and the liberty of conscience; haphazard additions to the lists of emigrants have everywhere struck down citizens who had never abandoned either their country or even their homes; in fact, great principles of social order have been violated.

To repair these errors and injustices a government founded on the sacred principles of liberty, equality, and the representative system has been proclaimed and recognized by the nation. It will be the constant desire of [this government] to heal all the wounds of France. Thus the disastrous law of the forced loan and the yet more disastrous law of hostages have been repealed; individuals deported without prior trial have been restored to their country and their families. . . . The Consuls of the Republic declare once again that freedom of worship is guaranteed by the Constitution; that no man can say to another: "You will follow this creed; you will worship only on such a day. . . ."

The Government will pardon; it will show mercy to repentance; indulgence will be complete and absolute. But it will strike down whoever may still dare, after this declaration, to resist the national sovereignty. . . .

[9] From J. M. Thompson, ed., Napoleon's Letters, p. 208.
[10] From J. E. Howard, ed., Letters and Documents, I, 332, 340.

TO GENERAL BRUNE, COMMANDER-IN-CHIEF OF THE ARMY OF THE WEST

Paris, January 14, 1800 [10]

The armistice concluded between General Hédouville and the chouans must last only until [January 21]. Georges [Cadoudal], who commands the[se] rebels in the Morbihan, is not included in it. . . . Break up Georges's bands. Seize his guns and his corn stocks (he has a great deal on the coast which he is selling to the English). In fact make the insurgents of the Morbihan feel the weight and horror of war. . . .

Diplomatic reasons of the greatest importance demand that [by the end of January] the English should know that considerable forces are in pursuit of Georges. . . .

The Constitution is suspended [throughout] the Departments of Ille-et-Vilaine, Loire-Inférieure, Côtes-du-Nord and Morbihan.

Welcome every individual who submits, but allow no further meeting of leaders; hold no kind of diplomatic parley.

Great tolerance for the priests: severe action against the larger communes to force them to guard themselves and protect the smaller. Do not spare communes which misbehave. Burn a few farmsteads and large villages in the Morbihan and begin to make examples. . . . Only if the war is made terrible for them will the inhabitants realize that their apathy is fatal to them and join against the brigands. . . .

PROCLAMATION TO THE ARMY

aboard *L'Orient*, off Alexandria,

June 22, 1798 [11]

Soldiers! You are about to undertake a conquest which will have an incalculable effect on civilization and on the pattern of trade in the world. You will deal England a savage blow. . . .

The people of this area are Mohammedans. The first article of their Creed is "There is no other God but God, and Mahomet is his Prophet." Don't contradict them. Behave as you do with the Jews, the Italians; respect their mufties and imams just as you did rabbis and bishops. Show for the ceremonies which the Koran prescribes the same tolerance which you have shown to convents and synagogues. . . . The Roman legions, remember, protected all religions. . . .

[11] From Napoleon, *Correspondance*, translated by M. Hutt.

CONVERSATIONS WITH GENERAL GOURGAUD

August 28, 1817 [12]

"I have been reading the Bible," [said the Emperor]. . . . "Jesus should have been hanged like scores of other fanatics who posed as the Prophet or the Messiah. . . . I prefer the religion of Mahomet: it is less ridiculous than ours."

WITH BERTRAND

March 27, 1821 [13]

"I am very glad that I have no religion," the Emperor remarked. "I find it a great consolation, as I have no imaginary terrors and no fear of the future." . . . In actual fact the Emperor died a Theist [says Bertrand], believing in a rewarding God, the principle of all things. Yet he stated . . . in his will . . . that he had died in the Catholic religion because he believed that to be [the right thing to do in terms of] public ethics.

AND WITH ROEDERER

August 18, 1800 [14]

"Morality? There's only one way to encourage morality, and that is to reestablish religion. Society cannot exist without some being richer than others, and this inequality cannot exist without religion. When one man is dying of hunger next door to another who is stuffing himself with food, the poor man simply cannot accept the disparity unless some authority exists which tells him 'God wishes it so. There have to be both rich and poor in this world: but . . . in heaven things will be different.' "

ADDRESS TO THE CLERGY OF MILAN

Milan Cathedral, June 5, 1800 [15]

Convinced that the Catholic, Apostolic and Roman religion is the only religion which can bring true happiness to a well-ordered society

[12] From G. Gourgaud, *St. Helena Journal, 1815–1818*, trans. S. Gillard (London, 1932), p. 259. Reprinted by permission of The Bodley Head.

Baron Gourgaud saved Napoleon's life at the Battle of Brienne and was asked by the Emperor to accompany him to St. Helena, where he stayed until 1818. He died, aged sixty-seven, just before the Second Empire was proclaimed in 1852.

[13] From *Memoirs of General Bertrand*, pp. 133, 181.

[14] From M. Vitrac, ed., *Autour de Bonaparte. Journal du comte P. L. Roederer* (Paris, 1909), pp. 18–19; translated by M. Hutt.

[15] From J. E. Howard, ed., *Letters and Documents*, I, 366–67.

and strengthen the foundations of a good government, I assure you that I shall devote myself to defending it at all times and by every means. I regard you, the ministers of that religion, which is indeed also my own, as my most dear friends. I declare that I shall regard as a disturber of the peace and enemy of the common good whoever commits the least outrage against our common religion or dares to offer the slightest insult towards your sacred persons. . . .

Modern philosophers have striven to persuade the French nation that the Catholic religion is the implacable enemy of every democratic system and republican form of government: hence this cruel persecution launched by the French Republic against th[at] religion and its ministers. . . . But experience has disillusioned the French and has convinced them that of all religions there is none which adapts itself as does the Catholic to different forms of government and which favours republican democratic government in particular, affirming its rightness and illuminating its principles. I, too, am a philosopher, and I know that no man can [be] virtuous and just in any society unless he knows whence he comes and whither he goes. Reason alone cannot help us there; without religion we move always among shadows; and the Catholic religion is the only one which throws certain and infallible light on the origin and end of man. No society can exist without morality: there is no good morality without religion; it is religion alone that gives to the State a firm and durable support. . . .

It is my firm intention, therefore, that the Catholic religion shall be preserved in its entirety, that it shall be publicly performed and that it shall enjoy this public exercise [in] full and inviolable freedom.

TO HIS UNCLE, CARDINAL FESCH, ARCHBISHOP OF LYON

Rouen, November 2, 1802 [16]
It is time that you were starting out for your diocese, without further delay. You should take with you a respectable but not luxurious number of servants, modelling your household on the best at Lyon—those of the prefect and the general commanding that district. Be careful what you do, but appoint as many constitutional priests as possible, and make certain of support from this party.[16a] In addition you must show great consideration and respect for the Pope, and for the virtues and (as he is your superior authority) the views of the Archbishop of Paris.

I wish you to send me your episcopal charge before it is published and printed. . . .

[16] From J. M. Thompson, ed., *Napoleon's Letters*, pp. 99–100.
[16a] The *constitutionnels* were those priests who accepted the reorganization referred to above p. 4 and p. 14 n. 4.

Do not forget that . . . everybody will see what you do. Be austere in your private life, keep up a proper state in public, and give all your time to the duties of your office. Profess not to meddle in politics: if they present you petitions for me, reply that you are a minister of religion, and of that alone. Don't give too much rein to your enthusiasm, even for the management of almshouses, or the care of the poor.

Your first business, and one that will occupy you for some months, is to administer the sacraments in your diocese, to conciliate and to get to know your priests, and to organize your Church. Lyon was once a great industrial centre, and contains a large number of priests formerly attached to a party in opposition to the State. Don't employ these men; or, if you cannot see how to avoid employing some of them, let me know what the trouble is, and I will have them moved elsewhere, on my own initiative. . . .

TO POPE PIUS VII

February 13, 1806 [17]

. . . Your Holiness is sovereign of Rome, but I am the Emperor. My enemies must be your enemies. It is therefore inappropriate for any representatives of Sardinia, England, Russia, or Sweden to reside in your States, nor is it right that vessels belonging to these powers should enter your ports.

As you are the head of our Church I shall continue to exhibit a filial deference for your Holiness; but I am accountable to God, who made use of my strength to reestablish religion. Am I supposed, without complaining, to let this work be compromised by the dilatoriness of Rome? . . . Those who let the [Church in] Germany remain in a state of anarchy will have to answer for this before God; those who delay sending bulls [of appointment] to my bishops . . . will have to answer for this before God. . . . If, in Rome, important matters like these are deliberately allowed to drag on and on, I, commissioned by God to watch over the interests of the faith, will be unable to ignore a situation which works contrary to the interests and the salvation of my people.

Most Holy Father, I know that your Holiness wants to do what is right; but you are surrounded by men who do *not* want to, men . . . who deliberately seek to create difficulties, not to resolve them. . . . I cannot allow matters to drag on for a year which ought to be cleared up in a fortnight. It was not by dozing away that I raised the status of the clergy . . . and reorganized religion in France, so that

[17] From Napoleon, *Correspondance*, translated by M. Hutt. On Eugène, see above p. 16 n. 8.

there is today no country in which it does more good or where it is more respected. Those who tell your Holiness anything different are deceiving you and are your enemies; they will draw down misfortunes upon them which will be fatal to them.

TO HIS STEPSON EUGÈNE, VICEROY OF THE KINGDOM OF ITALY

Dresden, July 22, 1807 [17]

Does the Pope think that the rights of the throne are less sacred in the eyes of God than those of the [papal] tiara?

TO COUNT DE CHAMPAGNY, MINISTER OF FOREIGN AFFAIRS

Schönbrunn, May 17, 1809 [18]

The Emperor intends to communicate the enclosed decrees, on the subject of the Papal States, to the Senate accompanied by a report from the Minister for Foreign Affairs.

His Majesty wishes this report to develop the motives laid down in the preamble [to the decrees] to prove that, when Charlemagne made the popes temporal sovereigns [circa A.D. 800], he meant them to remain vassals of the Empire; that nowadays, far from regarding themselves as vassals of the Empire, they refuse to belong to it at all; that the motive of Charlemagne's generosity to the popes was the good of Christianity, and that now they are becoming allies of the Protestants and of the enemies of Christ. . . . Under these circumstances the only possible course was to occupy Rome with troops.

This measure, though indispensable, excited endless protests and lasting enmity on the part of the head of religion against the most powerful prince in Christendom. . . .

There is only one way in which His Majesty can put an end to debates so contrary to the welfare of religion and of the Empire; and that is to revoke the Donation of Charlemagne, and to reduce the popes to their proper rank, by safeguarding the spiritual power from the passions that control the temporal power. . . .

A CONVERSATION WITH DR. O'MEARA

November 2, 1816 [19]

"Moreover I wanted to establish a universal liberty of conscience. My system was to have no predominant religion, but to allow perfect

[18] From J. M. Thompson, 2d., *Napoleon's Letters*, pp. 212–13.

[19] From B. E. O'Meara, *Napoleon in Exile, or a Voice from St. Helena: The Opinions and Reflections of Napoleon*, 2 vols. (London, 1822), I, 183–84.

liberty of conscience and of thought, to make all men equal, whether Protestant, Catholics, Mahometans, Deists, or others; so that their religion should have no influence in getting them employment; in fact, that it should neither be the means of serving nor of injuring them; and that no objection should be made to a man's getting a situation on the score of religion, provided he were fit for it in other respects. I made every thing independent of religion. All the tribunals were so. Marriages were independent of the priests; even the cemeteries were not left at their disposal, as they could not refuse interment to the body of any person, of whatsoever religion. My intention was to render everything belonging to the state and the constitution, purely civil and independent of any religion. I wished to deprive the priests of all influence and power in civil affairs, and to oblige them to confine themselves to their own spiritual matters, and meddle with nothing else."

3
Equality and Aristocracy

CONVERSATIONS WITH BERTRAND

January 27, 1821 [1]
"What France wants above all is equality," said the Emperor.
"What she does not want are the pretentiousness and the arrogance of
the aristocrat."

WITH LAS CASES

November 18–19, 1816 [2]
Equality of rights . . . was one of the points to which Napoleon
attached particular importance. And this regard for equality . . .
seemed to belong innately to his character. "I [was not always a
ruler]," he would say: "before I became a Sovereign, I remember [I
was] a subject; and I can never forget how powerfully the sentiment
of equality influences the mind, and animates the heart."
Once, when he was suggesting a project to be [drafted] by one of
his Counsellors of State, he said, "Let me charge you to respect liberty;
and above all, equality. With regard to liberty, it might be possible
to restrain it, in a case of extremity; circumstances might demand
and justify such a step: but heaven forbid that we should ever in-
fringe upon equality! It is the passion of the age; and I wish to continue to be the man of the age!"

AND WITH O'MEARA

August 27, 1816 [3]
"Instead of allowing the sons of peasants . . . to be eligible to be
made generals, as they were in my time, [the Bourbons] want to confine [the higher ranks] entirely to the old nobility. . . . I made most
of my [generals] *de la boue.* Wherever I found talent and courage I
rewarded it. My principle was 'careers open to talent.' "

[1] From *Memoirs of General Bertrand*, p. 29.
[2] From Las Cases, *Mémorial de Sainte Hélène.*
[3] From B. E. O'Meara, *Napoleon in Exile,* I, 102–3: ". . . *de la boue,*" translated
literally, means "out of mud."

TO HIS BROTHER, JÉRÔME, KING OF WESTPHALIA

Fontainebleau, November 15, 1807 [4]

I enclose the constitution for your Kingdom. You must faithfully observe it. I am concerned for the happiness of your subjects, not only as it affects your reputation, and my own, but also for its influence on the whole European situation.

Don't listen to those who say that your subjects are so accustomed to slavery that they will feel no gratitude for the benefits you give them. There is more intelligence in the Kingdom of Westphalia than they would have you believe; and your throne will never be firmly established except upon the trust and affection of the common people. What German opinion impatiently demands is that men of no rank, but of marked ability, shall have an equal claim upon your favour and your employment, and that every trace of serfdom, or of a feudal hierarchy between the sovereign and the lowest class of his subjects, shall be done away with. The benefits of the Code Napoléon, public trial, and the introduction of juries, will be the leading features of your Government. And to tell you the truth, I count more upon their effects, for the extension and consolidation of your rule, than upon the most resounding victories. I want your subjects to enjoy a degree of liberty, equality, and prosperity hitherto unknown to the German people. . . . Such a method of government will be a stronger barrier between you and Prussia than the Elbe, the fortresses, and the protection of France. What people will want to return under the arbitrary Prussian rule, once it has tasted the benefits of a wise and liberal administration? In Germany, as in France, Italy, and Spain, people long for equality and liberalism. I have been managing the affairs of Europe long enough now to know that the burden of the privileged classes was resented everywhere. Rule constitutionally. Even if reason, and the enlightenment of the age, were not sufficient cause, it would be good policy for one in your position; and you will find that the backing of public opinion gives you a great natural advantage over the absolute kings who are your neighbours.

CONVERSATION WITH O'MEARA

March 3, 1817 [5]

"J'ai toujours marché avec l'opinion de grandes masses et les évènements (I have always acted in accordance with the opinion of great masses, and with events). I have always taken little notice of the opinion of individuals, and a great deal of that of the public."

[4] From J. M. Thompson, ed., Napoleon's Letters, pp. 190–91.
[5] From B. E. O'Meara, Napoleon in Exile, I, 404.

The bishops had objected to shops remaining open on Sundays: the Minister for Public Worship therefore asked for a ruling—and got it:

Osterode March 5, 1807 [6]

It is contrary to divine law to stop men, who have needs to be met on a Sunday, just as on the other days of the week, from working for their living on the Sabbath. The government could only impose such a law if it distributed free food to all those who lack it. . . . The government, then, need do nothing on this subject. . . . And if I did have to take action, I would be more inclined to command that on Sundays shops should, once church services were over, be open and workmen back at work. Since people eat every day they must be allowed to work every day.

TO MELZI, VICE-PRESIDENT OF THE ITALIAN REPUBLIC

Paris, July 8, 1802 [6]

The draft law . . . on the freedom of the grain trade is quite inappropriate. You cannot make general rules to regulate grain supplies. . . . All a government can do is to permit or forbid the export of grain as circumstances dictate. Certainly grain prices must not be too low: but of the two evils, it is better to have prices which are too low than too high. Of the thousand things over which the working man and the landowner are divided, the price of grain is the one on which there is the sharpest opposition of interests. And therefore it is a matter—perhaps the only matter—on which the Government must always favor wage earners as against property owners: for unless this is done . . . the poorer people rise in revolt. . . .

CONVERSATIONS WITH O'MEARA

October 17, 1816 [7]

"I instituted the new nobility to crush the old one, and to satisfy the people, as the greatest part of those I ennobled had sprung from themselves—every private soldier had a right to [expect he could earn] the title of duke. I believe that I acted wrong in doing this, however, as it lessened that system of equality which pleased the people so much."

[6] From Napoleon, *Correspondance*, translated by M. Hutt.
[7] From B. E. O'Meara, *Napoleon in Exile*, I, 164.

WITH BERTRAND

February 19, 1821[8]
"Only an aristocracy is unchanging and in a position to laugh at liberty and at freedom of the press. Which is why I sought to create an aristocracy. I worked at it for fifteen years, and if today there exists a certain amount of stability in France, it is due to that."

WITH O'MEARA

March 3, 1817 [9]
"I have always been of opinion, that the sovereignty lay in the people. In fact, the imperial government was a kind of republic. Called to the head of it by the voice of the nation, my maxim was 'careers open to talent' without distinction of birth or fortune, and this system of equality is the reason that your [English] oligarchy hate me so much."

WITH CHAPTAL [10]

"Ambition," the Emperor said one day, "is what principally motivates men. You try hard so long as you hope to climb, but once you reach the top you can see nothing ahead of you. I created principalities to leave something for the senators and marshals to be ambitious about and thereby keep them dependent on me."

AND WITH O'MEARA AGAIN

August 27, 1816 [11]
On my return from Elba I saw an old woman hobbling along with the help of a crutch. I was not recognised. "Well, *ma bonne,* and where are you going? . . ." "*Ma foi,*" replied the old dame, "they tell me the emperor is here, and I want to see him before I die." "Bah," said I, "what do you want to see him for? What have you gained by him? He is a tyrant [just like] the others. You have only changed one tyrant for another, Louis for Napoleon." "*Mais, monsieur,* that may be; but, after all, he is the king of the *people,* and the Bourbons were the kings of the nobles. We have chosen *him,* and if we are to have a tyrant, let him be one chosen by ourselves." "There," said Napoleon, "you have the sentiments of the French nation expressed by an old woman."

[8] From *Memoirs of General Bertrand,* p. 71.
[9] From B. E. O'Meara, *Napoleon in Exile,* I, 405.
[10] From Count J. Chaptal, *Mes Souvenirs sur Napoléon* (Paris, 1893), p. 324; translated by K. Gladstone.
[11] From B. E. O'Meara, *Napoleon in Exile,* I, 105.

4
Governing and Commanding

[October 1818][1]

The revolution of 1789 was a general attack of the masses of the nation upon the privileged classes. The nobles occupied, either directly or indirectly, all judicial posts . . . and . . . enjoyed various feudal rights. They were exempt from paying taxes to the state, and yet they enjoyed . . . exclusive possession of all lucrative and honourable employments. The principal aim of the revolution was to abolish these privileges, to remove these abuses, to destroy what still remained of the ancient feudal edifice, to break the last links of the people's bondage, and to subject every citizen equally to support the expenses and charges of the state. It . . . established equality of rights. . . .

Before the revolution, France was composed of provinces, divided in an irregular manner, differing among one another both in extent and population. These provinces had . . . a great number of particular laws for the administration of civil and criminal justice. It was an assemblage of different states not yet [fused] together. The revolution destroyed all these little nations in order to form from them a great one. . . .

The States-General of 1789 and the Legislative Assembly (1791–92) . . . gave the death blow to the *ancien régime*.

The Constituent Assembly (1789–91) laid down principles and founded nothing.

The Convention (1792–95) made everything level; it allowed nothing of the *ancien régime* to remain; its passage, a veritable torrent of lava, destroyed all that it could . . . reach; it was splendid as the defender of national honour and independence . . . [but] it was atrocious as the administrator of France's internal affairs.

---

[1] From C. T. de Montholon, *History of the captivity of Napoleon at St. Helena* (London, 1846–47), III, 41–2, 47. The count remained on St. Helena throughout the period of Napoleon's exile; he died in 1853, at the age of seventy.

CONVERSATION WITH CAULAINCOURT

December, 1812 [2]

It is said that I love power. Well, has anyone, in any department, cause for complaint? Never have the prisons been so empty. Does anyone complain of a prefect without obtaining justice? Forty-five out of every fifty complaints are decided against the prefects. The government is strong, my hand is steady, and the officials are sensible that I shall not slacken the reins. So much the better for the people, for while this system traces out a definite path for each to follow, my watchfulness inspires the authorities with vigilance; officials fulfill their duties; all citizens and all forms of property are equally well protected. The roads have never been safer. Thanks to me there are no more squabbles, no more petty spites, no more parties. Such things are no longer known in France. I have never wished to be anyone's man, I have never sought support from public opinion nor from any class of men. I rely on myself, on the results of what I have successively created in the interests of France, on my institutions, on the moral effect of a government . . . that is not swayed by outside opinions. Whether as First Consul or as Emperor, I have been the people's king; I have governed for the nation and in its interests. . . . This is well known throughout France and the French people love me. I say French people, and by that I mean the nation. . . .

A CONVERSATION WITH THIBAUDEAU [3]

What makes a good general? The answer is those qualities which serve a man well in public life: acumen, shrewdness, mental finesse, administrative ability, eloquence, not the eloquence of a lawyer but the eloquence that rouses an army. Finally, understanding of other people. These are all civilian qualities and the general who is successful is the general who has them all. It is because he is thought to have the finest brain that the soldier obeys and respects him. You need only hear a soldier talking in camp; he has greater respect for the general who knows how to use his brain than for the general

---

[2] From J. Hanoteau, ed., *Memoirs of General Caulaincourt*, II, 249–50.

[3] From A. C. Thibaudeau, *Mémoires sur le Consulat, 1799–1804* (Paris, 1827), pp. 78–80; translated by K. Gladstone.

Thibaudeau was one of the regicides who had sat in the Convention and who became one of Napoleon's prefects. Born in 1765, he survived to sit in Napoleon III's Senate (d. 1854).

with the greatest courage. . . . Civil qualities are superior to mere force: bayonets are lowered before the priest who speaks in the name of heaven and before the man who really knows what he's talking about. . . . It is not because I am a general that I rule France, but because the nation believes that I have the civilian qualities needed for government. If the nation did not have this opinion of me, my government could not survive.

One should not use the standards of the past to reason about the present. There are thirty million of us, all connected by the ideas, the possessions, the interests we have. Three or four hundred thousand soldiers are nothing compared to this mass of people. And after all, the soldiers themselves are the children of civilians. The army is in fact the nation.

Take the military mind. You can see that the only law it is aware of is the law of force and that this is its sole term of reference. The civilian mind, on the contrary, is aware only of the general good. The soldier's method is to want to do everything like a despot, while the civilian's way is to submit everything to discussion, to verification, to reason. . . . Discussion generates the light of reason and understanding. I have no hesitation, therefore, in considering the civilian mind pre-eminent over the military mind.

NOTE DICTATED TO HIS BROTHER, LUCIEN, MINISTER OF HOME AFFAIRS

Paris, December 25, 1799 [4]

If I did not have to go to war, I should initiate the prosperity of France through the local authorities. If one is to regenerate a nation, it is much simpler to deal with its inhabitants a thousand at a time than to pursue the romantic ideal of individual welfare. Each [commune] in France represents 1,000 inhabitants. . . . The Minister will therefore begin by having a general inventory made of the 36,000 communes—this has always been wanting. . . . Local bodies will be divided into three classes: those which are in debt, those which just pay their way, and those which show a surplus. The second and third classes are in a minority, and there need be no hurry to deal with them. The point is to restore solvency to those which are in debt. . . . Once this inventory is drawn up, the prefects and the sub-prefects . . . will bring the whole force of the administration to bear upon the insolvent municipalities, and to get rid at once of any mayors . . . who do not see eye to eye with them as to local improvement

---

[4] From J. M. Thompson, ed., *Napoleon's Letters*, pp. 81, 83.

and regeneration. It will be the duty of the prefect to visit these bodies at least twice a year, and of the sub-prefect four times a year, under penalty of dismissal. He will make a monthly report to the Minister about each municipality, stating the results of what he has tried to do, and what still remains to be done.

I should like proposals for a prize for those mayors who have got their municipalities out of debt within two years: whereas, in the case of any municipality which is not solvent at the end of five years, the Government will nominate a special commission to take over its administration. . . .

TO THE COUNT OF MONTALIVET, MINISTER OF HOME AFFAIRS

Saint-Cloud, November 15, 1811 [4a]

I am going to hold a Council for Home Affairs once a week from November to February—fourteen meetings in all. The first subject to be dealt with will be . . . commerce and manufactures. Then we will take the different departments of your Ministry, in order. Three meetings can be devoted to the business of Roads and Bridges, and Public Works; three, at intervals of a fortnight, will deal with the balance-sheet of the city of Paris, and with towns with revenues of over a million a year, and with the auditing of deposit companies' accounts; two, also a fortnight apart, with . . . water works, prisons, and workhouses; one, with departmental indebtedness, and the budgeting for the one per cent. tax, both fixed and variable: that will leave other meetings to deal with new appointments to prefectures, and mayoralties of the approved towns, with mines, libraries, public education, sciences and arts, and the other subjects that fall under your department. . . . The accounts for 1810–11 will be examined, so that, if the grants allowed are inadequate, they can be supplemented wherever necessary. . . . After dealing with the accounts of each branch of the administration, we will consider the relevant legislation, and propose whatever changes may contribute towards ultimate perfection in every department. The minutes of these Council meetings, taken as a whole, should provide both a summary of the financial position . . . and a statement of the grounds for the changes and improvements carried out. The upshot of all the reports will be:

(1) a statement of the actual expenses for 1810
(2) an approximate statement of the expenses for 1811; and
(3) the budget for 1812.

[4a] From J. M. Thompson, ed., *Napoleon's Letters*, pp. 261–62.

NAPOLEON IN COMMITTEE

at Dusseldorf, 1811 [5]

[The Emperor] appointed a review of the troops at 8 A.M., a Council of Administration at 10, and a Council of State at 2 P.M. . . . I awaited the [first meeting] confidently as I fancied that the Emperor would come very well disposed towards it. I was mistaken. The meeting was stormy and I had to bear the brunt of it. . . . First the Emperor attacked me about my system of accounts, which he picked to pieces [in] his rough way, and made out to be ill arranged. I could only reply to him by reconstructing the business as I understood it myself, and as in my opinion everyone ought to understand it. . . . The Emperor would not give up, and summoned the director of the accounts of the grand-duchy [of Berg] to the sitting. . . . He worked out his answer exactly as I had done. "There is nothing to be done with these people," said the Emperor, harshly, "it is a conspiracy of disorder."

And this good German director answered, "No, Sire, be quite easy; there is no disorder. Your Majesty has not had time to see that it is all right."

The Emperor . . . [next] attacked me about the public debt, for its daily increase by indirect means, without his being informed. I answered that the debt could only increase in one way, and that very direct, by the pensions His Majesty was pleased to grant. . . .

"Again, what are these deposits that appear in section eight of the receipts, and increase in one year by more than twelve thousand pounds? . . . [Nothing but] disorder."

"Sire, . . . the ancient rules of the grand-duchy required that the receipts from estates owned by minors . . . should be lodged in the public treasury. Private persons are also allowed to place their capital there. When they wish to withdraw it they inform the Treasury . . . and it is repaid. . . . These sums bear an interest of four per cent. . . . but the Treasury [profits] by placing the funds in France. . . ."

At this moment the thunder broke. In vain I proved that the grand-duchy thus obtained profits which I . . . [noted] exactly in my accounts; in vain I . . . insisted . . . that I had found this arrangement . . . long established, that its suppression would be the rupture of a bond of honourable confidence between the Prince and his subjects,

[5] From *Life and Adventures of Count Beugnot*, trans. C. Yonge (London, 1871), I, 339–47.

The count (1761–1835) had sat in the Legislative Assembly and was one of the first prefects Napoleon appointed. In 1808 he was appointed Minister of Finance to Jérôme, King of Westphalia; he also watched over the finances of Berg from 1808 to 1810.

and that long use had rendered it necessary. The Emperor flew into a regular passion. . . . He wanted to see [every detail relating to] this fund. I begged the Emperor to order it to be verified that moment, and before I left the Council. I spoke these last words in a tone of great emotion, and those present saw I could hardly restrain my tears. The Emperor called on the Minister of the Interior to be so good as to tell him what he knew of the fund, [and he] answered that he could add nothing to what . . . I had just said; and he could only repeat that the suppression of this arrangement would have had a bad effect on the duchy. . . . The Emperor's anger resolved itself into an animated allocution on the dangers of credit, the ways . . . thus opened to the young Grand Duke, who on his accession would find a machine ready prepared to enable him to get hold of the fortune of his subjects. . . . Then came a digression on the foolish expenses that the German princes run into; and as an instance, an account of a day's sport given to him in the kingdom of Würtemberg, which was only a disgusting butchery, and had cost I do not know how many thousands of pounds.

Beugnot was, he says, glad to see the Emperor heading off on that tack: perhaps he would now ease up a bit—before the Council got on with a matter only too likely to lead to more "thunder," namely the question of authorizations for expenditure.

. . . It is well known that the expenses of the twelve months of the year were fixed once for all by the budget; but on the first of each month the Emperor issued orders for the payment to the different ministers of the sums considered necessary for . . . the month, and it was only in virtue of this order, and in exact accordance with the sums there stated, that the treasury cashed the orders of the ministers. This method had been applied to the grand-duchy. . . . As you can imagine, I never failed to forward on the 20th of each month . . . a note of the funds necessary for the various services during the ensuing month. . . . But sometimes, and especially during the last Austrian war . . . [the necessary orders for payment] had been delayed for two months. . . . Yet we encountered expenses which admitted of no delay, and I had taken upon myself to draw provisional orders upon the Treasury without authorisation; and it was a remarkable thing that these orders, though subsequently authorised, did not escape the Emperor's observation in the examination he made of the condition of the treasury three years afterwards. . . .

The Emperor, of course, wanted to know why the rules had been broken, and Beugnot explained, detailing the careful procedures he had always followed on such occasions.

A slight murmur [from those around the table] . . . made me believe that my answers had been considered satisfactory; and so perhaps they were by all except the Emperor.

"That is all very fine," replied His Majesty. "I know nothing that people cannot manage to justify by necessity, especially when they constitute themselves judges of that necessity. . . . The object of payment orders for the grand-duchy, as for . . . France . . . , is to keep the keys of both treasuries always in my pocket. When I sign a payment order I lend this key, and it may be legally used; but when I have not lent it, there is no other way of getting into the treasury but by breaking open the doors; and when doors are forced to obtain money, what is it called? It would be a fine thing to see the ministers of France and those of Italy . . . [grabbing] . . . public [money like] those of the grand-duchy, and every one making out credits for himself after his own fashion. It would be worse than the Tower of Babel!" . . . The hour appointed for the Council [of State] had struck. So the Emperor raised the siege, and left me quite convinced that it was the last time I should have the honour of working with him. So persuaded was I of this that I did not accompany him to the Council, where . . . [he amazed] the good Germans, as they did not know how he had become acquainted with their interests, and wondered at the superior manner in which he handled them. M. Fuschius said to me when he came from the Council, "Indeed, monsieur, I have read a great many things about the Emperor, and heard more, but I did not yet know him: he's more than a man."

"I . . . [agree]," I answered: "he's a devil."

Five or six persons were present when this remark slipped out; and it was repeated . . . to the Emperor; but he . . . said gaily, "He is right, for I kept him on hot coals all the morning."

I went home, told my wife my misfortune, and advised her to pack . . . for I was disgraced, and certainly a message would come to demand the return of my portfolio. We were mournfully considering our fate, when a messenger from the Emperor was announced. . . . I found a servant who brought me . . . an invitation to dinner with the Emperor. . . . [By dinner time] the feelings by which I had at first been agitated . . . had given place to . . . [a certain] resentment at the way I had been treated all the morning, and I went to the Emperor in a tolerably moody frame [of mind]. . . . I think if His Majesty had continued to hold the same tone to me I should not have diminished in any way the profound respect which I owed him, but should have begged him to set me at liberty. I entered with a sad and distrustful face. . . . I made two low bows, and kept apart. He came to me.

"Well, you numbskull, have you recovered your wits?"

I bowed lower, without having a word to answer. The Emperor

immediately took hold of my ear, which was a . . . mark of favour towards the man who had the luck to receive it. All was forgotten, repaired, embellished by this imperial gesture of familiarity. . . . I had in a moment returned to affection and gratitude.

The Emperor blamed me for having been so obstinate about the system of accounts, where I was wrong. I admitted . . . it; and if he had chosen he could have made me admit to faults even graver—and equally untrue.

IN CONVERSATION WITH CAULAINCOURT

December, 1812 [6]

You may not have been made much of in the Emperor's service, but at least you were sure that no intrigue or plot behind your back would poison his mind against you. . . . The more you were maligned to the Emperor the more persistent he was in . . . [establishing] the truth as to the faults alleged against you, and the more obstinate he showed himself in retaining you near him.

"I am my own minister," he often used to say. "It is I who conduct affairs. I am powerful enough to get the very best out of mediocre men. Probity, discretion and activity are all that I demand of a man."

[And Caulaincourt adds:] His low opinion of men in general rarely made the Emperor demand of them greater abilities or virtues than they actually [possessed].

OBSERVATIONS TO THE SENATE

December, 1812 [7]

Timid and cowardly soldiers . . . are the reason why nations lose their independence; but pusillanimous officials destroy the majesty of the law, the rights of the throne, and social order itself. When I undertook the regeneration of France, I prayed Providence to grant me a certain number of years. The work of destruction is the work of an instant; but to rebuild needs the help of time. What the state most needs, [he repeated], is courageous officials.

[6] From J. Hanoteau, ed., *Memoirs of General Caulaincourt*, II, 328–29.

[7] From *The Memoirs of Chancellor Pasquier*, trans. C. Roche (London, 1894), II, 51.

Napoleon had been incensed by the feeble (or treacherous) inactivity of some officials, including the prefect of the Seine Department, when conspirators had declared him, in October, to have died in Russia. Pasquier (1767–1862), a lawyer before the Revolution, was one of Napoleon's Counsellors of State and Louis XVIII's Minister of Justice.

TO HIS STEPSON, EUGÈNE, VICEROY OF THE KINGDOM OF ITALY [8]

Milan, June 5, 1805 [8]

By entrusting you with the government of Our Kingdom of Italy, we have given you proof of the respect your conduct has inspired in Us. But you are still at an age when one does not realize the perversity of men's hearts; I cannot therefore too strongly recommend to you prudence and circumspection. Our Italian subjects are more deceitful by nature than the citizens of France. The only way in which you can keep their respect, and serve their happiness, is by letting no one have your complete confidence, and by never telling anyone what you really think of the ministers and high officials of your court) Dissimulation, which comes naturally at a maturer age, has to be emphasized and inculcated at yours. If you ever find yourself speaking unnecessarily, and from the heart, say to yourself: "I have made a mistake," and don't do it again. Show respect for the nation you govern, and show it all the more as you discover less grounds for it. . . . The aim of your administration is the happiness of My Italian peoples; . . . you must . . . count yourself a failure unless the Italians believe that you love them. . . . Learn their language; frequent their society; single them out for special attention at public functions; like what they like, and approve what they approve.)

The less you talk, the better: you aren't well enough educated, and you haven't enough knowledge, to take part in informal debates. Learn to listen, and remember that silence is often as effective as a display of knowledge. Don't be ashamed to ask questions. Though a viceroy, you are only twenty-three; and however much people flatter you, in reality they all know your limitations and honour you less for what they believe you to be than for what they hope you will become. . . .

Don't preside often over the State Council; you have too little experience to do so successfully—though I see no objection to your attending it. . . . Anyhow, never make a speech there: they would listen to you, and would not answer you back: but they would see at once that you aren't competent to discuss business. So long as a prince holds his tongue, his power is incalculable; he should never talk, unless he knows he is the ablest man in the room. . . .

Work with your ministers twice a week—once with each of them separately, and once with them all together in Council. Half the battle will be won when your ministers and councillors realize that your only object in consulting them is to listen to reason and to prevent yourself being taken by surprise.

[8] From J. M. Thompson, ed., Napoleon's Letters, pp. 123–24.

AN INSTRUCTION FOR SENATORS

April, 1805 [9]

His Majesty desires you to go to your *senatorerie* before 21 May
to reside there continuously for three months, and to travel round all
the Departments . . . [in it]. The ostensible object both of your journey and of your residence will be to get to know the situation, character, condition, and value of the property from which the income of
your *senatorerie* is derived. Actually your most important duty will be
to supply Us with trustworthy and positive information on any point
which may interest the Government; and to this end, you will send Us
a direct report, once a week. . . .

You will realize that complete secrecy must be observed as to this
confidential mission. If it got about, all enlightened people would
avoid you, honest men would refuse to have any communication with
you, and you would have nothing to report but treacherous and mali-
cious denunciations. At the same time, the public officials, most of
whom deserve our confidence, would be discredited and discouraged,
and these special missions, which are meant to enlighten the Government, would be no better than an odious inquisition, tending to dis-
organize the public service.

(1) You are to discover what is the character, conduct, and capacity
of the public officials, both in the administrative and the judicial departments;

(2) What principles the clergy hold, and how much influence they
have;

(3) Who the outstanding men are in each part of your . . . [area],
in virtue of their character, wealth, opinions, and popular influence;
and to what class of society they belong.

You will draw up detailed returns of all information about persons,
basing your judgements upon genuine and established facts, and send
in these returns to Us.

(4) You will investigate, in the different classes and cantons, the
state of public opinion on (i) the Government; (ii) religion; (iii) conscription; (iv) the road tax; (v) the incidence of indirect taxation.

(5) You will notice whether there are any persons in hiding from
conscription; if so, how many; and whether a rising of any kind is to
be feared from this cause;

How the *gendarmerie* does its work; and what individual members
of it are noticeable either for their zeal, or for their neglect of duty;

The number and kinds of criminal offences, and whether they are
isolated acts, or the result of public gatherings;

[9] From J. M. Thompson, ed., *Napoleon's Letters*, pp. 117–19.

What is generally thought about the institution of the jury, and what its effect is upon criminal trials.

(6) You will look into the state of public education, both in the primary and secondary schools, and in the lycées, and inquire why some of these establishments are successful, and some slack. You will draw up one list of teachers of marked ability, and another of those who have done nothing to deserve public confidence.

(7) You will study the state of agriculture, commerce, and manufacture; and find out what individuals are distinguished by intelligence or success in these different spheres.

(8) The state of the food supply, and what is expected of this year's harvest.

(9) You will observe the conditions of the roads, and find out for what general or special reasons they deteriorate. . . .

You will send us separate memoirs . . . on all these subjects in succession.

TO HIS LIBRARIAN

Paris, July 23, 1801 [10]

Citizen Ripault is to see that he is supplied every day with all the papers that come out, except the eleven political papers. He will read them carefully, make an abstract of everything they contain likely to affect the public point of view, especially with regard to religion, philosophy, and political opinion. He will send me this abstract between five and six o'clock every day.

Once every ten days he will send me an analysis of all the books or pamphlets which have appeared during that period. . . .

He will take pains to procure copies of all the plays which are produced, and to analyse them for me. . . .

TO HIS BROTHER JOSEPH, EX-KING OF SPAIN

Reims, March 14, 1814 [11]

I will be master *everywhere* in France, as long as I have a breath in my body. Your character is quite different from mine. You like flattering people, and falling in with their ideas: I like people to please me, and to fall in with mine. I am master to-day, every bit as much as at Austerlitz.

[10] From J. M. Thompson, ed., *Napoleon's Letters*, p. 93.
[11] *Ibid.*, p. 302.

TO FOUCHÉ, MINISTER OF POLICE

Paris, April 5, 1800 [12]

The Consuls of the Republic intend that *Le Bien Informé, Hommes Libres* and *Défenseurs de la Patrie* shall cease publication, unless the proprietors procure editors of good character and of incorruptible patriotism. You must insist that every issue of these journals is signed by a recognized editor.

You are to instruct the Prefect of Police to take whatever steps are necessary:

(1) To prevent any bill-posting on the walls of Paris, or any [sale] of papers or pamphlets without a police licence;

(2) To prevent the print-dealers displaying . . . anything contrary to sound morals, or to the policy of the Government. . . .

Lastly, you are to inform M. [Tom] Paine that the police have information as to his suspicious behaviour, and that on the first complaint he will be sent back to America, the country to which he belongs.[13]

TO MARSHAL BERTHIER

Saint-Cloud, August 5, 1806 [14]

I imagine that you have arrested the Augsburg and Nuremberg booksellers. My intention is to bring them before a courtmartial, and to have them shot within twenty-four hours. It is no ordinary crime to spread defamatory writings in places occupied by the French armies, and to incite the inhabitants against them. It is high treason. The sentence must declare that, since, wherever an army may be, it is the duty of its commander to see to its safety, such and such individuals, having been found guilty of trying to rouse the inhabitants of Suabia against the French Army, are condemned to death. . . .

You are to have the sentence published all over Germany.

---

[12] *Ibid.*, pp. 86–87.

Joseph Fouché (b. 1759), Duke of Otranto, was another regicide. He succeeded in serving not only Napoleon but also Louis XVIII as Minister of Police before he died in 1820.

[13] "Do you call this a Republic?," asked Paine, disgusted, in 1802 (quoted in R. Palmer, *Age of the Democratic Revolution* [Princeton, 1964] II, 571), and he left for America.

[14] From J. M. Thompson, ed., *Napoleon's Letters*, p. 149.

Three men were condemned to death on August 25 for publishing a pamphlet deploring the French occupation of Germany; one of them, Palm, was shot. Berthier, Prince of Wagram, was for years Napoleon's chief of staff; having rallied, though, to the Bourbons in 1814, he neither rejoined nor fought against the Emperor on his return from Elba, but committed suicide.

NAPOLEON IN THE COUNCIL OF STATE

1806 [15]

. . . Of all our institutions public education is the most important. Everything depends on it, the present and the future. It is essential that the morals and the political ideas of the generation which is now growing up should no longer be dependent upon the news of the day or the circumstances of the moment. Above all we must secure unity: we must be able to cast a whole generation in the same mould. Men already differ sufficiently in their inclinations, their characters, and everything that education does not give and cannot reform. It is now our business to reorganize the teaching profession and to make it a career capable of attracting those to whom it appeals.

In the first stages of this career . . . it is essential that celibacy should be compulsory. In the lower ranks of the teaching hierarchy the heart must not be distracted by family ties nor the mind by care for the morrow. Marriage will be permitted in the higher ranks. . . . Finally, the career of public teaching . . . will provide posts at the top which will place those who hold them among the great dignitaries of the State.

Let us have a body of doctrine which does not vary and a body of teachers which does not die. No longer will masters transmit to their pupils their own principles and their own preferences, but the principles and sentiments drawn from the body of which they form part. How can we trust men who have formed themselves to form other men? What man can thread his way unaided through life without any light but his own . . . ?

A NOTE ON THE EDUCATION OF GIRLS

Finkenstein, May 15, 1807 [16]

The first problem that needs your attention is the employment and distribution of time. What are the girls brought up at Écouen going to be taught? You must begin with religion in all its strictness. Don't allow any compromise on this point. Religion is an all-important matter in a public school for girls. Whatever people may say, it is the mother's surest safeguard, and the husband's. What we ask of educa-

---

[15] From Marquis de Noailles, ed., *The Life and Memoirs of Count Molé*, 2 vols. (London, 1923), I, 61.

[16] From J. M. Thompson, ed., *Napoleon's Letters*, pp. 180–81.

The lycées, established in 1802 and of which there were thirty-seven in 1807, were intended to educate boys heading towards careers in the civil service, law, and other professions useful to the state, which controlled these secondary schools.

tion is not that girls should think, but that they should believe. The weakness of women's brains, the instability of their ideas, the place they will fill in society, their need for perpetual resignation . . . — all this can only be met by religion, and by religion of a gentle and charitable kind. . . . In the lycées I only prescribed the necessary minimum . . . of religious observance. At Écouen matters must be entirely different. Nearly all the knowledge taught there must be that of the gospel. I want the place to produce, not women of charm, but women of virtue. . . .

NAPOLEON TO THE EMPRESS JOSÉPHINE, AT MAINZ

Posen, December 3, 1806 [17]

I see [from your Nov. 27 letter] that you are really worked up about this. . . . I told you that . . . you could join me when, and only when, we were settled in our winter quarters: so you will have to wait a bit longer. The greater one becomes the less one can do as one pleases: events and circumstances determine one's actions. . . . Like other pretty women you think that what you want has to be: whereas I know that I am merely a slave—to a master totally lacking pity or sentiment. My master is the hard fact, how things are ["la nature des choses"].

Warsaw, January 23, 1807 [17]

Your letter of 15 Jan. has arrived. I cannot allow women to make such a journey—the roads are bad, deep in mud and dangerous. Return to Paris. . . . Perhaps I shall be there soon. I laughed when I read what you say about having married a husband in order to be with him: I in my innocence thought that the wife was made for her husband and the husband for his country, his family and for glory. Forgive my ignorance: you can always learn something from the ladies.

Adieu my dear. . . . Tell yourself "[His decision] proves how precious I am to him."

CONVERSATIONS WITH GOURGAUD

January 9, 1817 [18]

In France women are considered too highly. They should not be regarded as on equality with men. In reality they are nothing more than machines for producing children. . . . Disorder would [be] introduced into society if women abandoned the state of dependence which is their rightful position.

[17] From P. André, ed., *Oeuvres amoureuses de Napoleon* (Paris, 1912), pp. 123, 135; translated by M. Hutt.
[18] From G. Gourgaud, *St. Helena Journal*, p. 119.

WITH BERTRAND

January 26, 1821 [19]

Upon my return from the campaign of Wagram [1809] I was at the height of my fame and power. I was forty, and I was afraid that if I waited much longer I might not have any more children. I discussed the matter with the Empress. I explained to her that unless I had a child my dynasty [would be] without any foundation. My nephews could not replace me. . . . A child born to the purple, to the throne, in the Palace of the Tuileries, stood, in the eyes of the nation and of the people, for something quite different from my brother's son, who would naturally be of much less interest to them. Reasons of State and the continuation of my dynasty forced me to have a child. . . . She had been unable to give me any. . . . She could be sure that I would always treat her well. . . . If she wanted posterity to look upon her as an Empress . . . my dynasty must be firmly established, and for that to come about I, the Emperor, must have heirs.

"The divorce is necessary," I told her. "It will take place because I desire it. There are, however, two ways of going about it. Either with your consent or without it. Choose!" . . .

The Empress felt faint so I sent for her lady-in-waiting. For three days Joséphine pretend to be ill, and refused to take any food. I ignored the whole matter. Then one morning Joséphine sent for me. I found her attractively dressed as was her wont. She told me: "I have made up my mind. I agree to the divorce." In the course of our first conversation she had said: "Tell me, who is it you wish to marry?" "Good heavens, I have no idea," I replied.

TO HIS STEPSON EUGÈNE, VICEROY OF THE KINGDOM OF ITALY

Saint-Cloud, April 14, 1806 [20]

As regards the succession, it is not my custom to look to other people's advice for my political opinions; and my Italian subjects know me too well to forget that there is more in my little finger than in all their heads put together. In Paris, where people are more enlightened than in Italy, they hold their tongues, and bow to the judgment of a man who has proved that he saw further and more clearly than they did. I am surprised that in Italy they are less obliging.

[19] From *Memoirs of General Bertrand*, p. 27.
[20] From J. M. Thompson, ed., *Napoleon's Letters*, pp. 141, 243.
C. F. Lebrun had sat in the Estates General of 1789 and had been in prison during Robespierre's regime. He and Cambacérès replaced Sieyès and Ducos as the other two Consuls in December, 1799.

TO PRINCE LEBRUN, LIEUTENANT-GENERAL
OF THE EMPEROR IN HOLLAND

Paris, September 25, 1810 [20]

You speak to me of the grievances of the Amsterdam folk, of their anxieties, and of their discontent. Do these Dutchmen really take me for a Grand Pensionary Barnevelt? . . . I shall do what suits the interests of my Empire. I despise the clamour of madmen who think they know my interests better than I know them myself. . . . I did not take over the Government of Holland in order to consult the common people of Amsterdam, or to do what other people want. The French nation has been wise enough, at various times, to rely upon my judgment—you know that as well as anyone. My hope is that the Dutch will come to have the same opinion of me.

TO HIS BROTHER LOUIS, KING OF HOLLAND

Paris, April 3, 1810 [21]

It would not be appropriate to issue a proclamation to your people. Simply send a message to your parliament to say that the independence of Holland can exist only so long as it is not incompatible with the interests of France . . . and that unless care is taken to avoid thwarting the system [of trade] laid down by France, Holland may lose her independence. . . .

TO HIS STEPSON EUGÈNE, VICEROY OF THE KINGDOM OF ITALY

Saint-Cloud, August 23, 1810 [22]

I have received your letter. . . . All the raw silk from the Kingdom of Italy goes to England, for there are no silk factories in Germany. It is therefore quite natural that I should wish to divert it from this route to the advantage of my French manufacturers: otherwise my silk factories, one of the chief supports of French commerce, would suffer substantial losses. I cannot agree with your observations. My principle is: France first. You must never lose sight of the fact that, if English commerce is supreme on the high seas, it is due to her sea power: it is therefore to be expected that, as France is the strongest land power, she should claim commercial supremacy on the continent. . . .

[21] From Napoleon, *Correspondance*, translated by M. Hutt.
Three months later, Holland was annexed to France in order that the "continental system" might be properly enforced there.
[22] From J. M. Thompson, ed., *Napoleon's Letters*, pp. 241–42.

Piedmont . . . produces silk too; and there also I have prohibited its export to any country except France. Why should Piedmont be treated in one way, and the Kingdom of Italy in another? . . . I understand Italian affairs better than anyone else. It is no use for Italy to make plans that leave French prosperity out of account; she must face the fact that the interests of the two countries hang together. Above all, she must be careful not to give France any reason for annexing her; for if it paid France to do this, who could stop her? So make this your motto too: France first.

If I were to lose a great battle, a million . . . —nay, two million— [French] men . . . would flock to my banners, and every purse in the country would be opened for me; but my Kingdom of Italy would desert me. I find it odd, then, that there should be any unwillingness to help the French manufacturers in what is only another way of damaging the English.

A CONVERSATION WITH CAULAINCOURT

December, 1812 [23]

"Europe," [said Napoleon] "should think of only one enemy. And that enemy is the colossus of Russia!" I answered the Emperor frankly. "In fact it is Your Majesty they fear. . . . The [Powers] are afraid of a universal monarchy. Your dynasty is already spreading everywhere, and other dynasties fear to see it established . . . in their own countries. And what has stirred up the people even more than the Governments is the military regime imposed upon Germany under the administration of [Marshal Davout], Prince of Eckmühl."

The Emperor listened and replied not only without ill-humour but with real cordiality. . . . He smiled at the things which touched him nearest, maintaining an air of taking them in good part and of wishing to encourage me in saying all that I thought. At the things which doubtless seemed to him rather strongly expressed he reached for my ear to tweak it; and as he could not find it under my bonnet, my neck or my cheek received the pinch—a kindly rather than an irritable one. He was in such a good mood that he admitted the truth of some of the points I brought forward. Others he refuted. . . . He remarked that particular interests might here and there have been disturbed by police measures, or by combinations of circumstances which had nothing to do with the end he had in view. The people, however, were too enlightened, he said, not to see, from the very system on which the countries he had [taken over] were administered,

[23] From J. Hanoteau, ed., *Memoirs of General Caulaincourt*, II, 143–45, 149, 162–63.

that our laws, under which they now lived, offered real guarantees
to every citizen against all arbitrary action. He insisted that our administration was based upon principles that were broadly conceived,
noble, adapted to the ideas of the country, and suited to the real
needs of the people. He went on to say:

"I could treat them like conquered countries, but I administer
them [in the same way as I do] France. They are wrong to complain. It is the checks on trade that irk them. But those depend on
considerations of a higher order, to which the interests of France
must also yield. Only peace with England can end those inconveniences and their complaints. They need only be patient. Two
years of persevering effort . . . [and] England will be forced to conclude a peace consistent with the commercial rights of all nations.
Then they will forget the inconveniences they complain of, while
the consequent prosperity, and the state of affairs that will then be
established, will for the most part provide means for the prompt repair of all their losses. . . .

"It is said—and you are the first to say it, Caulaincourt—that I
abuse my power. I admit it, but I do it for the good of the Continent
at large. Now England thoroughly abuses her strength, the power
that comes from standing isolated among the tempests. And she does
so for her own good alone. . . . [She] would sacrifice every State in
Europe, even the whole world, to further . . . [her shopkeepers']
speculations. . . . The world will realize that in time: men's eyes will
be opened, but it will be too late. If I triumph over them, Europe
will bless me. If I fall, the mask of the English will fall soon after,
and the world will see that they have thought of nothing but themselves: that they have sacrificed the peace of a continent to their interests. . . .

"I'm not ambitious. Long nights, fatigue, war—I'm too old for all
that. I like my bed . . . as well as anyone. But I want to finish my
work. . . . I want to take advantage of this opportunity to wind up
the old quarrel between England and the Continent. Similar circumstances will never occur again. What seems to offend no one but me
to-day will offend the other rulers before long. Emotion and habits of
thought are against me. The Governments are blinded by prejudice
and favouritism. . . . I am the only one who can see it now because
the others are determined to shut their eyes to it. . . . But posterity
will judge between [us and] the verdict will be for the French. They
are fighting now, whatever the world may say, only for the general
good. It is therefore just that the flags of the Continent should stand
in line with ours. The French are fighting for the most sacred rights
of nations: the English are only defending their self-assumed privileges."

A CONVERSATION WITH MONTHOLON

at St. Helena[24]

France, by her geographical situation, the fertility of her soil, the energy and intelligence of her inhabitants, is the arbitress of European states. She is among the nations of Europe what the lion is amongst the other animals. . . . In 1793 and 1794, the whole of Europe formed a coalition against her; . . . 1,300,000 Frenchmen instantly flew to arms, from the love of their country, and not, as has been said, through fear of the guillotine. Europe was conquered—condemned to recognise the French republic, and to submit to the empire of those principles of liberty and equality by which France had just been regenerated. There is nothing great of which the French are not capable; danger electrifies them; . . . the love of glory is with them like a sixth sense. . . .

Those who are called to hold the reins of such a kingdom should comprehend the full value and bearing of the favourable position which France enjoys, and never suffer *a nation which was destined to be a sun, to degenerate into a satellite.*

The whole of my policy was uniformly directed by this opinion, both during the consulate and the empire. I was ambitious to effect the fusion of all the great interests of Europe, as that of parties had been effected in France—to become the arbiter between nations and their kings; but for this, it was first necessary to gain the confidence and the friendship of the latter, which could only be acquired at the expense of my popularity with the former. I knew it, but I felt myself to be all-powerful, and took little note of those murmurs which would have been soon replaced by gratitude, had the great work of my ambition been accomplished. It was with this view that, after the battle of Austerlitz, I . . . [let] Alexander [go, he having given] . . . his imperial word that he would . . . no longer interfere in the quarrels between Austria [and France]; that after Wagram I did not partition Austria; I could have done it—nothing would have been easier. . . .

I, however, believed the protestations of the Emperor Francis. I suffered the . . . crown to remain upon his head, but I was wrong. I committed a fault, also, in marrying the archduchess Marie-Louise, because from that day I looked upon the house of Austria as a part of my family. . . . Had I not reckoned on the integrity of the Austrian alliance, the war in Russia would not have taken place. It could have been avoided. . . . It would have been enough for that purpose not to have interfered with . . . her breaches of the treaty of Tilsit,

[24] From C. T. de Montholon, *Napoleon at St. Helena,* II, 1–5.

and to have allowed Russia to sell her natural products to England in exchange for English manufactures. This was the vital question in our quarrel.

Each of my victories was a diplomatic step on my road towards restoring peace to Europe. After the battle of Marengo, as well as after those of Austerlitz, Jena, Wagram, and Dresden, I always offered a general peace; and when 400,000 Frenchmen and allies of France were on the banks of the Niemen . . . I still stretched out the hand of a brother to the Emperor Alexander, and renewed to him the solemn declaration that none of my conquests beyond the natural limits of France were made or retained for any purpose other than that of compensation or exchange at a general peace.

Had I reigned twenty years longer, I would have shown the difference between a constitutional emperor and a king of France. The kings of France have never done anything save in the interests of their dynasty, and with a view [to] increasing their feudal power by the depression of the high nobility, the extinction of the great fiefs and their reunion with the crown. . . . I would have changed the face of France and of Europe. Archimedes promised to move the world, if they only furnished him with a fulcrum for his lever; I would have made a fulcrum for myself, wherever I could have [put into action] my energy, my perseverance, and my budgets. With budgets well employed, a world may be regenerated.

5
In the Field

October 27, 1799 [1]

Yesterday Bonaparte said to me, "There is no man more pusillanimous than I when I am planning a campaign. I purposely exaggerate all the dangers and all the calamities that the circumstances
make possible. I am in a thoroughly painful state of agitation. This
does not keep me from looking quite serene in front of my entourage.
. . . Once I have made up my mind, everything is forgotten except
what leads to success."

WITH MME. DE RÉMUSAT

1804 [2]

"Military science," said Bonaparte, "consists in calculating all
the chances accurately in the first place and then giving accident exactly, almost mathematically, its place in one's calculations. It is upon
this point that one must not deceive one's self and that a [fraction]
more or less may change everything. Now, the apportioning of accident and science cannot get into any head except that of a genius,
for genius must exist wherever there is a creation, and assuredly the
grandest improvisation of the human mind is the gift of existence to
that which has it not. Accident, hazard, chance, whatever you choose to
call it—a mystery to ordinary minds—becomes a reality to superior
men. Turenne did not think about it, and so he had nothing but
method. I think," he added with a smile, "I should have beaten him."

TO MARSHAL BERTHIER, HIS CHIEF OF STAFF

Boulogne Camp, August 28, 1805 [3]

I want you to have two portable boxes made, and divided into
compartments—one for me, and the other for yourself. They are to
be so arranged that one can find out at a glance, with the help of

[1] From J. C. Herold, *Mind of Napoleon*, p. 230.

[2] From Mme. de Rémusat, *Memoirs*, I, 202–3. Turenne was Louis XIV's great
general.

[3] From J. M. Thompson, ed., *Napoleon's Letters*, p. 129.

cards, the movements of all the Austrian troops, regiment by regiment, and battalion by battalion. . . . Divide them up into as many armies as the Austrians possess, and keep compartments for any troops the Emperor may have in Hungary, or Bohemia, or the interior of his states. Once a fortnight you are to send to me a list of the changes that have taken place during the previous two weeks. . . .

CONVERSATIONS WITH CHAPTAL[4]

Genius is sometimes only a form of inspiration which does not mature towards perfection. Most often, though, genius is the art of combining ideas, an art which is constantly being perfected by observation and experience. A good idea is not always combined with a good judgment, but a good judgment always presupposes a combination of good ideas.

AND WITH BERTRAND

January [6], 1821 [5]

In war . . . the difficult thing is to assess the enemy's strength. That is something that only comes with an instinct for war. There is no such thing as intellect in war, especially not at the speed with which we make war today. That was well enough in the days when a position was held for about two months. Prince Charles took a week to do what I carried out in a quarter of an hour.

Observation, calculation, cogitation—with all the available information at hand and with a clear sense of purposes and priorities (both of which shifted, or changed, as fresh intelligence data arrived)—we can see this process operating at Boulogne in August, 1805. We can also see Napoleon waiting for the right moment to make a decision—and then, the alternatives totally discarded, pressing single-mindedly forward with the scheme he had chosen.

For eighteen months the Army of England had waited in camps around Boulogne. For six months the Emperor had waited for the outcome of orders he had given that might result in Villeneuve's fleet commanding the Channel long enough for his army to cross it: and for two months he had been watching

---

[4] From J. Chaptal, *Souvenirs*, p. 324; translated by K. Gladstone.
[5] From *Memoirs of General Bertrand*, p. 4.
Archduke Charles was commander in chief of the Austrian army.

the Austrians prepare for yet another campaign, it seemed, against France. If he captured London, Vienna would back down: but if the invasion did not come off and Austria was allowed to complete her preparations, he might well find himself up against a dangerous situation in central Europe.

TO VICE-ADMIRAL VILLENEUVE

Boulogne Camp, August 22, 1805 [6]

I hope you have arrived at Brest. Start, without losing a moment, and sail up the Channel with all the ships you have. England is ours. We are all ready: every man is on board. Appear for twenty-four hours, and the thing is done.

AND TO VICE-ADMIRAL GANTEAUME

August 22, 1805 [7]

Villeneuve is coming to Brest. He will want to drop anchor there. Don't let him do this: instead both of you must sail at once. There is not a moment to lose.

TO VICE-ADMIRAL DECRÈS

Boulogne Camp, August 22, 1805 [8]

I don't believe Villeneuve has enough character to command a frigate [let alone a fleet]. The man has no energy, no moral courage. A couple of Spanish ships are in collision; a few of his men fall sick; or he has two days' head winds . . . [or] hears a rumour that Nelson has joined Calder—and at once all his plans are changed, though there is nothing in any of these things, taken separately. To add insult to injury, he gives no details about the composition of his fleet, and doesn't say a word as to what he is going to do or not to do. He is quite unused to war, and doesn't know how to conduct it. . . . If Villeneuve [has gone to] Cadiz, my intention is that, after adding to his fleet the six ships there, and taking on board two months' provisions, he should sail into the Channel. . . .

[6] From J. M. Thompson, ed., *Napoleon's Letters*, p. 129.
[7] Napoleon, *Correspondance*, translated by M. Hutt.
[8] From J. M. Thompson, ed., *Napoleon's Letters*, p. 128.
Decrès, Minister of the Navy, had informed Napoleon earlier in the day that despatches received suggested that Villeneuve, on leaving Ferrol, was not heading towards Brest as Napoleon wished.

TO TALLEYRAND, MINISTER OF FOREIGN AFFAIRS

August 23, 1805 [9]

The more I reflect on the European situation, the more I see the urgency of taking decisive action. The fact is, I have nothing to hope for from [having it out, in talks, with Vienna]: Austria will reply with fine phrases, in order to gain time, and to prevent my doing anything this winter. [And] this winter . . . she will sign her subsidy treaty . . . and in April I shall find 100,000 Russians in Poland, paid for . . . by England. . . . Then things will be in a pretty pass. So I have made up my mind.

My fleet [under Villeneuve] left Ferrol on 14 August. . . . If it obeys orders, joins the Brest fleet, and sails up the Channel, there is still time. If on the other hand my admirals hesitate . . . and fail in their task, I have no alternative but to wait [through] the winter [before getting my invasion] flotilla across. It is a risky operation, and it would be still more so if . . . the political situation obliged me to leave here [after all], in April. . . .

TO BERTHIER, HIS CHIEF OF STAFF

August 23, 1805 [10]

Tell General Marmont . . . that if the Ferrol fleet arrives I will invade England, but that . . . if it is delayed I will postpone that operation to another year. . . . Tell him to be ready to disembark the army . . . and march towards Mainz . . . within twenty-four hours of receiving further orders to this effect. . . .

TO CAMBACÉRÈS

August 24, 1805 [10]

. . . I still have no news of my combined fleets. . . .

TO DUROC

August 24, 1805 [10]

You will leave for Berlin . . . to conclude the projected treaty of alliance with Prussia as quickly as possible. . . .

[9] *Ibid.,* p. 129.
[10] From Napoleon, *Correspondance,* translated by M. Hutt.
Marmont commanded the Second Corps near Utrecht. Cambacérès, another regicide, had been a member of the Committee of Public Safety in 1793 and one of the directors in the regime that Napoleon ousted in 1799; in 1805 he was Chancellor of the Empire. Duroc, with Napoleon in Egypt and one of his helpers in Brumaire, was created duke of Frioul in 1808; on May 22, 1813, he was mortally wounded at Napoleon's side.

TO BERTHIER

August 26, 1805 [10]

. . . Prepare the necessary orders for General Marmont. . . .

PROCLAMATION TO THE ARMY

Pfaffenhofen, October 13, 1805 [10]

Soldiers, a month ago we were camped on the Channel coast, opposite England. But then a wicked coalition forced us to hurry to the Rhine. We crossed that river. . . . Since then . . . the Neckar, the Danube, and the Lech, all of them notorious obstacles, have been crossed without our march having been delayed by a day, by an hour, by a minute. . . . The enemy, deceived by the rapidity of our movements, has been completely outmaneuvered. . . .

Remember, were it not for the army which is in front of you we should be in London today, avenging six centuries of insults. . . . Remember tomorrow that you are fighting against the allies of England. . . .

ORDER OF THE DAY

Austerlitz, December 3, 1805 [11]

Soldiers! I am very pleased with you. To-day at Austerlitz you proved that you have the courage which I knew you had. You have covered the eagles on your flags with immortal glory. In less than four hours you smashed and routed an army of one hundred thousand men commanded by the Emperors of Russia and Austria. . . . Their much vaunted infantry, though greater in numbers, could not withstand the impact of your attack. Henceforward you need fear no rivals. And so it is that in two months this third coalition has been defeated and broken up. Peace cannot be far off now but, as I promised my people, I shall only make peace if it is backed up by guarantees and includes promises of compensation to our allies. . . .

Soldiers! When everything necessary has been done to guarantee the well-being and prosperity of our country, I shall lead you back to France and there I shall do all I can to take care of your interests. My people will rejoice to see you again and you will only need to say

[11] From Napoleon, *Correspondance*, translated by K. Gladstone.

"I was at the battle of Austerlitz" for them to respond *"Voilà un brave!"*

ORDER OF THE DAY

Schönbrunn, August 5, 1809 [12]
His Majesty wishes to express his displeasure with the Marshal Prince of Ponte-Corvo [Bernadotte] for his order of the day dated 7 July which contained the following:

"Saxons, on 5 July seven or eight thousand of you pierced the centre of the enemy front in spite of the resistance of forty thousand men. At dawn on 6 July you rejoined the battle with the same doggedness and, in the midst of the havoc wrought by the enemy artillery, your columns stood firm. Napoleon himself witnessed your devotion and he numbers you among his own warriors."

Quite apart from the fact that it is His Majesty who commands his army, it is His Majesty's task, and his alone, to apportion the degree of glory which each person merits.

His Majesty owes his success to French troops and not to foreigners. The order of the day of the Prince of Ponte-Corvo, tending to encourage pretensions on the part of troops which are, to say the least, mediocre, runs counter to the truth, counter to statesmanship and counter to national honour. Victory on the 5th was due to the forces of Marshals Masséna and Oudinot.

The forces of the Prince of Ponte-Corvo did not "stand firm." In fact they were the first to beat a retreat. . . .

His Majesty wishes this expression of his displeasure to serve as an example, so that no marshal will attribute to himself the glory which belongs to others. His Majesty commands that this present order of the day, which could adversely affect the morale of the Saxon army, remain secret. It will be communicated to the marshals only.

CONVERSATION WITH MOLÉ [13]

" 'Impossible'," he said to me one day, "is a word the meaning of which is wholly relative; every man has his *impossible,* according to his capacity. The impossible," he added with a smile, "is the spectre of the timid and the refuge of the coward. Believe me, in the mouth of power the word is only a confession of impotence."

[12] From Napoleon, *Correspondance,* translated by K. Gladstone.
[13] From Marquis de Noailles, ed., *The Life and Memoirs of Count Molé,* I, 149.

TO REAR-ADMIRAL DECRÉS, MINISTER FOR THE NAVY

Saint-Cloud, April 28, 1804 [14]

I am signing a decree to-day about naval construction. I will listen to no objections. Go through all the orders you have given twice a week, and see that they are carried out. If special measures are needed, let me know. I shall not regard any excuse as valid. Under proper management I could build thirty ships of the line in a year, if I needed them.

TO MARSHAL AUGEREAU, DUKE OF CASTIGLIONE

Nogent, February 21, 1814 [15]

What! six hours after the first troops from Spain had arrived you were still not in the field! Six hours' rest was quite enough. I won the skirmish at Nangis with dragoons who, coming from Spain, had not halted once since leaving Bayonne. You say the six battalions of the Nîmes division lack clothes, equipment, and are untrained. What a poor reason to give me! I have destroyed 80,000 of the enemy with conscripts so underequipped they haven't even got cartridge pouches! You've no money, you say. Well, where do you hope to draw money from? You can't have any until we have captured funds from the enemy. You lack draft-animals. Well, simply requisition them. You have no stores—this is too ridiculous. I order you to take the field twelve hours after receiving this letter. If you are still Augereau of Castiglione, keep the command; but if your sixty years weigh heavily on you, hand it over. . . .

A CONVERSATION WITH CHAPTAL

later than 1805 [16]

The Emperor was convinced that plain stubbornness often won battles. I have heard him relate how he fought General Alvinzy for five consecutive days without either side losing or gaining an advantage. "As I was younger and more stubborn," he said, "I did not doubt that he would end up by yielding me ground and it was only this conviction which made me stand firm. And on the fifth day at five o'clock in the afternoon he decided to order a retreat." The Emperor often used to say with an element of satisfaction that this

---

[14] From J. M. Thompson, ed., *Napoleon's Letters*, p. 107.
[15] From Napoleon, *Correspondance*, translated by M. Hutt.
[16] From J. Chaptal, *Souvenirs*, p. 301; translated by K. Gladstone.

General Alvinzy was the best commander he had ever had to fight and that this was why he had never spoken of him either ill or well in the Army's Bulletins, whereas he had praised [other enemy generals] whom he did not fear.

NAPOLEON AT BOULOGNE

July, 1804 [17]

One morning [at Boulogne] the Emperor signified his intention of reviewing the fleet, and gave orders for the ships to take up . . . positions, as the review was to be held right out at sea. [Then] he went out for his usual ride. . . . Everyone knew that the Emperor's wish was law, and, in his absence, Admiral Bruix was informed of it. He coolly replied that he was really very sorry, but that there could be no review that day. Consequently, not a vessel budged.

On coming back, the Emperor . . . was told of the Admiral's reply. . . . Stamping his foot violently, he sent for the Admiral. . . . "How is it, Admiral," said the Emperor, "that you have not carried out my instructions?"

"Sire," replied Bruix, respectfully but firmly, "an awful storm is brewing; Your Majesty can see that as well as I can. Does Your Majesty wish thus uselessly to imperil the lives of so many brave fellows?"

"Sir," exclaimed the Emperor, with increasing irritation, "I gave an order. Once more I ask, how is it you did not execute it? I alone am responsible for the consequences. Obey!"

"Sire, I shall *not* obey."

"Monsieur, you are an insolent fellow!"

And the Emperor, who still had his riding-whip in his hand, advanced towards the Admiral with a threatening gesture. Admiral Bruix, stepping back, gripped his sword-hilt.

"Have a care, Sire," said he, turning deadly pale.

All the onlookers grew cold with fear. For some time, with an arm uplifted, the Emperor stood motionless, glaring at the Admiral, who unflinchingly maintained his grim attitude. At last the Emperor flung away his whip, and M. Bruix relinquished his grasp of his sword-hilt as . . . he silently awaited the result of so terrible a scene.

"Vice-Admiral Magon," said the Emperor, "you will at once execute the movement which I ordered. As for you, sir," he continued, turning to Admiral Bruix, "you will leave Boulogne in twenty-four hours and withdraw to Holland. . . ."

[17] From *Memoirs of Constant* [*L. C. Wairy*], *the Emperor's Head Valet*, trans. Pinkerton (London, 1896), I, 214–17.

The Vice-Admiral proceeded to carry out the Emperor's instructions. Yet scarcely had the first dispositions been taken than the sea assumed a fearful aspect. . . . Thunder boomed incessantly in angry peals, and there came a great wind, which threw the vessels into grievous disorder. . . . In short, that which the Admiral foresaw occurred, and a most appalling tempest dispersed all the war-ships in such a way that their destruction seemed assured.

TO MARET, DUKE OF BASSANO, MINISTER OF FOREIGN AFFAIRS

Doubrovna, November 18, 1812 [18]
Since my last dispatch, our position has grown worse. Almost all our horses—30,000 of them—have perished as the result of the cold. . . . We have had to burn more than 300 guns, and a huge number of ammunition wagons. The cold weather has greatly increased the number of stragglers. The Cossacks have taken advantage of our complete lack of cavalry, and almost complete lack of artillery, to harass us, and to cut our communications, so that I am anxious about Marshal Ney, who stayed behind, with 3,000 men, to blow up Smolensk. Otherwise, given a few days' rest, some good food, (above all) horses, and a supply of artillery, we shall still make good. . . .

FAREWELL TO HIS GUARD

Fontainebleau, April 20, 1814 [19]
"Soldiers of my Old Guard, I bid you farewell. For twenty years you have been my constant companions on a path of honour and glory. . . . With men such as you our cause could not have been lost, but a protracted civil war would have ensued and the sufferings of France would thereby have been augmented. I have therefore sacrificed all our interests to those of the country. I depart: you, my friends, will continue to serve France, whose happiness has ever been the only subject of my thoughts, and still will be the sole object of my wishes! . . . Farewell, my comrades! I should wish to press you all to my bosom: let me, at least, embrace your standard!" . . . At these words . . . Napoleon kissed the flag. The silent admiration which

[18] From J. M. Thompson, ed., *Napoleon's Letters*, p. 274.
Maret had known Napoleon early in the Revolution, when he was a journalist. Secretary to the Consuls after Brumaire, he became Minister of Foreign Affairs in April, 1811. He died in 1839, at the age of seventy-five.
[19] From F. Fain, *Manuscript of 1814. Memoirs of the Invasion of France by the Allied Armies* (London, 1834), p. 267.
Baron Fain (1778–1836), Napoleon's archivist, served in the Council of State from 1811.

this moving scene inspired, was interrupted only by the occasional sobs of the soldiers. Napoleon made an effort to subdue the emotion by which he was powerfully agitated, and then added in a firm tone of voice, "Farewell, once more, my old comrades! Let this last kiss be impressed on all your hearts!" . . . Then rushing from amidst the group which surrounded him he hastily stepped into his carriage . . . and drove off.

PROCLAMATION TO THE ARMY

Bay of St. Jouan, March 1, 1815 [20]

Soldiers! In exile I heard your voice. Now I have landed [in France]. . . .

Your general, made king by the voice of the people and raised to the throne upon your shields, has returned: come and join him. Renounce the [Bourbon] colors which the nation has proscribed and which for twenty-five years have served to rally the enemies of France. Unfurl instead that tricolor which you carried in the day of our greatness! . . . Take up once more the eagles which you carried at Ulm, at Austerlitz, at Jena, Eylau, Friedland, Moscow. . . .

We must forget that we were the masters of the continent; but we must not let anyone meddle in our affairs. . . . Your rank, fortune, and glory, and those of your children, have no greater enemy than these [Bourbon] princes whom foreigners have imposed upon us. . . .

Soldiers, rally round the standard of your leader; his interests, his honor, his glory are the same, the very same, as your own. Victory will advance at the double. The eagle, bearing the national colors [of blue, white, red] will fly from steeple to steeple, right to the towers of Notre Dame [in Paris]. And then you will be able to show your scars with honor, then once again you will be able to boast of what you have done. You will be the liberators of your country . . . and in your old age . . . you will be able to say with pride . . . , "I cleansed Paris of the stain with which treason and the presence of the enemy there had sullied her." . . .

TO HIS BROTHER JOSEPH, EX-KING OF SPAIN

Philippeville, June 19, 1815 [21]

All is not lost. . . . When I reassemble my forces I shall have 150,000 men. [Then the] National Guard . . . will provide 100,000

---

[20] From Napoleon, *Correspondance*, translated by M. Hutt.
[21] I.e., the morrow of Waterloo. From J. M. Thompson, ed., *Napoleon's Letters*, pp. 307–8.

. . . and the regimental depots another 50,000. There is still time to retrieve the situation. . . . But people must help me, not deafen me with advice. . . .

The next letter was written after his first abdication, but it could just as well have been composed after Waterloo and before St. Helena:[22]

TO JOSÉPHINE

Fontainebleau, April 16, 1814 [23]

In exile I shall replace the sword by the pen. The history of my reign will be a curious one: I have been hitherto only in profile: now I will show myself full [face].

What a number of things I have to reveal! . . . Goodbye, my dear Joséphine: learn resignation as I have learned it, and never lose the memory of one who has never forgotten, and never will forget, you.

[22] Though not, of course, addressed to Joséphine, who died on May 29, 1814.
[23] From *The Letters of Napoleon to Marie-Louise,* ed. C. de la Roncière and P. Guedalla (London: Hutchinson Ltd., 1935), p. 265. Reprinted by permission of Hutchinson Ltd.

6
He Reflects

Osterode, March 27, 1802 [1]
All my life I have sacrificed everything—peace of mind, personal gain, happiness—everything to my destiny.

CONVERSATIONS WITH DR. O'MEARA

December 5, 1816 [2]
My [rise to power] . . . was not the result of intrigue or crime. It was owing to the peculiar circumstances of the times, and because I fought successfully against the enemies of my country. What is most extraordinary, though, and I believe unparalleled in history, is that I rose from being a private [individual] to the astonishing height of power I possessed without having committed a single crime to obtain it.

WITH LAS CASES

November 29–30, 1815 [3]
When I acquired the supreme direction of affairs, the wish was expressed that I might become a Washington. Words cost nothing; and no doubt those who were so ready to express that wish did so without any knowledge of places, persons or things. Had I been in America I would willingly have been a Washington—and I should have [shown] little merit in so being, for I do not see how I could reasonably have acted otherwise. But had Washington been in France, exposed to discord within and invasion from without, [he could not possibly] have been what he was in America. . . . I could only be a *crowned Washington*. It was only [as one of] a congress of kings, [the others] yielding or subdued, that I could play such a role. Only there and then could I successfully display Washington's moderation, disinterestedness, wisdom. I could not reasonably attain to this other

---

[1] From L. Cerf, ed., *Lettres de Napoléon*, p. 105; translated by M. Hutt.
[2] From B. E. O'Meara, *Napoleon in Exile*, I, 250.
[3] From Las Cases, *Mémorial de Sainte Hélène*.

than by means of *universal dictatorship*. To this I aspired. Can that be thought a crime? And can it really be believed that to resign such an authority would have been more than human nature could accomplish? . . . What could have checked me? . . . But it remained for me to win at Moscow . . . and to require prematurely of me that sacrifice for which the time had not arrived, [namely, my abdication], was a vulgar absurdity. . . .

September 2, 1816 [4]

"In what a situation was I placed!," continued the Emperor, [talking of the campaign in Saxony, 1813]. "I saw that France, her destinies, her principles, depended on me alone!" "Sire!," I ventured to observe, "this was the opinion generally entertained; and yet some parties reproached you for it, exclaiming with bitterness, 'Why must he connect everything with himself personally?' " "That was a vulgar accusation," resumed the Emperor warmly. "My situation was not one of my own choosing, nor did it arise out of any fault of mine; it was produced entirely by the nature and force of circumstances—by the conflict of two opposite orders of things. Would the individuals who held this language, if indeed they were sincere, have preferred to go back to the period preceding Brumaire, when our internal dissolution was complete, foreign invasion certain, and the destruction of France inevitable? From the moment when we decided on the concentration of power, which could alone save us; when we determined on the unity of doctrines and resources which rendered us a mighty nation, the destinies of France depended solely on the character, the measures, and the principles of him who had been invested with this accidental dictatorship: from that moment the public interest, *the State, was myself.* These words, which I addressed to men who were capable of understanding them, were strongly criticised by the narrow-minded and ill-disposed; but the enemy felt the full force of them, and therefore his first object was to effect my overthrow. The same outcry was raised against other words which I uttered in the sincerity of my heart: when I said that *France stood more in need of me than I stood in need of her,* this solid truth was declared to be merely excess of vanity. . . . The circumstances in which we were placed were extraordinary and totally new; it would be vain to seek for any parallel to them. I was myself the key-stone of an edifice totally new, and [lacking deep] foundations! Its stability depended on each of my battles! Had I been conquered at Marengo, France would have encountered all the disasters of 1814 and 1815, without those prodigies of glory which [followed after 1800] and which will be immortal. It was the same at Austerlitz and Jena, and again at Eylau and else-

[4] *Ibid.*

where. The vulgar did not fail to blame my ambition as the cause of all these wars. But they were not of my choosing; they were produced by the nature and force of events; they arose out of the conflict between the future and the past, [between France and] the coalition of our enemies, which obliged us to subdue them under pain of being subdued."

WITH A MEMBER OF THE COUNCIL OF STATE

in 1802 [5]

The First Consul: Now tell me: do you believe that these govments who have just signed peace with us will still remain our enemies?

State Counsellor: I find it hard to think otherwise.

First Consul: Then we must draw the consequence. If these governments . . . are going to go to war again one day it is better for us if we fight sooner rather than later. For every day that passes weakens the memory they have of their own recent defeats and diminishes the prestige which our own latest victories give us.

State Counsellor: But, Citizen Consul, what about the chance you have of taking advantage of peace to organize the state internally?

First Consul: I was coming to that, for I have certainly taken this [vital] matter into consideration. I proved even in the middle of war that I did not neglect the affairs of our institutions and the good internal functioning of the country. I will not stop there, for much remains to be done. But are military victories no longer necessary for creating an impression on the public and keeping a hold on the domestic front? Remember that a First Consul is not like those kings appointed by the grace of God who look upon their states as their inheritance. They are assisted in their rule by old habits of thought. To us these old habits are a hindrance. The French government today is quite unlike any other. Hated by its neighbours, forced to keep an eye on several groups of opponents at home, it has to resort to actions which create a great impression, and consequently it resorted to war. . . . My government must be the foremost [in all Europe]; otherwise it will be destroyed.

[5] From Thibaudeau, *Mémoires sur le Consulat,* pp. 390–93; translated by K. Gladstone.

WITH CHAPTAL

in 1811 or 1812 [6]

France does not really understand the situation I am in, and consequently misjudges what I do. The thrones of Europe are shared out between five or six families who resent seeing a Corsican sitting on one of them. I can only keep myself there by using force. . . . The moment I cease to be feared my Empire will collapse. . . . I simply cannot afford to let anyone threaten me without my striking back. The king who comes of an ancient line can ignore things which I, on the contrary, have to take seriously. . . . Louis XIV himself would have lost his throne towards the end of his life had he not been heir to a long line of kings. For kings like that, war is simply a matter of seizing territory or a fortress: for me there is always at stake in a war my very existence and that of the whole Empire. At home, too, my position is quite different from theirs . . . for no one contests the legitimacy of their right to rule, no one thinks of replacing them by someone else. . . . At home, as abroad, I reign because of the fear I inspire: and if I changed my system I should soon be dethroned.

WITH DR. O'MEARA

March 3, 1817 [7]

In spite of all the libels . . . I have no fear whatever about my fame. Posterity will do me justice. The truth will be known, and the good which I have done, with the faults which I have committed, will be compared. I am not uneasy about the result. Had I succeeded, I should have died with the reputation of the greatest man that ever existed. As it is, although I have failed, I shall be considered as an extraordinary man: my elevation was unparalleled, *because* unaccompanied by crime. I have fought fifty pitched battles, almost all of which I have gained. I have framed and carried into effect a code of laws, that will bear my name to the most distant [ages]. From nothing I raised myself to be the most powerful monarch in the world. Europe was at my feet.

WITH LAS CASES

September 30, 1816 [8]

"You wish to know the treasures of Napoleon?," [demanded the Emperor, stirred by accusations that he had amassed a colossal per-

---

[6] From Chaptal, *Souvenirs,* pp. 217–19; translated by M. Hutt.

[7] From B. E. O'Meara, *Napoleon in Exile,* I, 404–5.

[8] From Las Cases, *Mémorial de Sainte Hélène.*

sonal fortune]. "They are immense, it is true, but [none of them are hidden away]. They are: The noble harbours of Antwerp and Flushing, which are capable of containing the largest fleets . . . the harbour works at Dunkirk, Havre, and Nice,—the immense harbour of Cherbourg,—the maritime works at Venice,—the splendid roads from Antwerp to Amsterdam; from Bordeaux to Bayonne;—the passes of the Simplon, of Mount Cenis, of Mount Geneva, of the Corniche, which open communications through the Alps and which exceed in grandeur, in boldness, and in skill of execution, all the works of the Romans; the roads from the Pyrenees to the Alps, from Parma to Spezia, from Savona to Piedmont,—the bridges of Jena, Austerlitz, Des Arts, Sèvres, Tours, Lyons, Turin, of the Isère, of the Durance, of Bordeaux, Rouen, etc.—the canal which connects the Rhine with the Rhône and thus [links] the North Sea with the Mediterranean; the canal which connects the Scheldt with the Somme, and thus joins Paris and Amsterdam; the draining of the marshes of the Cotentin, of Rochefort,—the rebuilding of most of the churches destroyed during the Revolution,—the building of others,—the water supply of the city of Paris,—the numerous drains, the quays, the embellishments and the monuments of that great capital,—the embellishment of Rome,—the creation of many hundreds of cotton manufactories for spinning and for weaving, which employ several millions of workmen,—funds accumulated to establish upwards of 400 factories [making] sugar from beet-root,—numerous workshops for all kinds of *objets d'art*, etc.—fifty millions expended in repairing and beautifying the palaces belonging to the Crown,—sixty millions in furniture for the palaces belonging to the Crown in France, and in Holland, at Turin, and at Rome—the Napoleon Museum, filled with objects legitimately acquired, either by money or treaties of peace by virtue of which the *chefs d'oeuvres* it contains were given in lieu of territory or of contributions—several millions applied to the encouragement of agriculture, which is of paramount [importance] in France. . . . All these things form a treasure of several thousand millions which will endure for ages! *These* are the monuments that will confute calumny! [And furthermore] History will say that all these things were accomplished in the midst of perpetual wars, without having recourse to any loan, and whilst the national debt was diminishing every day, and that nearly fifty millions of taxes had been remitted."

and May 1, 1816

The historian of the Empire . . . will have an easy task, for the facts speak for themselves, they shine like the sun.

I closed the gulf of anarchy and cleared [away] chaos. I purified the Revolution, dignified Nations, and re-established Kings. I [stirred men to] emulation, rewarded every kind of merit, extended the [known] limits of glory—and that is something! On what point could I be assailed on which an historian could not defend me? For my intentions? As to these I can be absolved. For my despotism? But it can be demonstrated that dictatorship was absolutely necessary. Will it be said that I restricted liberty? It can be proved that licentiousness and anarchy . . . still [threatened] freedom. Shall I be accused of having been too fond of war? It can be shown that I was always [attacked] first. Will it be said that I aimed at universal monarchy? It can be proved that this was merely the result of fortuitous circumstances, that our enemies themselves led me, step by step, to this determination. Lastly, shall I be blamed for my ambition? This passion I [certainly] possessed and that in no small degree; but at the same time my ambition was of the loftiest and noblest kind that ever, perhaps, existed!—that of establishing and consecrating the [rule] of reason and the full exercise and complete enjoyment of all the human faculties! Here the historian will probably feel compelled to regret that such an ambition was not fulfilled . . . !

HIS DEATHBED INSTRUCTIONS TO HIS SON

April 17, 1821 [9]

Towards 3 p.m. the Emperor sent for me. When I entered the room, I found him sitting up, and the fire glancing in his eyes made me fear a fresh attack of fever. He perceived my uneasiness, and said kindly, "I am not worse, but my mind has been roused by talking with Bertrand about what my executors ought to say to my son, when they see him. Bertrand does not understand this: he and Lafayette have remained what they were in 1791, with their plans of an imaginary government, their English ideas, and their resolutions in the Estates-General; they only see in the revolution of 1789 a reform of abuses, and they refuse to acknowledge or perceive that it was in itself an entire social regeneration. In their eyes I have only established despotism, and acquired military glory. . . . You will understand me [though]; you have only to recall to your mind all that I have said and dictated to you concerning the ambition of my reign; but all this may, perhaps, be scattered . . . in your memory when the time comes for speaking of it; it is better, therefore, that I should, in a few words, give you a summary of the counsels which I bequeath to my son; you will be thus more easily enabled to detail my ideas to him. Write—

"My son should not think of avenging my death; he should profit by it. Let the remembrance of what I have done never leave his mind; let him always be, like me, every inch a Frenchman. The aim of all his

[9] From C. T. de Montholon, *Napoleon at St. Helena*, III, 181–93.

efforts should be, to reign by peace: he [must not] re-commence my wars out of pure love of imitation, and without any absolute necessity. . . . To do my work over again would be to suppose that I had done nothing; to complete it, on the contrary, would be to show the solidity of the basis, and explain the whole plan of an edifice which I had only roughly sketched. The same thing is not done twice in a century: I was obliged to hold down Europe by force: in the present day, the way is to convince her. I saved the revolution which was about to perish; I raised it from its ruins, and showed it to the world shining with glory. I have implanted new ideas in France and in Europe; they cannot disappear: let my son bring into blossom all that I have sown; let him develop all the elements of prosperity [latent] in the soil of France, and by these means he may yet be a great sovereign.

"The Bourbons will not maintain their position after my death; a reaction in my favour will take place everywhere, even in England; this will be a fine inheritance for my son. It is possible that the English, in order to efface the remembrance of their persecutions, will favour my son's return to France; but in order to enjoy a good understanding with England it is necessary, at all costs, to favour her commercial interests: this necessity leads to one of these two consequences—war with England, or a sharing of the commerce of the world with her. This second consequence is the only one possible in the present day. . . .

"I bequeath to my son sufficient strength and sympathy to enable him to continue my work by means of . . . conciliatory diplomacy. . . . But let not my son ever mount the throne by the aid of foreign influence; his aim should not be to fulfil a desire to reign, but to deserve the approbation of posterity. . . . If he remains in exile, let him marry one of my nieces. If France recalls him, let him seek the hand of a princess of Russia. . . .

"The French nation, when it is [handled correctly], is more easily governed than any other: its prompt and easy comprehension is unequalled; it immediately discerns who labours for, and who against it; but it is necessary always to speak to its senses, otherwise its uneasy spirit gnaws, ferments and explodes.

"My son will arrive after a time of civil troubles; . . . let him despise all parties, and only see the mass of the people; save for those who have betrayed their country, he ought to forget the previous conduct of all men, and reward talent, merit, and services wherever he finds them. . . .

"France is the country where the [leaders] of parties have the least influence; to rely on them is to build on sand. Great things can only be done in France by having the support of the mass of the people; and, besides, a government should always seek for support where it is really to be found. There are moral laws as inflexible and imperious as the physical ones. The Bourbons can only rely for support on the nobles and the priests, whatever may be the constitution which they are made to adopt. . . . I, on the contrary, relied on the mass of the people . . . I set the example of a government which favoured the interests of all. I did not govern by the help of, or solely for, either the nobles, the priests, the citizens, or the tradesmen; I governed for the whole community, for the whole family of the French nation. To divide the interests of a nation is to injure them all, and engender civil war. A thing indivisible by nature cannot be divided; it can only be mutilated. I attach no importance to the constitution, of the principal bases of which I have made a draft. Good to-day, it may be bad tomorrow; and, besides, nothing should be definitely settled on this point without the formal consent of the nation; but its fundamental principle should be universal suffrage.

"My nobility will afford no support to my son; I [needed] more than one generation to succeed in making them assume my colour, and preserve by tradition the sacred deposit of my moral conquests. From the year 1815, all the grandees openly espoused the opposite party. I did not feel I could rely either on my marshals or my nobility, not even on my colonels; but the mass of the people and the army, up to the grade of captain, were on my side. I was not deceived in feeling this confidence; they owe much to me: I was their true representative. My dictatorship was indispensable; and the proof of this is, that they always offered me more power than I desired. . . . It will not be the same with my son: his power will be disputed; he must anticipate every desire for liberty. It is, besides, easier, in ordinary times, to reign with the help of a parliament than alone: it takes a great part of your responsibility, and nothing is more easy than always to have the majority on your side. . . . The influence of the government in France is immense; and if it understands the way, it has no need of employing corruption in order to find support on all sides. The aim of a sovereign is not only to reign, but to diffuse instruction, morality, and well-being. . . .

"In my youth, I, too, entertained some illusions; but I soon recovered from them. The great orators who rule the assemblies by the brilliancy of their eloquence are in general men of the most mediocre political talents: they should not be opposed in their own way; for they have always more noisy words at command than you. Their eloquence should be opposed by a serious and logical argument; their strength lies in vagueness; they should be brought back to the reality of facts; practical arguments destroy them. In the council, there were men possessed of much more eloquence than I was: I always defeated them by this simple argument—*two and two make four*. France possesses very clever practical men; the only thing necessary is to find them, and to give them the means of doing the right job: such a one is at the plough, who ought to be in the council; and such another is minister, who ought to be at the plough. . . . From the agrarian law to the despotism of the Grand Turk, every system finds an apologist in France; let my son listen to them all, let him take everything at its true value, and surround himself by all the real talent of the country. The French people are influenced by two powerful passions, which seem opposed, but which, nevertheless, are derived from one and the same feeling—namely, a love of equality, and love of distinctions. A government can only satisfy these two desires by the most exact justice. The law and action of the government must be equal towards all; honours and rewards must be bestowed on the men who seem in the eyes of all to be the most worthy of them. . . .

"My son will be obliged to allow the liberty of the press: this is a necessity in the present day. In order to govern, it is not necessary to pursue a more or less perfect theory, but to build with the materials which are under one's hand; to submit to necessities, and profit by them. The liberty of the press ought to become, in the hands of the government, a powerful auxiliary in diffusing, through all the most distant corners of the empire, sound doctrines and good principles. But to leave it to itself would be [madness]. On the conclusion of a general peace, I would have instituted a Directory of the Press, composed of the ablest men of the country, and I would have diffused, even to the most distant hamlet, my ideas and my intentions. In the present day it is impossible to remain, as one might have done three hundred years ago, a quiet spectator of the transformations of society; now one must, under pain of death, either direct or hinder everything.

"My son ought to be a man of new ideas, [a man devoted to] the cause which I have made triumphant everywhere. He ought to establish institutions which may efface all traces of the feudal law, secure the dignity of man, and [nurture] those [seeds] of prosperity which have been [dormant] for centuries. He should propagate, in all those countries now uncivilized and barbarous, the benefits of Christianity and civilization. Such should be the aim of all my son's thoughts; such is the cause for which I die a martyr to the hatred of the oligarchs. . . . My enemies are the enemies of humanity; they desire to fetter the peoples, whom they regard like flocks of sheep; they endeavour to oppress France, and to make the stream flow backwards towards its source. Let them take care that it does not burst its bounds! With my son, all opposed interests may live in peace; new ideas can be diffused and gather strength, without any violent shock or the sacrifice of any victims; humanity will be spared dreadful misfortunes. But if the blind hatred of kings still pursues my blood after my death, I shall then be avenged, but cruelly avenged. Civilization will suffer in every way, and rivers of blood will be shed throughout the continent [as the peoples of Europe cast off their chains]. . . . The accession of my son is in the interests of nations, [too], as well as of kings. The only alternative to the ideas and principles for which we have fought, and which I have carried triumphantly through all difficulties, is slavery and confusion for France and for the whole of Europe. . . . Europe is progressing towards an inevitable transformation: to endeavor to retard this progress is to lose strength by a useless struggle; to favour it, is to strengthen the hopes and wishes of all.

"There are national aspirations which must be satisfied sooner or later, and it is towards this end that continual progress should be made. My son's position will not be exempt from immense difficulties; but let him do by general consent what I was compelled by circumstances to effect by force of arms. . . .

"So that my son may see whether his administration is good, or the contrary—whether his laws are in accordance with the manners of the country—let him have an annual report presented to him of the number of condemnations pronounced by the tribunals. If crimes and delinquencies increase in number, it is a proof that misery is on the increase, and that society is ill-governed: their diminution, on the other hand, is a proof of the contrary.

"Religious ideas have more influence than certain narrow-minded philosophers are willing to believe: they are capable of rendering great services to humanity. By standing well with the Pope, an influence may be maintained over the consciences of a hundred millions of men. Pius VII will be always well disposed towards my son: he is a tolerant and enlightened old man. Fatal circumstances embroiled our governments; I regret this deeply. . . .

"If you are permitted to return to France, you will still find many who have remained faithful to my memory. The best monument which they could raise to me would be to make a collection of all the ideas which I expressed in the council of state, for the administration of the empire; to collect all my instructions to my ministers; and to make a list of the works which I undertook, and of all the monuments which I raised in France and Italy. Maret, Daru, Mollien, Merlin, and Cambacérès may contribute to this work; it will . . . complement what I have charged Bignon to write on my foreign policy. . . . In what I have said in the council of state, a distinction must be made between measures good only for the moment, and those whose application is eternally true.

"Let my son often read and reflect on history; this is the only true philosophy. Let him read and meditate on the wars of the greatest captains; this is the only means of rightly learning the science of war.

"But all that you say to him, or all that he learns, will be of little use to him, if he has not in the depth of his heart that sacred fire, that love of good which alone can effect great things.

"I hope that he will be worthy of his destiny."

BERTRAND DESCRIBES HIS END

April 26, 1821 [10]

In the morning the Emperor had asked at least twenty times whether he might be allowed to have some coffee. But every time the answer had been: "No, Sire."

"Won't the doctors allow me just a spoonful?"

"No, Sire, not at present." He had been sick perhaps eight or nine times in the course of the day.

What thoughts sprang to mind at the sight of so great a change! Tears came to my eyes, as I looked at this man, formerly so terrifying, who had commanded so proudly, so absolutely, now reduced to begging for a spoonful of coffee, asking permission, obedient as a child, asking permission again and again without obtaining it. Repeatedly asking permission, and always unsuccessfully, yet without any signs of bad temper. At other periods of his illness he had sent his doctors to the devil and had done as he pleased. But now he was as docile as a child. That was what the Great Napoleon had become, a humble and an unhappy man.

May 3

Just before ten o'clock in the evening, Antommarchi gave him a biscuit dipped in wine. "Good, *bon.*" Then his flannel vest was changed, the blister on his abdomen was dressed, and the Emperor nearly fainted. He was very weak; with the eyes of a dying man, he looked at Montholon with an expression that inspired pity and seemed to say: "How can you torment me so cruelly?" [Late that night] he asked what his son was named. Twice his voice recovered its clearness. [After] eight o'clock he gave the appearance of having recovered his lucidity of mind, but he ceased to speak. Then he could no longer move his hand, but frequently opened his eyes that had become dull, dying and painful to see. . . .

May 5

At forty-nine minutes after five o'clock [in the evening] the Emperor breathed his last. During the last three minutes he sighed three times. . . .

At the moment of crisis there was a flicker of movement in the pupils of his eyes. Then there was a regular movement of the mouth, and of the chin to the forehead, of clockwork regularity. During the night the Emperor had spoken the name of his son before saying, "A la tête de l'Armée." The day before he had twice asked, "Comment s'appelle mon fils?" and Marchand [his valet] had replied, "Napoléon."

[10] From *Memoirs of General Bertrand*, pp. 226, 252, 260.

NAPOLEON VIEWED BY HIS CONTEMPORARIES

7

His Appearance

He was not, at first sight, all that striking—until you noticed his eyes and sensed the "field" around this compact dynamo. Electrical storms flashed, sometimes, out of this highly charged field: it could be dangerous, lethal even. But it was also magnetic, compelling—and sometimes tranquillizing in the sense that many, caught within its aura, felt their misgivings ebb away, while some, exposed to it long enough, seem to have had their critical faculties dulled (at least so far as "he" was concerned). Captain Maitland himself could not help remarking on the "extent [to which Napoleon] possess[ed] the power of pleasing" [1]—that is, when he wanted to; for on other occasions, as he himself remarked to Fain, he would switch on rages intended to cow and to frighten people.

Maitland had the Emperor aboard his ship for three weeks only.[2] The others who describe him in these extracts were (in a physical sense at least) close to him for long periods—his valet and "the only two persons," according to their master, "who were in my confidence in the service . . . of my private [office]." [3]

[1] Quoted in F. Markham, *Napoleon*, p. 125.

[2] From July 15, when Napoleon boarded the *Bellerophon* off Rochefort, until August 7, 1815, when, off Torbay, he transferred to the *Northumberland* for the voyage to St. Helena.

[3] Napoleon quoted in C. T. de Montholon, *History of the Captivity of Napoleon at St. Helena* (London, 1846–47), III, 39.

HIS SECRETARY MÉNEVAL, DESCRIBES HIM IN 1802 [4]

Napoleon was at this time moderately stout . . . about five feet two inches tall and well built. His head was big, his neck short and his shoulders broad. The size of his chest bespoke a robust constitution, less robust, however, than his mind. His legs were well shaped, his foot was small and well formed. His hand, and he was rather proud of it, was delicate, with tapering fingers. His forehead was high and broad, his eyes grey and penetrating; his nose was straight and well shaped. His teeth were fairly good, the mouth perfectly modelled, the upper lip slightly drawn down toward the corner of the mouth, and the chin slightly prominent. His skin was smooth and his complexion pale. His fine chestnut hair, which, until the time of the expedition to Egypt, he had worn long, cut square and covering his ears, was clipped short. The hair was thin on the upper part of the head, and left bare his forehead. The shape of his face and the *ensemble* of his features were remarkably regular. In one word, his head and shoulders were in no way inferior in nobility and dignity to the most beautiful bust which antiquity has bequeathed to us.

Of this portrait, which in its principal features underwent little alteration in the last years of his reign, I will add some particulars furnished by my long intimacy with him. When excited by any violent passion his face assumed an even terrible expression. [He screwed up] his forehead, his eyes flashed fire, his nostrils dilated. But these [brief spasms] . . . in no way brought disorder to his mind. He seemed to be able to control at will these explosions, which, by the way, as time went on, became less and less frequent. His head remained cool. Usually his expression was calm, meditative, and gently grave. When in a good humour, or when anxious to please, his expression was sweet and caressing, and his face was lighted up by a most beautiful smile. When with people he knew well his laugh was loud and mocking.

My portrait of Napoleon would be incomplete did I not mention the hat, without trimming or lace, which was ornamented by a little tricolour cockade, and the grey [overcoat] which covered the simple uniform of colonel of his guard. This hat and this [overcoat] [stood out] in the midst of the coats covered with gold and silver embroidery which were worn by his generals, and the officers of his household.

As a boy he gave no signs of what he was to be one day. As a matter of fact, it was not until he left the military school that he gave himself up with ardour to study. He has often told me that since that date he has regularly worked sixteen hours a day. Nevertheless, he already had

[4] From C. F. de Méneval, *Memoirs to Serve for the History of Napoleon I from 1802 to 1815*, translated by R. Sherard, 3 vols. (London, 1894), I, 105–9.

within him the germs of the qualities which were brought out by education, and which, under the influence of events, developed to the highest degree. These dominating qualities were pride, a sense of his dignity, a warlike instinct, a genius for form, the love of order and of discipline. . . . Those who knew Napoleon in his youth agree in saying that his nature was gentle, reserved, and pensive; that he had little taste for noisy pleasures, and more inclination for study than for polite accomplishments. He did, however, it is said, [pay tribute] to the muses. There are, we are assured, some pieces of poetry of his in existence, but these are only short, and . . . I have never heard that he admitted writing them. [Yet] Napoleon was a born poet. His lofty thoughts, the originality of his speech and his style, his proclamations, testify to a strong and fruitful imagination.

HIS VALET, IN ABOUT 1806 [5]

His head was very large, being twenty-two inches in circumference, long rather than broad, and, consequently, somewhat flat about the temples; it was extremely sensitive, and I used to put wadding in his hats, and keep them some days in my room to make them softer. His ears were small . . . and perfectly shaped. The Emperor's feet were very tender; I used to let his shoes be first worn by a valet whose foot was exactly the same size as the Emperor's.

He was five feet two and a quarter tall; his neck was rather short; he had stooping shoulders and a broad chest, with very little hair upon it; and well-shaped thighs and legs. His foot was small, the toes being entirely free from corns or bunions; his arms were well made, his hands and nails admirable in shape; he took the utmost care of his whole person without being dandified. He often used to bite his nails, but only slightly; it was a sign of his being impatient or preoccupied.

Later on, he grew much stouter, yet without losing anything of his comely shape; on the contrary, during the Empire he was handsomer than during the Consulate; his skin became very white and his complexion fresh-coloured.

During his moments, or rather, his long hours, of work and meditation, the Emperor had a curious habit of involuntarily shrugging his right shoulder in a rapid, nervous way, and this habit he had all his life, so that persons who did not know it took it for a sign of discontent or disapproval, anxiously wondering why and how they had managed to displease him.

The Emperor used to eat very fast; he hardly remained twelve minutes at table. When he had finished dinner he got up and went

[5] From the *Memoirs of Constant* [*L. C. Wairy*], *The Emperor's Head Valet*, trans. Pinkerton (London, 1896), I, 264–65.

into the drawing-room; but the Empress remained at table, and
motioned her guests to do likewise. . . .

ANOTHER "CONFIDENTIAL SECRETARY," FAIN, IN 1810 [6]

He was small, but well made. However, he was rather short in
the neck and perhaps already too stout. . . . There was never any
colour in his complexion. His cheeks were a dull white, which gave
him a full, pale face, but not with the pallor which denotes a sick
person.

I never saw him unwell enough to take to his bed. . . . I never
knew him to have anything wrong except a discomfort of the bladder,
which sometimes bothered him. I think the doctors ascribed this
trouble to the after effects of the . . . scabies he had caught and
neglected at the siege of Toulon.

His chestnut hair was cut short and worn flat on his head. He had
a round head, a broad and high forehead, greyish-blue eyes with a
mild expression, a well-shaped nose, a pleasingly cut mouth and fine
teeth.

His sight was not of the best. He helped it out with a pair of opera-
glasses he always carried.

He had a most fastidious sense of smell. I have seen him withdraw
from more than one servant who had no idea of the secret aversion
he had incurred.

When he was at work or preoccupied, the regularity of his features
easily assumed a tinge of imposing sternness. But in the relaxation of
intimacy his smile became very pleasant.

He seldom laughed. When he did, he shouted with laughter. But
it was more for ironic effect than in hearty mirth.

I may add that no human face ever changed more promptly in re-
sponse to varying states of mind. The very glance that had just been
benign would suddenly dart lightning.

He has been accused wrongly of an immoderate addiction to coffee
and snuff. He drank no more coffee than anyone else: [and he did
not inhale] his snuff. But he was constantly changing his snuff-box.
The moment he had [taken a pinch] he would turn the box upside
down and hand it to one of us, saying:

"Go and get me some snuff."

This was one of our regular errands. On the chest of drawers in
his bedroom we would find a row of snuff-boxes, prepared in advance
to last out . . . the day. . . .

[6] From the *Mémoires* of F. Fain; extract translated by K. John in J. Savant, ed.,
Napoleon in His Time (London, 1958), pp. 249–50. Reprinted by permission of
Putnam & Co. Ltd., London, and of Éditions Buchet-Chastel.

What has been said of his over-indulgence in baths is better founded. He took them too often, and too hot. It seems likely that he had this bad habit to thank for premature corpulence. At least one cannot impute it to [over-indulgence] for that man was certainly no lover of the table! He was abstemious, he lived frugally and ate fast. . . .

When he was strolling in his garden, he liked to walk slightly bent, with his hands in his pockets, or swaying, with his hands behind his back.

He could sleep when and as he pleased. Whatever his need of sleep, three or four hours would be enough. I used to see him get up again without effort as soon as he woke in the night, set to work, and then go back to bed and immediately back to sleep.

In summer he liked to take a siesta. As a rule, he slept about seven hours in the twenty-four. But it was always in several spells, broken off at will night or day. During the evacuation of Leipzig [in Oct., 1813] he got two hours' untroubled sleep in an armchair; the blowing up of the bridge awoke him.

THE CAPTAIN OF THE *BELLEROPHON*, JULY, 1815 [7]

Napoleon Buonaparte was . . . a remarkably strong, well built man . . . his limbs particularly well formed, with a fine ankle and very small foot, of which he seemed rather vain, as he always wore, while on board the ship, silk stockings and shoes. His hands were also very small and had the plumpness of a woman's rather than the robustness of a man's. His eyes light grey, teeth good: and when he smiled the expression of his countenance was highly pleasing: when under the influence of disappointment, however, it assumed a dark, gloomy cast. His hair was of very dark brown . . . and though a little thin on the top and front, had not a grey hair amongst it. His complexion was a very uncommon one, being of a light, sallow colour, differing from almost any other I ever met with. From his having become corpulent he had lost much of his personal activity and, if we are to give credit to those who attended him, a very considerable portion of his mental energy was also gone. It is certain his habits were very lethargic while he was on board the *Bellerophon*: for though he went to bed between eight and nine o'clock in the evening, and did not rise till about the same hour in the morning, he frequently fell asleep on the sofa in the cabin in the course of the day. His general appearance was that of a man rather older than he then was.

[7] From Captain F. L. Maitland, *Narrative of the Surrender of Buonaparte and of His Residence on Board H.M.S. "Bellerophon"* (London, 1826), pp. 208–210.

8
At Work

At least one of Napoleon's observations about himself would not have been controverted by anyone, friend or enemy —"work is my element." [1] This man, who "in [his] prime," as he recalled, "was able to dictate to four secretaries at once—and keep them exceedingly busy," this man was never at rest. [2] Before his health deteriorated, even his occasional indolence masked unremitting activity—internal, cerebral activity, the planning and calculating that made him formidable both in the field and in the council chamber. All of the extracts which follow testify to the demonic energy of what Odeleben, one of his adjutants, calls his "ever-restless spirit": but it will be noted that the administrators quoted are not unreservedly enthusiastic about the desirability of such a spirit presiding over the destinies of France and Europe. They were, it is true, writing with hindsight, after the collapse of the Empire. And perhaps a certain caution is one aspect of the civil-service mentality—though it must be observed that these were not low-level hacks and as such wedded to safe routines. Chaptal (1756–1832) was a distinguished chemist whose administrative talents had been recognized by the Committee of Public Safety in 1793. From 1800 to 1804 and again in 1815, he held ministerial office, as did Mollien, Minister of Finance from 1806 to 1815. Both entered Napoleon's service via the Council of State, and so did Roederer. Born in the same year as Mollien (1754), he had been a lawyer before 1789, and prominent in Parisian politics during the early years of the Revolution. And so did Molé (1781–1855), a member of a long-distinguished legal family, whose father had been executed in the Terror, and who became a prefect and Director-General of Roads and Bridges from 1809 to 1815.

[1] Quoted in H. A. L. Fisher, *Napoleon*, p. 148.
[2] Napoleon quoted in *Memoirs of General Bertrand*, p. 196.

AN ADJUTANT ON THE GENERAL STAFF
DURING THE CAMPAIGN OF 1813 [3]

The fatigue and labour undergone by the adjutants, the secretaries, the orderly officers, in short, by all who were about Napoleon, from the Grand Equerry to the meanest of his valets, is beyond belief. A man of illustrious birth, for instance, General Narbonne, was obliged during the latter period of the campaign to sleep on straw, or on two chairs, in Napoleon's ante-chamber, where he did the duty of adjutant; in that situation he was obliged constantly to be at his post, in order to awaken him, seven or eight times during the night, whenever any despatch or report of consequence arrived which required that he should be immediately acquainted with it. In this ante-chamber all those who were on duty slept upon straw. Often, when a forced march or battle was expected, the ante-chamber was filled with all those who were likely to be called for by Napoleon. It resembled then the belly of the Trojan horse.

Sometimes Napoleon would work through the night. [His servant] brought him coffee, and he walked up and down his cabinet . . . in a dressing gown, his head wrapped round with a . . . silk handkerchief, [something like] a turban. He talked and dictated incessantly. . . . Usually he worked till four in the morning, then he slept, or at least ruminated for a couple of hours.

When I speak of Napoleon's "cabinet" during the campaign, the largest and most convenient room in the house must be understood. . . . He attached more importance to it, than to the room which he inhabited himself. And when Napoleon bivouacked with his troops another tent was pitched close to his own, to serve as the cabinet. . . . In the middle of the room was placed a large table, on which was spread the best map that could be obtained of the [area and] pins with various coloured heads were thrust into it, to point out the situation of the different *corps d'armée* of the French or those of the enemy. . . . During the night the map was surrounded by twenty or thirty candles, in the midst of which was placed a compass. When the Emperor mounted his horse, Caulaincourt, the Grand Equerry, carried the map. . . . He was always at Napoleon's elbow . . . ready to present it to him whenever he exclaimed *"la carte!,"* "the map!"

At the four corners of the sanctuary were placed small tables for the secretaries. . . . Napoleon . . . most commonly dictated to them dressed in a green uniform, often with his hat upon his head, pacing

[3] From Baron von Odeleben, *A Circumstantial Narrative of the Campaign in Saxony in the Year 1813,* trans. A. Kempe (London, 1820), I, 142–77.

up and down his apartment. Accustomed to have every thing which he conceived executed with the greatest promptitude, no one could write fast enough for him. . . . It is incredible how fast he dictated, and what a facility his secretaries had acquired in following him with the pen. . . . These secretaries . . . were like so many strings attached to the administrative war departments . . . as well as to the other authorities of France, to whom the orders of Napoleon were directly issued. It is really astonishing how he made so small a number of persons suffice for such a load of business without impeding its regular course. . . .

[It was Caulaincourt who] opend . . . the despatches which the couriers brought . . . and he gave Napoleon everything that immediately concerned him, whether he were on the march or had taken up his quarters. When he was in his carriage . . . Caulaincourt hastily alighted from his horse, took the courier aside, opened the mail, galloped after Napoleon, handed him the despatches; after which, a quantity of envelopes were seen flying from each side of his carriage. . . . [In the carriage, too, were] thrust all the papers that he had not had time to read in his cabinet. . . . He amused himself by looking over them when he was travelling, if the [lie] of the country were well known or immaterial to him. All useless reports were cut up and thrown out of the carriage window, the pieces . . . flying in the air like a swarm of bees. Probably Berthier was intrusted with destroying [such reports . . . though] perhaps Napoleon amused himself by doing it, for he was not able to remain still for an instant. When Berthier and he had nothing to discuss, and he was tired of playing with the tassel of the carriage window, his majesty fell asleep. To avoid this sort of *ennui,* when there were neither reports, lists, nor statements to submit to him, the pockets of the carriage were filled with journals and other periodical publications from Paris. Scarcely had he time rapidly to skim through them than they were sent flying [out of the carriage window]. . . . And when there were neither journals, nor periodical publications, the carriage was filled with novels, and even with very voluminous romances. . . . But this kind of reading was not much relished by Napoleon, who liked works of a solid description; if the first pages did not please him, the unfortunate books were thrown out of the carriage window. . . .

The activity of an ever-restless spirit, whose supreme happiness consisted in the various alarms and continuous occupations of war, set aside all idea of regularity and stated times of employment. Everything at headquarters was done [without warning], yet each individual was obliged to be ready instantly to fulfil his task. . . . In all operations the principal plan emanated from Napoleon . . . and to the last word which he dictated in his cabinet, was attached the sudden order, "The carriage—To horse!" Then all those who were to follow him [were galvanised into] motion as if they had [received] an electric [shock]. . . .

[When travelling] Caulaincourt . . . rode on horseback at the right-hand side of the carriage. General Guyot, or some officer [near] him in rank, was on the left, with the adjutants on duty, equerries, orderly officers, pages and the chargers for Napoleon and Berthier . . . [while behind them came] twenty-four *chasseurs,* under the command of an officer. These arrangements . . . were . . . observed on every occasion with the greatest exactness. . . . Only officers of elevated rank had the privilege of approaching the sides of the carriage, or following immediately behind it. Thus the [cohort] hurried on like a tempest, day or night. . . . When Napoleon stopped, his saddle horses had to do the same; and four *chasseurs* [from] the escort alighted, fixed bayonets . . . and formed the corners of a square about him. The same thing was done, when any necessity of nature obliged him to alight from his carriage; and when he halted to take a turn on foot, in order to observe the enemy, then the square was enlarged, and the page on duty came forward, and brought a telescope, which Bonaparte placed upon his or Caulaincourt's shoulders.

When circumstances obliged the Emperor to remain, either early in the morning or at night, for some time in the open air, the *chasseurs* prepared a large fire for him. This fire was always supplied with an extraordinary quantity of wood: large logs were burnt, to serve as a sort of signal pointing out the spot where he was.

Berthier was his companion on these occasions, as well as at table. All the rest kept at a certain distance, forming a semi-circle. Napoleon walked up and down, either alone, absorbed in thought, or conversing with Berthier, awaiting perhaps the sound of cannon or other signals from his generals. When he began to be weary, he took snuff, or amused himself with kicking the pebbles about with his foot, or pushing the wood towards the fire. He could not rest a moment without doing something.

BARON MÉNEVAL AGAIN [4]

When some lengthy answer was rendered necessary by the reading of a report or despatch; when some spontaneous idea was suggested to him by his observations or comparisons; or when this idea, having sprung up in his mind, elaborated by his meditations, had reached its maturity, and the moment to set it in motion had arrived,

[4] From his *Memoirs,* I, 372–78.

Napoleon could not keep still. He collected his thoughts, and concentrated his attention on the subject which was occupying him. He would rise slowly, and begin to walk slowly up and down the whole length of the room in which he found himself. This walk lasted through the whole of his dictation. As he entered upon his subject, his voice [took on] a more animated tone and he began to twist his right arm and pull at the trimmings of his sleeve with his hand. At such times, he did not speak any faster than before, and his walk remained slow and measured.

He had no difficulty in finding words to express his thoughts. Sometimes incorrect, these very errors added to the energy of his language. . . . Nor were they frequent, and were only left uncorrected when, the despatch having to be sent off at once, time was short. In his speeches to the Senate and to the Legislative corps; in his proclamations; in his letters to sovereigns; and in the diplomatic notes which he made his ministers write, his style was polished, and suited to its subject.

Napoleon rarely wrote himself. Writing tired him; his hand could not follow the rapidity of his thoughts; he only took up the pen when by chance he happened to be alone and had to put the first rush of an idea on to paper; but after writing some lines he used to stop and throw away his pen. He would then go out to call his secretary or the Secretary of State or General Duroc,[5] or sometimes the aide-de-camp on duty, according to the kind of work in which he was engaged. He made use of the first who answered his call, without irritation, but rather with a visible satisfaction at being relieved from his trouble.

His writing was a collection of letters unconnected with each other, and unreadable. Half the letters to each word were wanting, he could not read his own writing, or would not take the trouble to do so. If he was asked for some explanation he would take his draft and tear it up, or throw it into the fire, and dictate it over again—the same ideas, it is true, but couched in different language and a different style.

Although he could detect faults in the spelling of others his own spelling left much to be desired. It was negligence which had become a habit, he did not want to break or tangle the thread of his thoughts by paying attention to the details of spelling. Napoleon also used to make mistakes in figures, absolute and positive as arithmetic has to be. He could have worked out the most complicated mathematical problems, and yet he could rarely total up a sum correctly. It is fair to add that these errors were not always made without intention. For example, in calculating the number of men who were to make up

[5] See above, p. 60.

his regiments, he always used to increase the sum total. One can hardly believe that in doing so he wanted to deceive himself, but he often thought it useful to exaggerate the strength of his armies. It was no use pointing out any mistake of this kind; he refused to admit it.

It is said that Voltaire used to have a number of desks in his room, on one of which was a poem which he had begun, on another a tragedy, on others, a piece of historical writing, and a pamphlet: and that he used to pass from one kind of composition to another as the spirit moved him. Napoleon would, at one sitting, deal in turn with matters relating to war, to diplomacy, to finance, to commerce, to public works, and so on; and rested from one kind of work by engaging in another. Every branch of the government was with him the object of a special, complete and sustained attention; no confusion of ideas, no fatigue, and no desire to shorten the hours of labour, ever [showed]. Napoleon used to explain the clearness of his mind, and his faculty of being able at will to prolong his work, by saying that the various subjects were arranged in his head, as though in a cupboard. "When I want to interrupt one piece of work," he used to say, "I close the drawer in which it is, and I open another. The two pieces of business never get mixed up together, and never trouble or tire me. When I want to go to sleep, I [just] close up all the drawers."

The initiative in the drafting of all laws and regulations almost always came from Napoleon. His ideas of amelioration, improvement, and construction kept his ministers [fully] occupied in prescribing and supervising the numerous details of execution. If any regret can be expressed on this subject, it is that the unceasing activity of the finest intellect which has ever been granted to a human being, should have accustomed his agents to await his inspiration and to distrust themselves; and that in consequence, so many men of talent should have found themselves paralysed and taken by surprise in moments of danger.

He used sometimes to spend whole days without doing any work, yet without leaving the palace, or even his work-room. In these days of leisure—[or rather] apparent leisure, for it usually concealed an increase of cerebral activity—Napoleon appeared embarrassed how to spend his time. He would go and spend an hour with the Empress, then he would return and, sitting down on the settee, would sleep, or appear to sleep for a few minutes. He would then come and seat himself on the corner of my writing-table [and] speak to me of all sorts of disconnected subjects, of himself, of his constitution, of me, or of some plan that he had in his head. He would glance through the titles of his books, saying a word of praise or of blame on the authors, and would linger with preference over the tragedies of Corneille, "Zaïre" or Voltaire's "The Death of Cæsar." . . . He would read tirades from these tragedies, aloud, then would shut up the book and walk up and down reciting verses from "The Death of Cæsar." [Among] the passages which he recited with the greatest pleasure, [was] the following:

> J'ai servi, commandé, vaincu quarante années;
> Du monde, entre mes mains, j'ai vu les destinées;
> Et j'ai toujours connu qu'en chaque événement,
> Le destin des États dépendait d'un moment! . . .

When he was tired of reading or reciting he would begin to sing loudly but [out of tune]. One of his favourite songs was about a girl who was cured by her lover of a sting from a winged insect. It consisted of one verse only. It ended with this line:

> A kiss from his lips was the doctor in this case.

When he was in a more serious frame of mind, he used to sing verses from the Revolutionary hymns and songs, such as the *Chant du Départ* or *Veillons au salut de l'Empire*; or he would hum these two lines:

> The man who wishes to bring the world under his sway
> Must begin with his own country.

[Did he intend this to apply to himself?] I believe that he understood his country's happiness otherwise. All the powers of his ambition were strained to render the French nation great and prosperous. . . . Her greatness was the object of all his thoughts, the opinion that she had of him was his constant preoccupation, although outwardly he seemed to be indifferent to popularity.

COUNT CHAPTAL[6]

When Bonaparte took the reins of government, not only was he profoundly ignorant of the principles of administration, of jurisprudence, of geography, etc., but he knew nothing whatever of the government that had existed before the Revolution. . . . Military glory alone had carried him to the supreme eminence. That alone sur-

[6] From his *Souvenirs*, pp. 224–35, 325–27, translated by K. Gladstone; and, in J Savant, ed., *Napoleon in His Time*, pp. 131–33, 143, trans. K. John; the latter reprinted by permission of Putnam & Co. Ltd., London and Éditions Buchet-Chastel

rounded him with all the glamour of enthusiasm and illusion. And it supported him to the end.

Bonaparte had one virtue which is more unusual the higher a man has risen. He was not ashamed of knowing so little of the details of general administration. He put many questions, asking the definition and sense of the most ordinary words. He incited discussion, and kept it going till his opinion was formed. . . .

In the four years of the Consulate he held several councils every day. There all questions of administration, finance and jurisprudence were debated in turn. And as he was gifted with great acumen, he would often throw in profound comments, judicious reflections, which astonished those who had most experience in these matters.

The councils often went on till five in the morning, since he was never known to abandon a question till his [mind was made up]. And on this head he was somewhat difficult, rarely contenting himself with the opinion offered him by his most enlightened advisers. At that time the ministers and the Council of State had some power over him. As his judgment was not yet formed on most subjects, he permitted argument, and it was then possible to enlighten him, and even to carry the opinion expressed in his presence. Accordingly, this period was marked by achievements in statute law, administration and finance which have been admired by all Europe and will long be the pride of France.

But as soon as Bonaparte had acquired settled views, right or wrong, on all questions of government, he ceased to consult anyone, or if he did so, it was no longer to embrace the opinions offered him. He always followed his own ideas. His opinion was his one rule of conduct. He made bitter [fun] of all who expressed a view different from his. He tried to hold them up to ridicule, and would often say, tapping himself on the head, that "this sound instrument was more useful to him than the advice of men who were supposed to be educated and experienced."

Only those who observed this period of four years can have a just idea of the changes that took place in the First Consul. Till then he had sought to gather round him the ablest minds of every party. Soon he began to think the choice of his agents immaterial. So he called indiscriminately to his council and to leading posts in the government those whom favour or intrigue might suggest, thinking himself strong enough to rule and govern single-handed. He even made a point of removing all who had ability or character enough to be irksome. He wanted flunkeys and not advisers, and had thus managed to isolate himself completely. By now the ministers were only head clerks. The Council of State was reduced to shaping decrees of which he was sole author. He [regulated] even the most petty details. All

about him were timid and passive. They studied the will of the
oracle and performed it blindly.

Once he had reached the point of concentrating the whole government in himself and taking counsel only with himself, Bonaparte
hit on the idea of moulding a generation of satellites. . . . [So he]
started a nursery of five or six hundred young men, whom he appointed in turn to every office. One saw a young man of twenty-two
placed at the head of a department; others set to administer conquered territory. . . . Not all these young men had either the capacity
or the prestige required. But he thought them devoted to his person
and government, and that was enough. He applied the same principles
to the organisation of the army. . . . In his last years his aim was
much less to make use of ability than to reward devotion to his person.

This conduct of Bonaparte's had no small share in alienating the
minds of the French. . . . But because Napoleon had gathered all
the reins of power into his own hands, he wanted servile and passive
tools in the provinces to carry out his wishes. He thought he was
powerful enough to govern everything in this way. . . .

When Bonaparte came to power, the factions which had formed
in the Revolution were at full strength. Everyone had sided with one
or other of these factions, and, as each in turn had been predominant,
there was a deal of bitterness about, with enemies bent on paying
each other back. All this split the French into a number of factions,
so that everywhere there were violent feelings, while nowhere was
there love of the country.

In this difficult situation, Bonaparte decided on a policy of unifica-
tion, of fusion. Men who had been at loggerheads for ten years, men
who detested each other, were set by Bonaparte to serve alongside
one another. . . . And he carried out this same policy of "fusion" in
every country he came to rule. . . . Bonaparte viewed in the same
light men who belonged to the classes which had once been privileged
and men who had come to the fore during the Revolution. There
was no one class of persons to whom he gave honours and in this respect there was perfect equality around him. The supporters of the
Revolution, however, were constantly opposed to his surrounding
himself with members of the old privileged classes. They remained
unconvinced that the latter were acting in good faith; and they considered them spies on the lookout for a stroke of misfortune which
would enable them to regain their former privileges. Bonaparte did
not share their fears, however, for he believed he was powerful enough
to hold everyone in check and rule over them all. It never occurred to
him that he could be overthrown. . . . Perhaps it was this conviction
that constantly made him go to extremes and led him continually
to put his crown at risk. Fortune had served him so well that he had

come to believe that what he called his "star" would never fade. . . .

Napoleon was at times free and easy in conversation. But if the other person took advantage of this to criticise him or attack any of his principles, he abruptly changed his tone and set out to humiliate rather than argue with him. One had to be constantly on guard against his false air of good-nature. The men who knew him best, those who were his most regular companions, like Duroc and Berthier, never deviated from the proprieties. He played frequently at all sorts of games, but he was always cheating. He [insisted on being] paid, but used to give back the money his conscience told him he had won unfairly. . . .

No one was at ease in dealing with Napoleon, because no one could rely on a spirit of kindliness or indulgence. The smallest mishap, the slightest negligence sent him into a fury, and he had no consideration for those who were in daily touch with him, so that they were always on thorns, afraid of displeasing or of taking responsibility for decisions that might annoy him. As a result they spent their whole time getting his orders on the most trifling points, and executing them without modification, and even then might think themselves lucky if they had not to bear the blame for the ineptitude of some measures he had ordered himself.

His court was truly a slave-galley, where every man pulled as he was bid.

COUNT MOLÉ [7]

Napoleon's face seen at such close quarters, struck me even more forcibly than the idea I had formed of it. I have always believed in faces. His was in keeping with his whole history. His head was superb and unlike any other. . . . In the [size of] his skull, the formation of his splendid forehead, the setting of his eyes, his sculptured lips, the droop at the corners of his mouth, the beautiful proportions of his face and the regularity of his features, but above all in his glance, piercing and veiled rather than gentle, and his smile, more contemptuous than pleasant, and mocking rather than friendly—in all this, as I have said, I thought I could recognize all the qualities which raise a man above his fellows and make him fit to rule them, but none of the qualities or virtues which make him liked, or even simply respected, in all the circumstances of life. . . .

Those who heard some of [Napoleon's] speeches in public were always talking of his *jerky* phrasing. The adjective is far more appropriate to his processes of thought. Sitting hunched up in the chair in which he presided over the Council of State, composed, lost in

[7] From his *Memoirs*, pp. 57, 79–80, 84–85, 148–49, 309.

thought to the point of forgetting where he was and even those to whom he was speaking, his eyes fixed on nothing; that long, small gold snuff box which he was always mechanically opening to help himself to a pinch of snuff, and last but not least the mechanical movement of his arm in handing back the snuff box to the chamberlain, who soon filled it up and returned it—all this was so eminently the picture of a man meditating in solitude that all the eyes fixed on his face observed him in silence, and everyone took care to make no noise for fear of disturbing an internal process of which the end and product were awaited with curiosity.

As soon as his thought took shape he let it fall from his lips, indifferent to the form in which it was clothed. Contemptuous of all set rules, placing himself above the conventions, he regarded as the privilege of his superiority over other men the right of thinking aloud and letting his brain conceive and his mouth utter, relying on the attention and respect with which his slightest word was received by his hearers, the most eminent of whom felt themselves a long way inferior to him. He had no fear of finding himself contradicting himself. With his ingenuity in discovering subtle and plausible reasons in support of all opinions, he attached less importance to selecting them well than to proving that [he had thought about] every aspect of every question, and that there was not a single idea they could suggest which had not already occurred to him.

But in the heat of debate, and sometimes under the influence of contrariness—for he usually liked the discussion to be free and full—he was led on to support both the *pro* and the *con*. His position in the Council between two parties which hated each other thus became for him something which [is too risky for men of ordinary talents], a matter of tactics and skill. Moreover, these two parties, amazed at such a display of resource and ingenuity [deployed in order] to bring them together, instead of breaking them, persuaded themselves more and more that even if he did not give them entire satisfaction, he would at any rate save them from being delivered to their adversaries or humiliated before them. . . .

In short, I would say of the Council of State and the members of that assembly what has been said with so much truth of our great armies, and the generals who commanded them—that when Napoleon was at their head they became irresistible and the generals under his orders all seemed great captains; but that when he was absent, those armies had difficulty in holding their own, and his lieutenants quarrelled, were jealous of each other and could do nothing. The long horseshoe table of the Council of State, with its array of men of such varied origins and opinions—not one of whom could be described as a great mind or of exceptional talents—was simply transformed when the organizing genius appeared on a dais at the end of the horseshoe. Under his hand it then became a clavier from which he drew sweet sounds and graceful improvisations, the result being due far less to the instrument than to him who had the secret of playing it.

I would say the same of all those whom Napoleon employed both in the Civil Service and in the Army: by putting them into the right place and simply asking of them what they knew and what they could do, he doubled their accomplishments and their success. After Napoleon's fall I saw the same men employed under the Restoration; they no longer justified the idea they had given one of themselves. One can often compare men to the figure "0" which owes all its importance to the number preceding it. . . . Without Napoleon we have seen what became of his lieutenants, Counsellors of State and so many others who shone only in the reflection of his glory and genius. . . .

Master of France and of Europe by victories, he had brought all parties and all interests, those who had suffered and those who had [been in the ascendant], victims and executioners alike, to abdicate in his favour. Indestructible convictions and the most fervent of passions lapsed into silence and held their hand, waiting for the time when the Supreme Being should think fit to recall the colossus He had sent upon earth to accomplish His designs.

The era of pacification at home and social and political reorganization had begun and ended with the Consulate. It was then that far-seeing minds realized that there was a great weakness behind all these gifts, gifts so well calculated to dazzle the world. It was the infirmity of refusing to believe in the limitations, those remorseless frontiers, of human nature and activity. It is a curious thing that Napoleon, whose good sense [amounted to] genius, never discovered the point at which the impossible begins.

The more I saw of him, the greater was my conviction that he thought only of satisfying his own desires and adding incessantly to his own glory and greatness. The slightest obstacle enraged him: he would sacrifice everything to overcome it, and in his satisfaction at discovering that whenever a collision occurred nothing could withstand his power or his will, when it came to choosing between the present and the future he preferred the present as the more certain and subject to his will. In a word he thought less of leaving a race, or a dynasty, behind him than a name which should have no rival and a glory which could never be excelled. . . .

His treatment of Spain and the head of the Catholic world had shown that an immoral action or abuse of power was nothing to him so long as he attained his object. But more than anything else it was his expedition to Russia and his scheme for a continental blockade which made it plain to everyone, even his oldest colleagues, that death alone could set a limit to his plans and put a curb on his ambition. . . .

May I conclude what I have to say about him with one last reflection. The beginning of his career was stamped with greatness because, in his rapid ascent from obscurity to the pinnacle of glory and power, he had recourse only to what was heroic and great about him, his character and intellect. The middle period was rich with marvels because with the help of his omnipotence he could give his genius free rein. The end was miserable because his heart was hard and his spirit petty, and heart and spirit alone make a man a hero in adversity.

COUNT ROEDERER [8]

What characterizes Bonaparte's mind is the power and steadfastness of his concentration. He can spend eighteen hours at a time working either at the same thing or at different things. I have never seen him mentally fatigued. His mind always remained resilient even when he was physically tired—or when he was angry. I have never known him wander from the matter in hand, least of all from the matter under discussion back to the last piece of business or on to the next. News from Egypt, whether good or bad, never diverted his attention from discussions on the Civil Code; nor did the Civil Code distract him when he turned to formulate plans to safeguard Egypt. There never was a man more fully engaged in what he was doing, a man more capable of refusing to consider an idea if it came at the wrong moment—or more assiduous and intent upon thinking an idea through when he reckoned the time was right to consider it. . . .

One remarkable thing about his government was the way in which those who were mediocre felt talented, while those who were talented felt mediocre. This was because he inspired the former and stunned the latter.

COUNT MOLLIEN [9]

When I first worked for the First Consul I found it exceedingly difficult to sort out my ideas about him. I am sure that I was not the only person to think him one of the great enigmas of history. . . .

[8] From *Autour de Bonaparte: Journal du Comte P. L. Roederer*, ed., M. Vitrac (Paris, 1909), pp. 93–95; translated by K. Gladstone.

[9] From F. Mollien, *Mémoires d'un ministre du Trésor Public 1780–1815*, ed. C. Gomel (Paris, 1898), I, 316–17; III, 2–5; translated by K. Gladstone.

The closer I came to this astonishing man, and the more I observed him, the less I was able to interpret his character and bring him into proper perspective. I found it difficult to understand the combination of authority and simplicity in his character, his ability to cause those who met him to respond, at one and the same time, in a variety of ways to his own personality, making them feel respect for his position, admiration for the diversity of his talents and a sort of fear caused by his boundless power. People were puzzled . . . by the way he mistrusted men with long and excellent records of service, whereas he was apparently prepared to trust someone as new as myself to give an opinion about the other men whom he had chosen to occupy key positions in the state. I understood this to stem from his wish, indeed his positive need, to appear as the only person who was really indispensable to the state, and . . . to whittle down the importance of anyone near him who might even partially usurp this position. And I suspect that this intention was more an instinctive reaction on his part than a calculated policy.

There can be no doubt that his inexhaustible genius, the audacity and speed of his plans, often confounded the routine and conventional preparations of his enemies. And similarly there can be no doubt that some of his greatest achievements can be explained by that persistence, that diligence which he exhibited and which caused all those who carried out his orders to work in a zealous and dedicated manner. The very difficulties of carrying out these orders roused and spurred his men on. What a host of different obstacles, considered insurmountable before, were cleared away during this period! And yet Napoleon at the height of his power misjudged in himself and in others the limits of what men can hope to achieve. He often used to say that he found the role of king too easy and that he had taken over the job of prime minister. But difficulties arose when this prime minister had the world in his power and wanted to direct everything that happened, whether in Madrid, Vienna, Berlin or the French capital itself. On one occasion, in a year when food was short, when he was involved in military operations at the far end of Europe, he wanted to attend, in person, to the supply of rations to the several hundred thousand men under his command and simultaneously to see to the provisioning of Paris and the major cities of France. . . . Then on the same day he pronounced upon the municipal budgets of several French towns, decided the fate of two or three kingdoms in Germany, and all this while simultaneously trying to work out what foreign governments were planning . . . and coping with a very large and varied correspondence.

Although there can be no doubt that his decrees, decisions and letters reveal the same characteristic clarity and precision which come from practice and skill in commanding men, it is easy to imagine how many matters of great importance could be jeopardised by this mass of orders and measures which often focused on one purpose at the expense of all the others. . . . One can see how modifications were necessary before the orders could be implemented and how variations in interpreting them could occur. Finally, the state of constant war inevitably disturbed and led to uncertainty in business transactions. As a result, even though an aura of glory encompassed France in this period, the prosperity which she so richly deserved was not achieved.

This government, which did not let itself be hampered by any form of criticism, certainly created a brilliant effect, while the strong administration implanted in France impressed foreigners. . . . It was an effective way to guarantee prompt obedience to the firm will of the man who organized and directed it. Napoleon rather enjoyed being admired by other rulers for the accuracy and ease with which, in the large and complicated mechanism of government, every movement eventually reached back to him as if he were its origin and end. But it was impossible for this government, which every year increased its territory through new conquests, relentless endeavour and endless new undertakings, not to neglect, on occasion, duties which, though merely routine, are nevertheless considered essential by men today.

9

As Leader

As Molé says, Napoleon could stir men into showing greater zeal and competence than they had thought themselves capable of. And he could very often command loyalty, even devotion—particularly in the army. His bravery and dash at Lodi had earned him an approving nickname, "the little corporal"; his wandering round the campfires at night, the license to speak to him freely which he gave seasoned rankers, served to keep him in touch, as it were, with his soldiers; while his care for their interests and his victories stirred devotion in men whose only moments of glory had been when they had shared his. There were thousands for whom, after 1815, life became too safe, too dull—too "unheroic" (I am thinking of Stendhal).[1]

BY ONE OF HIS GUARD[2]

[It] was 25 November [1812. At last] the head of the column appeared . . . a few on horseback, but the greater part on foot. . . . Those on foot dragged themselves painfully along, almost all of them having their feet frozen and wrapped in rags or in bits of sheepskin, and all nearly dying of hunger. Afterwards came the débris [of what had been] the Cavalry of the Guard. The Emperor came next, on foot, and carrying a baton. He wore a large cloak lined with fur, a dark-red velvet cap with black fox fur on his head. Murat walked on foot at his right, and on his left the Prince Eugène, Viceroy of Italy.[3]

[1] See below, p. 100 n. 4.

[2] From the *Memoirs of Sgt. Bourgogne 1812–13*, ed. J. Fortescue (London, 1930), pp. 194–97.

Bourgogne joined the Light Infantry of the Guard in 1805 and had fought in Spain, Austria, and Poland before this campaign. Picart was a Grenadier of the Guard.

[3] Murat, the cavalryman who had helped Napoleon on 13 Vendémiaire year IV and on 18 Brumaire year VIII, was rewarded for his splendid services in war by being given the Duchy of Berg, the Kingdom of Naples and Sicily—and the hand of Napoleon's sister Annunziata, rebaptized Caroline. In 1814 this innkeeper's son —encouraged by his wife and by Fouché—fought for the allies against Prince Eugène, hoping thereby to conserve his kingdom. It was in vain. So in 1815 he came out for Napoleon, but was captured and shot on October 18, 1815. He was then forty-eight.

Next came the Marshals whose corps had been nearly annihilated. . . .

After them came the Imperial Guard on foot, marching also in order. Poor Picart, [my companion], who had not seen the army for a month, gazed in silence. . . . Great tears fell from his eyes, rolled down his cheeks, and froze in his moustache. Then, turning to me, he said: "I don't know, *mon pays*, if I am awake or dreaming. It breaks my heart to see our Emperor on foot, his baton in his hand. He, so great, who made us all so proud of him!" He went on: "Did you notice how he looked at us?"

The Emperor had turned his head towards us as he passed. He looked at us as he always looked at the men of his Guard when he met them. He seemed, in this hour of misfortune, to inspire us by his glance with confidence and courage. Picart declared that the Emperor had recognised him, which was quite possible. Poor Picart forgot all his own miseries, and now only thought of the Emperor, and of the comrades he longed to see.

At last the Grenadiers appeared . . . [and] after them came more than 30,000 men, almost all with their feet and hands frozen. Many of them walked leaning on sticks; generals, colonels, other officers, privates, men on horseback, men on foot, men of all the different nations making up our army, passed in a confused rabble, covered with cloaks and coats all torn and burnt, wrapped in bits of cloth, in sheepskins, in everything they could lay their hands on to keep out the cold. They walked silently without complaining, keeping themselves as ready as they could for any possible struggle with the enemy. The Emperor in our midst inspired us with confidence, and found resources to save us yet. There he was—always the great genius; however miserable we might be, with him we were always sure of victory in the end.

BY A WRITER WHO HAD TAKEN PART
IN SEVERAL CAMPAIGNS 1800–13 [4]

I feel something like religious awe as I write the first sentence of a life of Napoleon. For this is the history of the greatest man who has lived since Cæsar, or since perhaps even Alexander. . . .

At the beginning of the new era there was great enthusiasm for the ideals of the Republic and equally great contempt and hatred of the ways of the kings whom we were fighting. Even the military conduct

[4] Namely "Stendhal," Henri Beyle. Translated by K. Gladstone, from pp. 15–18 of the undated Nilsson (Paris) edition of his *Les temps héroïques de Napoléon: la vie de Napoléon—fragments*. The author of *Le Rouge et le Noir* (1830) and *La Chartreuse de Parme* (1839) was eighteen when he went on the first of the campaigns, which took him to Italy (1800), Germany (1806), and Russia (1812). He died in 1842.

of their troops contributed to the feeling of many of our soldiers in 1794 that the French were the only rational beings alive in the world. In our view the people in the rest of Europe who were fighting in order to remain in chains were just pitiable fools or crooks in the pay of the despots who were attacking us. We considered Pitt and Cobourg . . . as the leaders of these crooks and as the personification of all that was corrupt and stupid in the world. We had at that time a deep sense of faith which permeated all we did and which I can no longer detect in our life today. We had no form of religion in 1794; our spirit expressed itself in our belief in the idea of *saving our country*. We saw everything else, like clothes, food or promotion, as utterly unimportant. Because there was no special class in our society, the idea of "being successful in society," so characteristic of the French, simply did not exist. Our eyes used to fill with tears when in the street we saw an inscription on the wall in honour of the young drummer Barra:[5] while . . . numerous civic ceremonies and celebrations strengthened our faith in our single idea of *serving our country*.

This idea was our religion. When Napoleon appeared and put an end to the series of defeats to which we were exposed by the feeble government of the Directory, we considered his dictatorship solely in terms of its *military value* to France. He won victories for us and we judged all his actions by the standards of the religion which we felt in our hearts: what we valued in his dictatorship was *service being done our country*.

Later we were sometimes unfaithful to this religion, but whenever something momentous happened our faith returned. It was like the power that Catholicism wields over its believers at such times.

Things were different for the men born around 1790. When in 1805 at the age of fifteen, they began to open their eyes, the first things to strike them were the velvet and the plumed headdresses worn by the dukes and counts recently ennobled by Napoleon. But we, the old servants of our country, had nothing but contempt for the puerile ambition and ludicrous enthusiasm of this new generation. Among the older men there were many at Court who considered such things to be a caprice on the part of Napoleon, a caprice they condemned. Some even considered it a dangerous whim, while not one in fifty believed it would last. And such men, quite unlike the younger generation, only recaptured the dash and success of the first Italian campaigns of 1796 when the Emperor was away with the army. I shall relate in due course the repugnance felt by the army in Boulogne in 1804 when the cross of the Legion of Honour was first awarded. . . .

Thus it was that there were men who genuinely loved Napoleon

[5] Aged thirteen, this boy had chosen to die rather than save himself by failing to sound the alarm when an attack was launched.

but who, when they were alone at Court and out of Savary's hearing,[6] would admit no other criterion save that of "serving the country" for judging the Emperor's actions. These men included Duroc, Lavalette, Lannes and a few others. They most certainly would have included Desaix and Cafarelli-Dufalga. And strangely enough Napoleon himself was one of them too, for he cared for France with the devotion of a man in love.

BY AN ENGLISH ADMIRER [7]

He very seldom spoke, but when he did, smiled, in some sort, agreeably. He looked about him, not knitting, but joining his eyebrows as if to see more minutely, and went through the whole tedious ceremony with an air of sedate impatience. As the front columns of each regiment passed him, he lifted the first finger of his left hand quickly to his hat, to return the salute, but did not move either his hat or his head. As the regiments advanced, they shouted, some loudly, some feebly, *"vive l'Empereur,"* and many soldiers ran out of their ranks with petitions, which were taken by the grenadier on the Emperor's left hand. [Suddenly] an ill-looking fellow, with a sword by his side, ran from the crowd of spectators, and rushed directly towards the Emperor. He was within arm's length, when the grenadier jumped forwards and, seizing him by the collar, pushed him back. Napoleon did not move a muscle of his body; not a line, not a shade of his face shifted for an instant. Perfectly unstartled, he beckoned the soldiers to let loose their prisoner; and the poor fellow approaching so close as almost to touch his person in front, talked to him for some time with eager gestures, and his hand on his heart. The Emperor heard him without interruption, and then gave him an answer, which sent him away apparently much satisfied with his audience. I see Napoleon at this moment. The unruffled calmness of his countenance, at the first movement of the soldier, relaxing softly into a look of attention and of kindness, will never be erased from my memory. We are not stocks, nor stones, nor Tories. I am not ashamed to say, that on recovering

[6] Savary, soldier son of a soldier father, became Duke of Rovigo, and in 1810 Minister of Police. Lavalette and Lannes were both twenty in 1789. The former had shone at Arcola and in Egypt, became a Counsellor of State and a count in 1808. Lannes, Duke of Montebello, served in Italy in '96, in Egypt, at Ulm and Austerlitz, and at Jena and Friedland. Mortally wounded at Aspern-Essling, he died on May 31, 1809. Cafarelli-Dufalga had been killed ten years before that; and Desaix had fallen at Marengo. For Duroc see above p. 60.

[7] Namely Byron's friend J. Cam Hobhouse, Lord Broughton, who describes a review on April 16, 1815 in *The Substance of Some Letters Written . . . [from] Paris During the Last Reign of the Emperor Napoleon* (London, 1816), I, 38-9.

from my first surprise, I found my eyes somewhat moistened; a weakness that never fails to overpower some persons, when alone and unrestrained by ridicule, at the perusal of any trait of unmixed heroism, especially of that undaunted tranquillity of mind, which formed and finished the master-spirits of antiquity.

10
As Enemy

But not everyone who met him was captivated. Nor did everyone feel that the Napoleonic style of society and the state was the only one, a model to be imposed throughout Europe. Czar Alexander, it is true, was bewitched by him in their talks at Tilsit; and Mme. de Staël, despite her account, also had her three years of admiration. Then disenchantment broke her dream, which gave way, in all sincerity, to a principled repudiation of almost everything he stood for. And what was Napoleon's attitude to this monstrosity, a female intellectual who loved to meddle in politics? "Let [the] hussy . . . keep quiet . . . or else . . . I shall crush her." [1] *But then he also tried to crush Alexander and Britain—and they too witnessed his downfall (though with an exultation untempered by her sadness at the knowledge that Waterloo was a defeat for France as well as for the Tyrant). As for Metternich, he had reckoned in 1813 that such a defeat could, and should, be avoided by the Emperor's surrendering every conquest beyond the "natural frontiers," the Rhine, the Alps, and the Pyrenees. Was this realistic, or was it the scheme of a master-diplomat out to brand Napoleon as the only obstacle to peace? Metternich must have been near the conclusion reached by the historian Vandal, that such a retreat, while there still glimmered the faintest hope of victory, was quite "beyond the capacity of [the Emperor's] character."* [2] *As Molé observed, "he never discovered the point at which the impossible begins."*

BY AN "IDÉOLOGUE" [3]

Bonaparte made himself remarkable by his character and capacity as much as by his actions. . . . In [the] style [of the proclamations he issued in Italy] there reigned a spirit of moderation and dignity, which formed a contrast with the revolutionary bitterness of the civil leaders

---

[1] Quoted in J. C. Herold, *Mistress to an Age: the Life of Madame de Staël* (London, 1959), pp. 156, 225.

[2] Apropos not of 1813, but 1802. Quoted in Markham, *Napoleon*, p. 95.

[3] Namely Germaine de Staël (1766–1817), daughter of Necker, the great financier who was Louis XVI's popular Minister of Finance in 1789. A "constitutionalist," she narrowly escaped being murdered in the September Massacres of 1792. Exiled

of France. He was said to be much attached to his wife, whose character was full of gentleness; people took delight in ascribing to him all the generous qualities which give a pleasing relief to extraordinary talents. Besides, the nation was so weary of oppressors who borrowed the name of liberty, and of oppressed persons who regretted the loss of arbitrary power, that admiration knew not what to attach itself to, and Bonaparte seemed to unite all that was fitted to take it captive.

It was with this sentiment, at least, that I saw him for the first time at Paris [in the autumn of 1797]. I could not find words to reply to him, when he came to me to say that he had sought my father at Coppet, and that he regretted having passed into Switzerland without seeing him. But, when I was a little recovered from the confusion of admiration, a strongly marked sentiment of fear followed. Bonaparte, at that time, had no power; he was even believed to be not a little threatened by the captious suspicions of the Directory; so that the fear which he inspired was caused only by the singular effect of his person on almost all who approached him. I had seen men highly worthy of esteem; I had likewise seen monsters of ferocity: there was nothing in the effect which Bonaparte produced on me, that could bring back to my recollection either the one or the other. I soon perceived, in the different opportunities which I had of meeting him during his stay at Paris, that his character could not be defined by the words which we commonly use; he was neither good, nor violent, nor gentle, nor cruel, after the manner of individuals of whom we have any knowledge. Such a being had no fellow. His cast of character, his understanding, his language, were stamped with the impress of an unknown nature. . . .

Far from recovering my confidence by seeing Bonaparte more frequently, he intimidated me more and more. I had a confused feeling that no emotion could influence him. . . . He never believed in exalted sentiments either in individuals or in nations: he considered the expression of these sentiments as hypocrisy. . . . [He was always] more willing to pardon a selfish calculation than a disinterested opinion: it was by the bad side of the human heart that he reckoned on acquiring the command of it. . . .

He regarded a human being as an action or a thing, not as a fellow creature. He did not hate any more than he loved; for him nothing existed but himself; all other creatures were cyphers. He was an able

for being too "royalist" under the Directory, she was again in 1803 exiled by Napoleon for being too "republican," and her great work, *De l'Allemagne* (1813), was seized and pulped (Savary told her it was "un-French"). This extract is taken from her *Considerations on the Principal Events of the French Revolution*, 3 vols. (London, 1821), II, 195–99, 257–59, 326–30, 381–86; III, 159–62, 322–23, 390–91. The first edition of this work appeared in 1818. On paragraphs two to five of the passage quoted, see Parker, "The Formation of Napoleon's Character," *French Historical Studies*, VII (1971), 23, n59.

chess-player, and the human race was the opponent to whom he proposed to give check-mate. His successes depended as much on the qualities which he lacked as on the talents which he possessed. Neither pity, nor religion, nor attachment to any idea whatsoever, could [deflect] him from his principal direction. He was for his self-interest what the just man should be for virtue; if the end had been good, his perseverance would have been noble.

Every time that I heard him speak, I was struck with his superior [qualities. . . . His conversation] indicated a fine perception of circumstances, such as the sportsman has of the game which he pursues; sometimes he related the events of his life in a very interesting manner; he had even somewhat of the Italian imagination in narratives which allowed of gaiety. Yet nothing could triumph over my invincible aversion for what I perceived in him. I felt in his soul a cold sharp-edged sword, which froze the wound that it inflicted; I perceived in his understanding a profound irony, from which nothing great or beautiful, not even his own glory, could escape; for he despised the nation whose votes he wanted, and no spark of generous enthusiasm was mingled with his desire to astonish the human race. . . .

Whether Napoleon lives or dies, whether he re-appears or not on the continent of Europe, one single motive leads me to speak of him; it is the ardent desire that the friends of liberty should entirely separate their cause from his, and that they should be careful not to confound the principles of the Revolution with those of the imperial government. . . .

[For] the triumph of Bonaparte in Europe, as well as in France, was founded on a [huge confidence trick, which many people have still not seen through]. The nations persisted in considering him the defender of their rights, at the very moment when he was their greatest enemy. The strength of the French Revolution, of which he had been the inheritor, was immense, because it was composed of the will of the French, and of the secret desires of other nations. Napoleon made use of this power against the old governments for a number of years, before the people discovered that their interest was not his object. Although Bonaparte destroyed republics, and stimulated kings and princes to acts of tyranny, in opposition even to their own natural moderation, it was still believed that all this would end in liberty. . . . [As for] the French, [they] long believed that the imperial government would preserve them from the institutions of the old régime, which to them are peculiarly odious. [But] they also long confounded the cause of the Revolution with that of a new master. . . .

[In fact] there is no counter-revolution more fatal to liberty than that which he accomplished. . . .

When Bonaparte put himself at the head of the French people, the whole nation desired a free and constitutional government. The nobility, long exiled from France, aspired only to return in peace to their homes; the Catholic clergy called for toleration; and a revolution had taken place in the public mind. Europe was willing to resign to France the frontier of the Rhine and the Alps; and the only thing that remained was to secure these advantages by repairing the evils which the acquisition of them had brought along with it. But Bonaparte conceived the idea of effecting a counter-revolution to his own advantage by retaining in the state nothing new except himself. He re-established the throne, the clergy, and the nobility; a monarchy, as Mr. Pitt said, without legitimacy and without limitation; a clergy, who were only the preachers of despotism; a nobility composed of old and new families, who [served no useful function] in the state [but] only as a gaudy decoration of arbitrary power.

Bonaparte opened the door to ancient prejudices, flattering himself that he could arrest them precisely at the point which suited his omnipotence. [And] from the moment that his soul became so grovelling as to see no grandeur except in despotism, it was perhaps impossible for him to do without continual war; for what would a despot be without military glory in a country like France? [And] would the nation be oppressed [at home] without giving it the fatal compensation of ruling abroad in its turn? Absolute power is the scourge of the human race. . . . [And] if the principles of liberty are destroyed in Europe, it is only because he eradicated them from the mind of nations.

How did Bonaparte establish his tyranny? The answer, to Mme. de Staël, lies in the combination of his character and the circumstances of the time—and his character was that of an egotistical Machiavellian. As for the circumstances:

One circumstance, which was singularly favourable to the power of Bonaparte, was that [after] ten years of tumult . . . nobody in France could believe his situation secure. Thousands of Frenchmen were on the list of emigrants, thousands more had acquired [property confiscated from the nobility and the Church]; thousands were proscribed as priests or nobles; and thousands of others were afraid of being so for what they had done in the Revolution. Bonaparte, who constantly marched between two opposite interests, took care not to [put an end to these worries] by fixed laws, which would enable every man to know his rights. To this or that man he gave back his property; from this or that other he took it away for ever. Sometimes he restored the estate of the father to the son, or that of the elder brother to the younger, according to whether he was satisfied or dissatisfied with their personal attachment to him. There was not a Frenchman who had not something big to ask of the government; and the First Consul reserved to himself, under some pretext or other, the power of disposing of the lot of each and every one. . . . A singular concurrence of circumstances placed the laws of the period of terror, and the military force created by republican enthusiasm, at the disposal of one man. What an inheritance for an able despot!

The party among the French who sought to resist the continually increasing power of the First Consul, had to invoke liberty in order to struggle against him with success. But at this word the aristocrats and the enemies of the Revolution raised the alarm of Jacobinism, and thus seconded the tyranny; [while to reassure] the Jacobins, pamphlets were poured forth which declared that there was no reason to apprehend that Bonaparte meant to resemble Cæsar, Cromwell, or Monk— obsolete roles, it was said, which were no longer suitable to the age. . . .

[Once Bonaparte had established his tyranny, continues Mme. de Staël], it was necessary to satisfy the ambitions of all who would support it. The taxes of the whole of Europe scarcely afforded a sufficient supply of money; and so Bonaparte sought other treasures in vanity.

The principal moving power of the French Revolution was the love of equality. Equality in the eye of the law partakes of justice, and consequently of liberty; but the desire of annihilating every rank superior [to one's own] is one of the [unpleasant aspects] of self-love. Bonaparte well knew the influence of this failing in France, and he availed himself of it. The men who had shared in the Revolution were not willing that there should be classes above them. Bonaparte rallied them round his standard by promising them the titles and dignities of which they had stripped the nobles. "Do you wish for equality?" said he to them. "I will do better still, I will give you inequality in your own favour." . . . An English caricature represents Bonaparte as cutting up the red cap of liberty into shreds, to make a grand *cordon* of the legion of honour. How exact an image of the nobility invented by Bonaparte, who could boast of nothing but the favour of their master! . . .

[But] it was not enough to have degraded the republican party by entirely changing its nature; Bonaparte wished also to deprive the royalists of that dignity which they owed to their perseverance and their misfortunes. He gave the greater part of the offices of his household to nobles of the old regime: he thus flattered the new race by mingling them with the old, and, as he himself united the vanity of an upstart to the gigantic talents of a conqueror, he loved the flattery of the courtiers of the former reign because they were more skilful in that art than the new men, whatever might be the eagerness of the latter to distinguish themselves in the same career. . . .

It is pretended that, in discussions in the Council of State, Napoleon displayed a universal sagacity. I have some doubts of the ability ascribed to a man who is all-powerful; one is not, however, master of Europe for fifteen years, without having a piercing view of men and things. But there was in the mind of Bonaparte an incoherence, which is a marked feature of those who do not range their thoughts under the law of duty. The power of commanding had been given by nature to Bonaparte; but he made himself obeyed only by degrading those whom he subjected. Yet his successes are astonishing; his failures more astonishing still. What he performed, aided by the energy of the nation, is admirable: the state of torpor in which he left it can scarcely be conceived. The multitude of men of talents whom he employed is extraordinary; but the characters whom he debased have done more harm to the cause of liberty than the service that could be rendered to it by all the powers of intelligence. To him, above all, may be applied the fine image of despotism, in [Montesquieu's] *Esprit des Lois*: "he cut the tree down by its roots to obtain its fruit." And perhaps he has even dried up the soil. . . .

Different opinions may be entertained of his genius and of his qualities: there is about this man something enigmatical which prolongs curiosity. Every one represents him under different colours, and each may be right, according to the point of view from which he beholds him; those who seek to concentrate his portrait in a few words, can give only a false idea of him. To attain some general result, we must pursue different ways: it is a labyrinth, but a labyrinth that has a clue —egotism. Those who knew him personally may have found him in domestic life possessing a kind of goodness which the world certainly never perceived. The devoted attachment of some truly generous friends is what speaks the most in his favour. Time will bring to light the principal traits of his character; and those who are willing to admire every extraordinary man, have a right to think him such. But to France he never could, and never can, bring any thing but desolation.

God preserve us then from him, and for ever!

THE LONDON *TIMES*, JULY 5, 1821 [4]

Thus terminates in exile and in prison the most extraordinary life yet known to political history. The vicissitudes of such a life, in-

---

[4] Reprinted in the issue dated August 16, 1969, and used here by permission of Times Newspapers Ltd.

deed, are the most valuable lessons which history can furnish. Connected with, and founded in, the principles of his character, the varieties of fortune which Bonaparte experienced are of a nature to illustrate the most useful maxims of benevolence, patriotism, or discretion. They embrace both extremes of the condition of man in society, and therefore address themselves to all ranks of human beings.

But Bonaparte was our enemy—our defeated enemy—and as Englishmen we must not tarnish our triumphs over the living warrior, by unmanly injustice towards the dead. The details of his life are notorious, and we omit them. The community of which Bonaparte was in his early days a member, and the military education which he received, may, independently of any original bias of character, have laid the foundation of the greatness to which he attained, and of that mischievous application of unbridled power, through which he fell very nearly to the level whence he first had started. Nothing could be more corrupt than the morals of military society among the French before the Revolution—nothing more selfish or contracted than the views (at all times) of a thoroughbred military adventurer.

Bonaparte came into active life, with as much (but we have no reason to think a larger share of) lax morality and pure selfishness as others of his age and calling. The public crisis into which he was thrown gave to profound selfishness the form of insatiable ambition. With talents and enterprise beyond all comparison greater than any against which he had to contend, he overthrew whatever opposed his progress. Thus, ambition in him was more conspicuous than in others, only because it was more successful.

He became a sovereign. How, then, was this pupil of a military school prepared to exercise the functions of sovereignty? An officer, as such, has no idea of divided power. His patriotism is simply love of his troops and his profession. He will obey commands—he will issue them —but in both cases those commands are absolute. Talk to him of deliberation, of debate, of freedom of action, of speech, nay of opinion, his *feeling* is that the body to which any of these privileges shall be accessible must fall into confusion and be speedily destroyed.

Whatever pretexts may have been resorted to by Bonaparte—whatever Jacobin yells he may have joined in to assist his own advance towards power—every subsequent act of his life assures us that military prepossessions in which he was educated, became those by which he was influenced as a statesman: and we are well persuaded of his conviction, that it was impossible for any country, above all for France, to be governed otherwise than by one sole authority—undivided and unlimited.

It may, we confess, be no satisfaction to the French, nor any great consolation to the rest of Europe, to know through what means it was, or by what vicious training, that Bonaparte was fitted, nay, predestined almost, to be a scourge and destroyer of the rights of nations, instead of employing a power irresistible, and which in such a cause none would have felt disposed to resist, for the promotion of knowledge, peace and liberty throughout the world.

In hinting at what we conceive to be the fact, however, we are bound by regard for truth; our business is not to apologize for Bonaparte; but so far as may be done within the brief limits of a newspaper, to analyse and faithfully describe him. The factions also which he was compelled to crush, and whose overthrow obtained for him the gratitude of his country, still threatened a resurrection when the compressing force should be withdrawn. Hence were pretexts furnished on behalf of despotism of which men more enlightened and better constituted than Bonaparte might not soon have discovered the fallacy.

Raised to empire at home, his ambition sought for itself fresh alignment; and foreign conquest was at once tempting and easy. Here the natural reflection will obtrude itself—what might not this extraordinary being have effected for the happiness of mankind, and for his own everlasting fame and grandeur, had he used but a moiety of the force or perseverance in generous efforts to relieve the oppressed, which he wasted in rendering himself the monopolist and patron of oppression!

But he had left himself no resource. He had extinguished liberty in France, and had no hold upon his subjects but their love of military glory. Conquest therefore succeeded to conquest, until nothing capable of subjugation was left to be subdued. Insolence and rapacity in the victor produced among the enslaved nations impatience of their misery and a thirst for vengeance. Injustice undermined itself, and Bonaparte, with his unseasoned empire, fell together, the pageant of a day.

His military administration was marked by strict and impartial justice. He had the art, in an eminent degree, of inciting the emulation and gaining the affections of his troops. He was steady and faithful in his friendships, and not vindictive on occasions where it was in his power to be so with impunity.

Of the deceased Emperor's intellectual and characteristic ascendancy over men, all the French, and some of other nations besides the French who had an opportunity of approaching him, can bear witness. He seems to have possessed the talent, not merely of command, but, when he pleased, of conciliation and persuasion. With regard to his religious sentiments, they were perhaps of the same standard as those of other Frenchmen starting into manhood at a time when infidel writings had so domineered over the popular mind that revealed religion was become a public laughing stock; and in a country where the pure Christian faith was perplexed with subtleties, overloaded by mummeries, and scandalized and discountenanced by a general looseness of morals.

Upon the whole, Bonaparte will go down to posterity as a man who, having more good at his disposal than any other potentate of any former age, had actually applied his immense means to the production of a greater share of mischief and misery to his fellow-creatures—one who, on the basis of French liberty, might have founded that of every other state in Europe—but who [instead] carried on a series of aggressions against foreign states to divert the minds of his own subjects from the sense of their domestic slavery; thus imposing on foreign nations a necessity for arming to shake off his yoke and affording to foreign despots a pretext for following his example. . . .

BY CZAR ALEXANDER I [5]

His Majesty replied that Napoleon was a man who would not scruple to use any means whatever so long as he attained his object. . . . "He is a man who in the midst of the greatest troubles keeps a cool head: his fits of passion are only meant to intimidate people and are often the fruit of calculation. He does nothing without thoroughly considering the consequences of his acts. . . . One of his favourite sayings is that nothing should be undertaken without a plan. In his opinion there is no difficulty that cannot be overcome if you find the right mode of proceeding. Once that is found, the rest is easy; while if the simplest matter possible is undertaken without finding the method of doing it, all is spoilt and no result is obtained. His health is excellent; no one can bear fatigue and hard work better than he does; but he requires eight hours sleep a day, though he does not keep regular hours. He is not eloquent either in speech or in writing; I have heard him dictate letters in an abrupt and unconnected style. . . ."

It is clear that Alexander understands him thoroughly; that Napoleon has preserved a marked influence over his mind; and that he greatly fears him. . . .

BY METTERNICH [6]

My opinion of Napoleon has never varied. I have seen and studied him in the moments of his greatest success; I have seen and

[5] In conversation, December, 1809, with his friend and adviser, Prince Adam Czartoryski. From the latter's *Memoirs,* trans. A. Gielgud (London, 1888), II, 199–200.

[6] From "Napoleon Bonaparte, a Portrait" (1820), in volume I, pp. 269–87 of his *Memoirs,* ed. R. Metternich, trans. A. Napier (London, 1880).

"For nearly half a century the most formidable enemy of the militant French Revolution" (to quote J. M. Thompson, *Napoleon Bonaparte, His Rise and Fall* [Oxford, 1958], p. 293), Metternich (1773–1859) was Austria's Minister of Foreign Affairs from 1809 until he was forced to resign by the Viennese revolution of March, 1848.

followed him in those of his decline; and though he may have attempted to induce me to form wrong conclusions about him—as it was often his interest to do—he has never succeeded. I may then flatter myself with having seized the essential traits of his character, and with having formed an impartial judgment with respect to it, while the great majority of his contemporaries have seen only the brilliant sides and the defective or evil sides of a man whom the force of circumstances and great personal qualities raised to a height of power unexampled in modern history.

Endeavouring with a rare sagacity and an indefatigable perseverance to make the most of what half a century of events seemed to have prepared in his favour; animated by a spirit of domination as active as clear-sighted; skilful in appreciating every advantage which the circumstances of the moment offered to his ambition; knowing how to turn to his own advantage with remarkable skill the faults and weaknesses of others, Bonaparte was left alone on the battle-field where blind passions and furious factions had raged and disputed for ten years, and at last confiscated to his own advantage the whole Revolution.

The judgment is often influenced by first impressions. I had never seen Napoleon till the audience which he gave me when [in August, 1806] I delivered my credentials [as Austria's ambassador to France]. I found him standing in the middle of one of the rooms, with the Minister for Foreign Affairs and six other members of the Court. His attitude seemed to me to show constraint and even embarrassment. His short, broad figure, negligent dress, and marked endeavour to make an imposing effect, combined to weaken in me the feeling of grandeur naturally attached to the idea of a man before whom the world trembled. This impression has never been entirely effaced from my mind: possibly it helped to show me the man as he was, behind the masks with which he knew how to cover himself. In his fits of passion, in his brusque interpellations, I saw prepared scenes, studied and calculated to produce a certain effect on the person to whom he was speaking.

In my relations with Napoleon, what at first struck me most was the remarkable perspicuity and grand simplicity of his mind and its processes. Conversation with him always had a charm for me, difficult to define. Seizing the essential point of subjects, stripping them of useless accessories, developing his thought and never ceasing to elaborate it till he had made it perfectly clear and conclusive, always finding the fitting word for the thing, or inventing one where the usage of the language had not created it, his conversation was always full of interest. He did not converse, he talked; by the wealth of his ideas and the facility of his elocution, he was able to lead the conversation, and one of his habitual expressions was, "I see what you want; you wish to come to such or such a point; well, let us go straight to it."

Yet he did not fail to listen to the remarks and objections which were addressed to him; he accepted them, questioned them, or opposed them, without losing the tone or overstepping the bounds of a business discussion; and I have never felt the least difficulty in saying to him what I believed to be the truth, even when it was not likely to please him.

Whilst in his conceptions all was clear and precise, in what required action he knew neither difficulty nor uncertainty. In practice, as in discussion, he went straight to the end in view without being delayed by considerations which he treated as secondary, and of which he perhaps too often disdained the importance. The most direct line to the object he desired to reach was that which he chose, and which he followed to the end; but then, being no slave to his plans, he knew how to give them up or modify them the moment that his point of view changed, or new combinations gave him the means of attaining his purpose more effectually by a different path.

He had little scientific knowledge, although his partisans encouraged the belief that he was a profound mathematician. But his natural abilities made up for his want of knowledge. He became a legislator and administrator, as he became a great soldier, by following his own instinct. The turn of his mind always led him towards the positive; he disliked vague ideas, and hated equally the dreams of visionaries and the abstraction of idealists. He valued only those sciences which can be controlled and verified by the senses or which rest on observation and experience. He had the greatest contempt for the false philosophy and the false philanthropy of the eighteenth century.

Napoleon was not irreligious in the ordinary sense of the word. He condemned Deism as the result of rash speculation. He looked on Christianity as the basis of all real civilisation; and considered Catholicism as the form of worship most favourable to the maintenance of order and the true tranquillity of the moral world. Personally indifferent to religious practices, he respected them too much to permit the slightest ridicule of those who followed them. It is possible that religion was, with him, more the result of an enlightened policy than an affair of sentiment; but whatever may have been the secret of his heart, he took care never to betray it. His opinions of men were concentrated in one idea which, unhappily for him, had in his mind gained the force of an axiom. He was persuaded that no man was guided or could be guided by any motive other than that of interest. He did not deny the existence of virtue and honour; but he maintained that neither of these sentiments had ever been the chief guide of any but those whom he called dreamers, and to whom, by this title, he in his own mind denied the existence of the requisite faculty for taking a successful part in the affairs of society. I had long arguments with him on . . . this point . . . but I never succeeded in moving him.

He was gifted with a particular knack of recognising those men who could be useful to him. He discovered in them very quickly the way by which he could best attach them to his interest, and he took care to join their fortune to his own, involving them in such a way as to cut off the possibility of retreat to other engagements. He had, above all, studied the national character of the French, and the history of his life proved that he understood it rightly. He privately regarded the Parisians as children. Having reproached him one day with the palpable falsehoods which formed the chief part of his Bulletins, he said to me with a smile, "They are not written for you; and Parisians will believe anything." . . .

It frequently happened that he turned his conversation into historical discussions. These discussions generally revealed his imperfect knowledge of facts, but an extreme sagacity in appreciating causes and foreseeing consequences. And he had, moreover, charged his memory with a collection of names and facts sufficiently copious to impose on those whose studies had been still less thorough than his own. His heroes were Alexander, Cæsar and, above all, Charlemagne. He was singularly occupied with his claim to be the successor of Charlemagne by right and title. He would lose himself in interminable discussions with me in endeavouring to sustain this paradox by the feeblest reasoning.

One thing which he always regretted extremely was that he could not invoke the principle of Legitimacy as the basis of his power. Few men have been so profoundly conscious as he was that authority deprived of this foundation is precarious and fragile, and open to attack. He never lost an opportunity of anxiously protesting against those who imagined that he occupied the throne as a usurper. "The throne of France," he said to me once, "was vacant. Louis XVI had not been able to maintain himself. If I had been in his place, the Revolution —notwithstanding the immense progress it had made in men's minds in the preceding reign—would never have been consummated. The King overthrown, the Republic was master of the soil of France. It is that which I have replaced. The old throne of France is buried under its rubble. I had to found a new régime. The Bourbons could not reign over this creation. I am new, like the Empire; there is, therefore, a perfect [affinity] between the Empire and myself." . . .

He was also much impressed with the idea of deriving the origin of supreme authority from the Divinity. He said to me one day, shortly after his marriage [on April 2, 1810] with the Archduchess [Marie-Louise of Austria], "I see that the Empress, in writing to her father, addresses her letter *to His Sacred and Imperial Majesty*. Is this title customary with you?" I told him that it was. Napoleon then replied, in a grave tone: "It is a fine custom, and a good expression. Power comes from God, and it is that alone which places it beyond the attacks of men. Hence I shall adopt the title some day." . . .

Napoleon looked upon himself as a being isolated from the rest of the world, made to govern it, and to direct every one according to his own will. He had no other regard for men than a foreman in a factory feels for his workpeople. The person to whom he was most attached was Duroc. "He loves me as a dog loves his master," was the expression he used in speaking to me about him. Berthier's feeling for him he compared to that of a child's nurse.[7] These comparisons, far from being opposed to his theory of the motives which actuate men, were the natural consequence of it, for where he met with sentiments which he could not explain simply by interest, he attributed them to a kind of instinct.

Napoleon [certainly] believed in fortune, and who has made the trial of it that he has? He liked to boast of his good star; but he did not deceive himself about himself: and, what is more, he did not care to grant too large a share to fortune in considering his elevation. I have often heard him say: "They call me lucky, because I am able; it is weak men who accuse the strong of good fortune." . . .

In private life, without being amiable, he was good-natured, and even carried indulgence to the point of weakness. A good son and good kinsman, with those little peculiarities that are met with more particularly in the Italian *bourgeoisie*, he allowed the extravagant courses of some of his relations without using sufficient strength of will to stop them, even when it would have been clearly to his interest to do so. His sisters, in particular, got from him everything that they wanted.

Simple and even easy as he was in private life, he showed himself to little advantage in [society]. It is difficult to imagine anything more awkward than Napoleon's manner in a drawing-room. The pains which he took to correct the faults of his nature and education only served to make his deficiencies more evident. I am satisfied that he would have made great sacrifices to add to his height and give dignity to his appearance, which became more common as his corpulence increased. His costumes were designed to form a contrast by comparison with the circle which surrounded him, either by their extreme simplicity or by their extreme magnificence. It is certain that he made Talma, the actor, come to teach him particular attitudes. Out of his mouth there never came one graceful or even a well-turned speech

---

[7] On Duroc and Berthier, see above p. 60 and p. 48 n. 14.

to a woman, although the effort to make one was often expressed on his face and in the sound of his voice. He spoke to ladies only of their dress, of which he declared himself a severe judge, or perhaps of the number of their children, and one of his usual questions was if they had nursed their children themselves, a question which he commonly phrased in terms seldom used in polite society. His feeling against women who mixed in politics or affairs almost amounted to hatred.

In order to judge this extraordinary man, we must follow him upon the grand stage for which he was born. Fortune had no doubt done much for Napoleon; but by the force of his character, the activity and lucidity of his mind, and by his military genius, he had risen to the level of the position which she had destined for him. Having but one passion, that of power, he never lost either his time or his means on those objects which might have diverted him from his aim. Master of himself, he soon became master of men and events. In whatever era he had appeared he would have played a prominent part. But the epoch when he first entered on his career was particularly fitted to facilitate his elevation. Surrounded by individuals who, in the midst of a world in ruins, walked at random without any fixed guidance, given up to all kinds of ambition and greed, he alone was able to form a plan, hold it fast, and conduct it to its conclusion. It was in the course of the second campaign in Italy that he conceived the one which was to carry him to the summit of power. "When I was young," he said to me, "I was revolutionary from ignorance and ambition. Now at the age of reason, I have followed its counsels and my own instinct, and I have crushed the Revolution."

He was so accustomed to think of himself as necessary for the maintenance of the system he had created that in the end he no longer understood how the world could go on without him. I have no doubt that he spoke from a deep and thorough conviction when, in our conversation at Dresden in 1813, he said to me these very words: "I shall perish, perhaps; but in my fall I shall drag down thrones, and with them the whole of society!" The prodigious successes of which his life was full had doubtless ended by blinding him; but up to the time of the campaign of 1812, when he for the first time succumbed under the weight of illusions, he never lost sight of the profound calculations by which he had so often conquered. . . .

The question has often been asked, Whether Napoleon was radically good or bad? It has always seemed to me that these epithets, as they are generally understood, are not applicable to a character such as his. Constantly occupied with one sole object, given up day and night to the task of holding the helm of an empire which, by progressive encroachments, had finished by including the interests of a great part of Europe, he never recoiled from fear of the wounds he might cause, nor even from the immense amount of individual suffering inseparable from the execution of his projects. As a war-chariot crushes everything which it meets on its way, Napoleon thought of nothing but to advance. Disinterested generosity he had none; he only dispensed his favours and kindnesses in proportion to the value he put on the utility of those who received them. He treated others as he thought himself treated by them. He accepted all services, without scrutinising either the motives, the opinions, or the antecedents of those who offered them to him, except to make use of them for his own purposes.

Napoleon had two aspects. As a private man, he was easy tempered and tractable, without being either good or bad. In his public capacity he admitted no sentiment; he was never influenced either by affection or by hatred. He crushed or removed his enemies, without thinking of anything but the necessity or advisability of getting rid of them. This object gained, he forgot them entirely and injured them no more.

Many useless attempts have been made, and much learning vainly expended in order to compare Napoleon to such or such of his predecessors in the career of conquest and political revolution. The mania for parallels has been a real evil for history; it has shed a false light on the most remarkable characters, and has often quite distorted the point of view from which they ought to be regarded. It is impossible to judge of a man when separated from the setting in which he was placed, and the circumstances which combined to act upon him. Even if nature were pleased to create two individuals absolutely alike, their development in periods and situations which admit of no analogy would necessarily efface the first resemblance and confuse the unskilful painter who wishes to reproduce it. The true historian, he who is aware of the infinitely varied elements which ought to enter into the composition of his pictures, will gladly give up the vain idea of comparing Napoleon to the heroes of antiquity, the barbarian conquerors of the Middle Ages, a great king of the last century, or a usurper of the stamp of Cromwell. . . . [Such comparisons] inevitably falsify the truth of history.

Napoleon's system of conquests was likewise unique. The object of the universal domination to which he aspired was not the concentration of an enormous region in the immediate hands of the government, but the establishing of a central supremacy over the states of Europe, after the ideal disfigured and exaggerated in the Empire of Charlemagne. If momentary considerations made him abandon this system, if they led him to appropriate or to incorporate with French territory countries which, in his own interest, he ought not to have touched, these measures, far from advancing the development of the great plan which he had really in his mind, only served to overturn and destroy it. This plan would have been extended to the Church. He wished to make Paris the seat of Catholicism, and to detach the Pope from all temporal interests, while assuring to him spiritual supremacy under the ægis of Imperial France.

In these political and military combinations, Napoleon did not fail to reckon largely on the weakness and errors of his adversaries. It must be confessed that a long experience only too well justified him in following this principle. But it is also certain that he abused it, and that the habit of despising the means and capabilities of his adversaries was one of the principal causes of his downfall. The Alliance of 1813 destroyed him, because he was never able to persuade himself that the members of a coalition could remain united and persevere in a given course of action.

The opinion of the world is still divided, and perhaps will always be, on the question, Whether Napoleon did in fact deserve to be called a great man? It would be impossible to dispute the great qualities of one who, rising from obscurity, has become in a few years the strongest and most powerful of his contemporaries. But strength, power, and superiority are more or less relative terms. To appreciate properly the degree of genius which has been required for a man to dominate his age, it is necessary to have the measure of that age. This is the point from which opinions with regard to Napoleon diverge so essentially. If the era of the Revolution was, as its admirers think, the most brilliant, the most glorious epoch of modern history, Napoleon, who was able to take the first place in it, and to keep it for fifteen years, was, certainly, one of the greatest men who have ever appeared. If, on the contrary, he only had to move like a meteor above the mists of a general dissolution; if he found nothing around him but the *débris* of a ruined social order . . . ; if he only had to combat a resistance weakened by universal lassitude, feeble rivalries, ignoble passions [and] adversaries everywhere disunited and paralysed by their disagreements, the splendour of his success diminishes with the facility with which he obtained it. Now as, in our opinion, this was really the state of things, we are in no danger of exaggerating the idea of Napoleon's grandeur—while still acknowledging that there was something extraordinary and imposing in his career.

The vast edifice which he had constructed was exclusively the work of his hands, and he was himself the keystone of the arch. But this gigantic construction was essentially wanting in its foundation; the materials of which it was composed were nothing but the ruins of other buildings; some were rotten from decay, others had never possessed any consistency from their very beginning. The keystone of the arch has been withdrawn, and the whole edifice has fallen in.

Such is, in a few words, the history of the French Empire. Conceived and created by Napoleon, it only existed in him; and with him it was extinguished.

NAPOLEON IN HISTORY

Thousands of books and articles have been written about Napoleon and the watershed decades with which his life coincided—decades when Europe changed, in important respects, from what it had been into something our generation can recognize as familiar. Whether, of course, individuals approved or deplored what had taken place affected the way they judged events in those formative decades, and hence the way they viewed the man whose life and work were spliced into them. Besides (and another reason for disagreement about him), there were so many facets to the man and his policies that he could neither be admired nor deplored in toto save by someone obsessed with one part to the exclusion of the whole. The result has been, inevitably, a plethora of biographies whose flavor is affected, not merely by the sources available to their writers, but also by those writers' attitudes toward liberty, order, religion, French interests (and Europe's)—these and a dozen more shibboleth concepts. This is not a question of simple personal bias. Such concepts divide men still, a fact which, given that historians cannot escape being part of mankind, means that their books must in some ways mirror the preoccupations and priorities of the societies they are part of. "It is impossible," as Geyl says at the beginning of his fascinating study of the varying ways in which Napoleon has been portrayed, "It is impossible that two historians, especially two historians living in different periods, should see any historical personality in the same light." [1] Consequently, we can hardly expect that, however professional training and scholarship manage to curb the errors and excesses attributable to personal bias, a definitive biography of Napoleon will ever appear.

Thiers was less a professional historian than a professional politician.[2] Nevertheless, some of the strength of his monumental Histoire du Consulat et de l'Empire[3] *stems from his use of Na-*

---

[1] P. Geyl, *Napoleon, For and Against* (London, 1957), p. 15.

[2] To borrow Rudé's phrase, *Robespierre* (Englewood Cliffs, N.J.: Prentice-Hall, Inc., 1967), p. 131.

[3] 20 vols. (Paris, 1845–62).

poleon's correspondence as well as the memoirs—always a dangerous source to rely on. By and large this History strengthened the "Legend"; for even if this parliamentary liberal was bound to find much to criticize in the Emperor's style, the Consul's achievement stirred in him an admiration which colors the whole of his powerful narrative. This was an immensely influential history, and it remained so even after Taine had launched his corrosive attack on the egoist who had stifled initiative by his methods and by institutions which still fettered the French, as he saw it, in his generation.[4] To this "bitterly disillusioned heir of Mme. de Staël"[5] the Emperor was antinational and not, as his nephew insisted, the hero whose "glory was a national possession."[6] But after France's defeat by the Prussians in 1870, after the ordinariness of the Third Republic became established, it was hardly surprising that there was a powerful current of admiration for the glory and order and the decisiveness that marked the fifteen years after Brumaire—that, despite Taine, a run of substantial books should have been on the whole favorable to Napoleon. Madelin's work may be seen, perhaps, as the culmination of this tendency.[7]

But a very different attitude was beginning to show even while those admiring books were being published. Professional academic historians were beginning to take a hand, their conclusions being informed by research in the archives which, from the late-nineteenth century, has been the hallmark of "real" history. Not that the sources used—and used properly—are the sole determinant of a book's flavor; and the usual "stance" of French professors has been, on the whole, republican, lay, and democratic. Thus for Aulard, the first incumbent of the Chair of the History of the French Revolution, Napoleon was the preeminent destroyer of the lay Republic that the Revolution had created.[8] And for Lefebvre, too, that Republic stood for something fine; it was invested with a sort of moral quality—and also a demo-

---

[4] Taine's character study of Napoleon first appeared in the *Revue des Deux-Mondes* in 1887, a revised version of which appeared in his 1891 book (see below p. 134–42).

[5] Geyl's phrase, *Napoleon, For and Against*, p. 133.

[6] In his *Napoléon et ses détracteurs* (Paris, 1887).

Prince Napoleon, who had edited his uncle's *Correspondance*, was the son of Jérôme Bonaparte.

[7] Namely his *Histoire du Consulat et de l'Empire*, 16 vols. (Paris, 1937–54).

The extract given below comes from a somewhat earlier work first published in Paris in 1932–33.

[8] His *Histoire Politique de la Révolution Française* appeared in 1901, subtitled *Origines et développement de la Démocratie et de la République, 1789–1804.*

cratic quality.[9] *For his republic was that of the Jacobins, not the post-Thermidor regime dominated by the bourgeoisie whose interests Bonaparte fostered while (and this was Aulard's point) carefully keeping them and the* petit peuple *apart. But while Lefebvre must be considered "against" and not "for" Napoleon, there is, as Geyl observes,*[10] *an absence of* parti pris *in his work which (given its other qualities of learning and lucidity) lifts it out of the run of merely "good books" and into the status of a classic. There is a sense of perspective, a "situating" of the man, as well as evaluation. This is good history. We are bound to hope, with Soboul, that this example is one that historians will, in the closing years of this century, follow as they write on Napoleon. For they will continue to write about this wonderful, terrible man: in the words with which Geyl concludes his book, "the argument will go on."* [11]

[9] G. Lefebvre (1874–1959) published the first edition of his *Napoléon* in Paris in 1935. He too held the Chair which Aulard had occupied; A. Soboul is currently its incumbent.

[10] *Napoleon, For and Against,* pp 421–22.

[11] *Ibid.,* p. 449.

11

Adolphe Thiers (1845-62)[1]

The republican government in 1795 had imposed peace on Spain, Prussia, and Northern Germany, but remained engaged in war with Austria and England, when there suddenly appeared in the army of the Alps a young artillery officer, of small stature, shy, but haughty expression of face, striking, but eccentric turn of mind, alternately taciturn or lavishly loquacious, one moment disgraced under the Republic, and then banished into the bureaux of the Directory, where he attracted attention by his just and profound opinions on every phase of the war, which procured him the command of Paris on the 13 Vendémiaire, and soon after the command of the troops in Italy. Reappearing suddenly amongst the army as commander-in-chief, he immediately impressed an extraordinary momentum on events, crossed the Alps, invaded Lombardy, conquered in succession the different armies of Austria, forced her to acknowledge

[1] From *The Consulate and Empire of France,* trans. D. Campbell and J. Stebbing (London, 1893–94), II, 166, 174–75; IV, 590–92; VII, 69; X, 258–65; XII, 432–35.

our conquests, and obliged her to subscribe to the immense losses she had sustained. He thus gave peace to the continent, and his astonishing deeds he expressed in language entirely new by its originality and grandeur, a language that may be called military eloquence. That this extraordinary young man should appear like a meteor on this disturbed and bloody horizon without attracting every eye and chaining every heart would have been impossible. Even had France been ice-cold, which she never was, she would have been captivated. She was bewitched, and the entire world with her.

Of all the powers to whom the Revolution had thrown down the gauntlet, one only remained to be conquered. This was England. . . . The Directory, looking for an occupation for the conqueror of Italy, and believing him to be not only the greatest captain of the century, but the most fruitful in resources, commissioned him to [undertake the defeat of] our eternal rival. Young Bonaparte determined to attack England in the east. It was he who suggested the expedition to Egypt, crossed the Mediterranean, conquered the Mamelukes at the Pyramids, the Janissaries at Aboukir, and having become master of Egypt, abandoned himself during some months to wondrous dreams, which embraced at the same time both the east and the west.[2] Learning suddenly that, thanks to its anarchical nature, the Directory had been engaged in a fresh war, which through incapacity was badly managed, General Bonaparte abandoned Egypt, crossed the sea a second time, and by his sudden appearance surprised and delighted a France that was plunged in desolation. He was no more prompt to covet supreme power than France was to offer it; for seeing his mode of directing war, administering conquered provinces, in a word, his manner of managing everything, France had recognised in him a great political as well as a great military chief. Having become First Consul, he signed within two years a continental peace at Lunéville, a naval peace at Amiens. . . . He gave peace to France and to Europe, and allowed the wearied world to breathe after twelve years of blood-spilling. . . .

Nor were his achievements limited to the restoration of peace between the nations of Europe: he also recreated peace within French society:

He reconciled the Roman Church with the French Republic and put an end to the evils of schism. His efforts to make the highroads

---

[2] Or so Napoleon said later, on St. Helena; but in fact it is most unlikely that in the winter of 1798–99 he seriously considered an expedition to India. See J. C. Herold, *Bonaparte in Egypt* (London, 1962), p. 219.

safe and practicable for travellers; to activate commerce and industry; to introduce order into the finances and regularity into our administration; to [prepare] a code of civil laws adapted to our manners; in short, to organise French society in all its parts, had been neither less constant nor less successful. . . . In the Council of State, which had previously been discussing [the proposed Civil Code] article by article, for several months, the First Consul had displayed a method, a clearness, frequently a depth of views, which were a matter of astonishment to every one. They were not surprised to find an administrator, for that quality is indispensable to a great general; but that he should possess the quality of legislator did appear extraordinary. His knowledge of this subject was rapidly acquired. Interesting himself in everything because he comprehended everything, he asked for some law books, and especially for the materials prepared at the time of the Convention [with a view to producing a] Civil Code. He had devoured them, like those books of religious controversy with which he had provided himself when engaged upon the Concordat. Classing in his head the general principles of civil law, combining with these few rapidly collected notions his profound knowledge of man, his perfect clearness of understanding, he had soon qualified himself for directing that important business, and he had even furnished the discussion with a great number of just, new, and profound ideas. Sometimes an insufficient acquaintance with these subjects caused him to support strange ideas: but he soon suffered himself to be led back to the truth by the learned men who surrounded him, and he was the master of them all when it was necessary to draw from the conflict of contrary opinions the most natural and the most rational conclusion. The principal service rendered by the First Consul was that of bringing to the completion of this fine monument a firm mind and persevering application, and thereby conquering the two great difficulties which had hitherto baffled preceding attempts, the infinite diversity of opinions, and the impossibility of proceeding uninterruptedly with the business amidst the agitations of the time. When the discussion had been long, diffuse, obstinate, the First Consul was able to sum up and to decide it by a word; and, moreover, he obliged everybody else to work by working himself for whole days together. . . . The public was astounded, and became accustomed to consider him as the sole author of everything good and great that was done in France. . . .

The first book of the Civil Code was finished. The pacification of France and its internal reorganisation were thus proceeding at an equal pace. Though all the evil was not repaired, though all the good was not accomplished, yet the comparison of the present with the past filled men's minds with satisfaction and hope. All the good effected was ascribed to the First Consul, and not unjustly; for, according to the testimony of his assiduous fellow-labourer, Cambacérès, he directed the whole of the proceedings, attended himself to the details, and *did more in every department than those to whom it was specially committed.*

The man who governed France from 1799 to 1815 had, no doubt, in his career, intoxicating days of glory, but, assuredly, neither he nor France ever witnessed days like these, days when greatness was accompanied . . . by that wisdom which holds out a hope of duration. He had just given [France], after victory, a most glorious peace; he had given [her], after chaos, complete order; he had still left a certain liberty, not all the liberty that was desirable, but as much, at least, as was possible on the morrow of a sanguinary revolution; to all the parties he had done good. . . . Finally, Europe, reconciled with the Republic, feeling without saying that she had been wrong in wishing to interfere in a revolution which did not concern her, and that the unparalleled greatness of France was the just consequence of an unjust aggression heroically repulsed, Europe eagerly came to lay her homage at the feet of the First Consul. . . .

Who could prevent such a man from peacefully enjoying the happiness he had procured others and himself? Some penetrating minds, seeing his devouring activity, experienced a kind of involuntary terror; but the generation of that time gave themselves up to him with blind confidence; and indeed it would be difficult in listening to this young man to doubt his profound wisdom. There was not a single event of the terrible French Revolution that had not deeply penetrated his mind, and added largely to his knowledge of human nature. He spoke of regicide and the effusion of human blood with horror. He considered party spirit a wild and detestable manifestation, and wished to put an end to it by tranquillising the Vendée, and recalling the emigrants. . . . He re-opened the churches, and attended mass. He had a horror of disordered finances, paper money, bankruptcy, and treated with contempt these flatterers of the populace who had abolished indirect taxation. Besides, in eloquent diatribes against Mr. Pitt, inserted in the *Moniteur,* he decried war, which was his profession, his glory, his power, and said he would be very glad if Mr. Pitt and his adherents were sent to bivouac on blood-stained battlefields, and learn what war really was. Lastly, what bitter raillery did he not pour forth against the inventors of a universal republic who wished to submit all Europe to a single power, and moreover wished to model his government on [some blueprint] drawn from their own brain! Who could teach anything to this young man, so well instructed by the events of the French Revolution? Alas! he was so wise, so thoughtful, when called upon to judge the passions of others; but when it became necessary to resist his own, what was he?

Now the young consul possessed everything his heart could desire, and satisfied every hope the world had formed of him. His power was limitless, in virtue not only of the laws, but of the adhesion of the nation. He was invested with supreme power for life, which ought to be sufficient for a man who was a husband but not a father; he had also the privilege of choosing his successor, a privilege that allowed him to consult at the same time the interest of the public and gratify his personal affections. As to France, she had, thanks to the Revolution and to him, a position which she had never held before, and which she was never again to hold, even when she commanded from Cadiz to Lübeck. Her frontiers were the Alps, the Rhine, the Scheldt; in fact, all that she could wish for the maintenance of her safety and her power, [because] acquisitions beyond these limits were contrary to the indications of nature and the principles of sound policy. France had emancipated Italy to the Adige, taking care to indemnify in Germany the Austrian princes who formerly had appanages in Italy. Acknowledging the necessity of the papal authority in matters of faith and its high utility in politics, France had restored the Pope, who was indebted to her for the safety and respect he enjoyed, and from her he expected the restoration of all his States. France wisely despised the powerless anger of the Neapolitan Bourbons. She had arranged the affairs of Switzerland with admirable wisdom. Recognising both the great and little cantons, the aristocratic and democratic cantons, because they all existed, obliging them to live in peace and on terms of equality, in a word, putting into execution in the Alps the principles of 1789 she [provided], in the Act of Mediation [1803], the model of all the future constitutions of Switzerland. But it was in Germany especially that the profound wisdom of the consular policy was most eminently displayed. There were German princes stripped of their States by the cession of the left bank of the Rhine to France; there were Austrian princes stripped of their patrimony by the emancipation of Italy. The First Consul never thought of leaving either without compensation, or allowing Germany to remain unorganised. The French Revolution had already established in France the principle of secularisation by the alienation of ecclesiastical property, and extending the principle to Germany, getting it recognised there, furnished ample means of indemnifying the deposed princes. With what remained of the States of the Archbishops of Trèves, of Mayence, of Cologne, and with those of some other ecclesiastical princes, the First Consul collected [the territories needed] to indemnify all the royal families that had suffered loss, and maintain in Germany a wise equilibrium. . . . Not having at that time adopted the principle of writing treaties with his sword alone, he associated in his work Prussia, who was induced to assist through motives of interest, Russia, through self-love, and Austria, influenced by the example of the two other powers. By these means he succeeded in procuring the adoption of the Recess of 1803, a masterpiece of practical and profound policy. This Recess, in fact, re-established in Germany order, peace, and content, and prepared for us the only alliance at that time desirable and possible, that [with] Prussia. France was at that moment so powerful, so dreaded, that with the alliance of one continental State she was certain of the submission of the others; and once the continent was submissive, England would be obliged to swallow in silence her vexation at seeing her rival so great. [As for] Austria, by treating her with respect, by never pushing her to extremities, France was sure of her support. . . . With regard to England, only one difficulty remained to be overcome—[she needed to be] humoured to induce her to pardon us all the glory we had acquired in a few years; and this was possible. A word of flattery from his lips would be sure to touch to the quick the heart of haughty Albion. . . .

What, then, had he to wish more for himself or for France, he, the happy mortal who had become her head? Nothing but to persevere in this policy, which was that of force rendered supportable by moderation. No man ever enjoyed so many diverse species of glory as the conqueror of Rivoli, of the Pyramids, of Marengo—the author of the Concordat, of the treaties of Lunéville and Amiens, of the Act of Mediation, of the Recess of 1803, of the Civil Code, and of the recall of the emigrants. If one merit were wanted to complete the *fasces* of his merits, it was perhaps that he had not given liberty to France. But . . . to the generation of 1800 liberty was only another name for the scaffold, for schism, for the Vendean war, for bankruptcy, for confiscation. The only species of liberty at that time suited to France was the moderation of a great man. But alas! the moderation of a great man, endowed with unlimited power, even were he at the same time endowed with every gift of genius, is this not the most chimerical of all revolutionary chimeras?

But misplaced liberty produces evils as great as does her total absence. This man, at that time so worthy of admiration, was by the very fact of possessing absolute power on the brink of an abyss. In fact, within a few months after the peace of Amiens had been signed . . . his language, sparkling with genius and redolent of ambition, offended the pride of the English; his devouring activity disturbed their peace. He sent an army to St. Domingo, he publicly sent Colonel Sebastiani into Turkey, Colonel Savary into Egypt, and General Decaen into India, charged with missions which it would be very difficult to construe as scientific missions. . . . From that moment the gauntlet was thrown down between the warrior who represented, in his own person, the French Revolution, and the English people, whose jealousy had not been sufficiently soothed. Thus Napoleon, who had been the sage peacemaker in 1802, became the inciter of a general war, merely because he was not able to subdue his passions. But he, like Alexander or Caesar, was a man of genius, and genius is forgiven much and [for a] long [time] by Fortune. . . .

In the general war, then, which recommenced in 1803, Napoleon was again triumphantly successful. Austria was again defeated, Prussia broken at Jena and the Czar brought to the conference table at Tilsit. Thiers continues:

Never had greater lustre surrounded the person and the name of Napoleon; never had greater apparent power been acquired for his imperial sceptre. From the straits of Gibraltar to the Vistula, from the mountains of Bohemia to the North Sea, from the Alps to the Adriatic, he ruled either directly or indirectly, either personally or by princes, who were some of them his creatures, the others his dependants. Beyond were allies or subjugated enemies, England alone excepted. Thus almost the whole continent was under his sway; for Russia, after resisting him for a moment, had warmly adopted his designs, and Austria found herself forced to suffer them to be accomplished, and even threatened with being compelled to concur in them. England, in short, was about to be placed between the acceptance of peace and a war with the whole world.

Such was the external appearance of that gigantic power: it had in it enough to dazzle the world, and it did actually dazzle it; but the reality was less solid than brilliant. A moment's cool reflection would have sufficed to convince one's self of this. Napoleon, diverted from his struggle with England by the third coalition, drawn from the shores of the Channel to those of the Danube, had punished the house of Austria by taking from it, in consequence of the campaign of Austerlitz, the Venetian States, the Tyrol, Suabia, and had thus enlarged the territory of Italy, aggrandised our allies of South Germany, removed the Austrian frontier from ours. So far, so good—for to finish the territorial emancipation of Italy, to secure friends in Germany, to place [buffers] between Austria and France, was certainly consistent with sound policy. But in the intoxication produced by the prodigious campaign of 1805, to change arbitrarily the face of Europe, and instead of being content to modify the past, instead of keeping up for our profit the old rivalry of Prussia and Austria by advantages granted to the one over the other—to wrest the German sceptre from Austria without giving it to Prussia; to create, by the title of Confederation of the Rhine, a pretended French Germany . . . to attempt the restoration of Poland, having in one's rear Prussia, vanquished but fuming, Austria secretly implacable—all this, admirable as a military work, was, as a political work, imprudent, extravagant, chimerical. After having aggravated by the treaty of Tilsit the [resentment felt in] Germany; after having half reconstituted Prussia, instead of restoring or destroying her entirely; after having, in like manner, half reconstituted Poland, and done everything in an incomplete manner, because at these distances time pressed, strength began to fail, Napoleon made irreconcilable enemies, impotent or doubtful friends, raised, in short, an immense edifice, in which everything was new from bottom to top, an edifice run up so rapidly that the foundation had not had time to settle, the mortar to harden.

But if everything is censurable, in our opinion, in the political work of Tilsit, brilliant as it may appear, all is admirable, on the contrary, in the conduct of the military operations [leading up to that settlement]. . . . Everyone will ask himself how it was possible to display so much prudence in war, so little in politics. The answer is easy—in war Napoleon was guided by his genius, in politics by his passions. . . .

Fortune, nevertheless, continued to "forgive" (or at least to spare) this "genius," and even if Spain was not subdued in 1808, Austria was beaten again in the following year. But in the end:

The victory of Wagram, though not equalling those of Austerlitz, Jena and Friedland in [terms of] the grandeur of its trophies, . . . the victory of Wagram, completed by the marriage with Marie-Louise, replaced Napoleon at his highest degree of power; and if prudence had gradually repaired the great fault of the war in Spain, the [illusory hopes placed in that marriage might have been realised. But for this to have happened] something would have had to be changed which was less changeable than destiny—the character of a man [would] have had to be changed, and that man was Napoleon. . . .

Greatness! there is no lack of that in [the man] who succeeded Frederick [as *the* great commander] and surpassed him in the admiration he excited, and the destruction he caused! It was reserved for the French Revolution, destined to change the aspect of European society, to produce a man who would fix the attention of the world as powerfully as Charlemagne, Cæsar, Hannibal, and Alexander. He possessed every qualification that could strike, attract, and fix the attention of mankind, whether we consider the greatness of the part he was destined to perform, the vastness of the political convulsions he caused, the splendour, extent, and profundity of his genius, or his majestic gravity of thought. This son of a Corsican gentleman . . . had, at thirty years of age . . . already run through a most extraordinary career. Become pacific for a while, he by his laws laid the basis of modern society; but again yielding to the impulses of his restless genius, he once more attacked Europe, vanquished her in three battles, Austerlitz, Jena, and Friedland, set up and threw down kingdoms, placed the crown of Charlemagne on his head, and when kings came to offer him their daughters, chose the descendant of the Cæsars, who presented him with a son that seemed destined to wear the most brilliant crown in the universe. He advanced from Cadiz to Moscow, where he was subjected to the greatest catastrophe on record, rose again, but was again defeated, and confined in a small island, from which he emerged with a few hundred faithful soldiers, recovered the crown of France in twenty days, struggled again against an exasperated Europe, sank for the last time at Waterloo, and having sustained greater wars than those of the Roman empire, went to die on an island, bound, by the fear and hatred of kings, bound like Prometheus to a rock. This son of a poor Corsican nobleman has indeed played in the world the parts of Alexander, Hannibal, Cæsar, and Charlemagne! He possessed as much genius as the greatest amongst them; acquired as much fame as the most celebrated, and unfortunately shed more blood than any of them. From a moral point of view, he is inferior to the best of these great men, but superior to the worst. His ambition was not as futile as that of Alexander, nor as depraved as that of Cæsar; but it was not as respectable as Hannibal's, who sacrificed himself to save his country the misfortune of being conquered. His ambition was that usual with conquerors who seek to rule after having aggrandised their native land. Still he loved France and cherished her glory as dearly as his own. As a ruler he sought what was right, but sought it as a despot; nor did he pursue it with the consistency or religious perseverance of Charlemagne. In variety of talents he was inferior to Cæsar, who, being compelled to win over his fellow-citizens before ruling them, had to learn how to persuade as well as how to fight, and could speak, write, and act with a certain simple majesty. Napoleon, on the other hand, having acquired power by warfare, had no need of oratory, nor possibly, though endowed with natural eloquence, could he ever have acquired it, since he never would have taken the trouble of patiently analysing his thoughts in presence of a deliberative assembly; but he could write, as he thought, with force and dignity, though he was sometimes a little declamatory like his mother, the French Revolution: he argued with more force than Cæsar, but could not narrate with his extreme simplicity or exquisite taste. He was inferior to the Roman dictator in the variety of his talents, but superior as a general, both by his peculiar military genius, and by the daring profundity and inexhaustible fertility of his plans, in which he had but one equal or superior (which we cannot decide) —Hannibal—for he was as daring, as prudent, as subtle, as inventive, as terrible, and as obstinate as the Carthaginian general, with one advantage, of living at a later period. Succeeding to Hannibal, Cæsar, the Nassaus, Gustavus Adolphus, Condé, Turenne, and Frederick, he brought military art to its ultimate perfection. God alone can estimate the respective merits of such men; all we can do is to sketch some prominent traits of their wonderful characters.

Napoleon has claims on us Frenchmen, claims which we can neither disavow nor forget, to whatever party we may be attached by birth, conviction, or interest. Certainly in organising our society by the Civil Code, and regulating our administration according to its conditions, he did not give us the political form in which French society was to repose indefinitely, and live peacefully, prosperously, and free; he did not give us liberty, which is still due to us from his heirs; but on the morrow of the French Revolution he could do no more than restore order, and we must thank him for having given us, with that, our civil and administrative organisation. Unfortunately for him and us, he diminished our greatness; but he left us glory, which constitutes moral power, and which in time will restore material greatness. He was by his genius fitted for France, and France for him. What they did together could not have been accomplished by the French army without him, nor by him without the French army. Author of our reverses, but companion of our exploits, we must judge him with severity; but at the same time we must entertain for him the sentiments of soldiers for the general who [for years] conducted them to victory. Let us study his great deeds, which are our own; let us learn from him, if we are soldiers, the art of guiding armies; if we are statesmen, how to govern empires; let us learn, above all, from his faults; let us avoid his example and learn to love moderate greatness, that which is attainable, and is durable because not insupportable to others; in a word, let us learn moderation from this most ambitious of men. Let us, as citizens, draw this last and memorable lesson from his life —that however great, wise, or boundless the genius of any man may be, the destiny of a country should never be entirely entrusted to his power. We most assuredly are not of the number of those who blame Napoleon for wresting France on the 18 Brumaire from the hands of the Directory, in which she might have perished; but it does not follow that because it was well to wrest the country from weak and corrupt hands, that it should have been delivered over unconditionally into the daring and powerful grasp of the conqueror of Rivoli and

Marengo. If any nation ever had an excuse for placing herself in the power of one man, it was France when in 1800 she adopted Napoleon as her chief. It was no pretended anarchy that was raised as a bugbear to terrify the nation into chains. Alas, no! thousands of innocent lives had been sacrificed on the scaffold, in the prisons. The horrors of barbarism had suddenly reappeared in the midst of a terrified civilisation, and even when these horrors had for some time subsided, the French Revolution continued to oscillate between the axe of the executioners, from whom it had been wrested, and the stultified emigrants who wished to effect a retrograde movement over a blood-stained path towards an unattainable Past, and all this whilst the threatening swords of foreigners flashed above the chaos.

At this very time there returned from the East a young hero, full of genius, who had conquered nature and men wherever he had appeared, and who, wise and moderate, seemed formed to captivate the world. There never was a better excuse for entrusting power to a single man, for never was terror more real than that which pervaded French society, never was genius greater than that to which Frenchmen turned for protection. [But] after a few years this great wise man became mad, mad with a different but not less disastrous frenzy than that of '93, a frenzy that immolated a million lives on the battlefield, roused all Europe against France, which was left vanquished on the field, weltering in blood, and stripped of the fruits of twenty years of victory. . . . Who could have foreseen that the wise man of 1800 would become the madman of 1812 and 1813? Yes, it might have been foreseen by anyone who remembered that the possession of unlimited power is always accompanied by an incurable frenzy—the ambition that aims at grasping everything because everything is within its reach—and that this frenzy often leads to the commission of evil by the same person who had before wielded the same power to do good. The life of this great man, so instructive for soldiers, rulers, and politicians, contains a lesson also for citizens. It teaches them that they ought never to abandon their country to the power of one man, no matter who he may be, no matter under what circumstances! This is the cry that springs from my heart, the sincere wish I utter, as I conclude this long history of our triumphs and our reverses: a wish which I hope will penetrate the heart of every Frenchman, and persuade him never to sacrifice his liberty, nor run the risk of doing so, by abusing it.

12

Hippolyte Taine (1891)[1]

Napoleon was so exceptional an individual that he defies classification. The singularity of his temperament and outlook and the qualities of his mind and imagination make it seem as though he was cast in a different form and substance from that of his fellow citizens and contemporaries. He was obviously neither a Frenchman nor a man of the eighteenth century. He seems to belong to another race, to another age. One immediately detects something foreign about him, something Italianate but something elusive too. . . . And in actual fact he was descended from the great Italians, those men of action round about the year 1400, military adventurers whose blood and mental and moral outlook he inherited. . . .

During the Italian Renaissance men felt more keenly and intensely, acted more impulsively and emotionally and were more impetuous and resolute than they are today. These characteristics reappear in this great survivor from the fifteenth century. There had never been, even in the Malatesta and Borgia families, a man with such an excitable and impulsive nature. He was the most irritable, the most easily angered man imaginable, all the more so since he often exhibited a violent temper quite deliberately. Unleashed at the right moment, especially when there were people present, his temper aroused such terror that it enabled him to extort concessions from people and maintain discipline. His outbursts of rage, part deliberate and part spontaneous, served his interests as much as they served to discharge his pent-up emotions, and he turned this to account whenever he needed to make an example of someone or wanted to ensure that his entourage kept on their toes. The people and the army thought of him as being imperturbable, but save on the battlefield, when he wore an inscrutable mask, and at official functions, when he assumed the dignified air the occasion demanded, his manner usually corresponded exactly with his inner state of mind. Sometimes his inner self erupted, giving a sudden, spontaneous effect to whatever he was doing. . . .

He was a terribly impatient man. When dressing, he used to throw any garment which did not suit him onto the floor or into the fire. He would get carried along by his thoughts at such a speed that his

[1] From *Les Origines de la France contemporaine*, vol. v: *Le régime moderne* (Paris, 1891), pp. 5–116; translated by K. Gladstone.

handwriting consisted of a string of unconnected and indecipherable marks which he could not understand when he reread it. Most of the time, therefore, he dictated, but so fast that his secretaries could scarcely keep up with him. When he was in conversation a tremendous torrent of words rushed out; and sometimes the pressure of dammed-up thoughts and feelings inside him became so great that he would burst into a stream of extravagant and foolish talk which was quite uncalled for and out of place. In this way the businesslike, thoughtful stateman could sometimes turn into a ranting improviser and polemist. Even at meetings of the Council of State he would let himself go, forgetting the matter under consideration and launching out left and right into digressions and abuse and proof of the rightness of what he was saying. He would carry on for two or three hours, hammering home his point, repeating himself, determined to win over or simply beat down his listeners; and he would finish up by asking them if he was not right—for he always tried to force everyone to agree with him. When, however, he reflected upon the way in which such agreement had been achieved, he knew perfectly well just what it was worth and, pointing to his chair, he would say, "It is very easy to be clever when you are sitting there." All the same he had enjoyed seeming clever, even though he had simply behaved as his feelings impelled him to do: for his feelings governed him more than he controlled them.

A strange thing in such a man of war and statesman was that he often cried when overwhelmed by his feelings. He had seen thousands of men die and had killed millions, and yet he could still weep after the battles at Wagram and Bautzen or at the deathbed of an old companion in arms. His valet recalled how he had seen him crying over his breakfast after he had left [the dying] Maréchal Lannes:[2] big tears rolled down his cheeks onto his plate. A few words or even just an idea affected him almost as deeply as the physical shock of actually seeing a mangled corpse. In 1806 when he was about to leave for the army and was saying goodbye to Joséphine, his sorrow so overwhelmed him that he broke down and shortly afterwards had an attack of vomiting. He experienced a similar breakdown and vomiting fit in 1809 when he decided to divorce Joséphine. He was upset the whole night long, more vulnerable even than her. "My darling Joséphine, I will never be able to leave you," he cried, as he pulled her back into his arms. Absolutely governed by his feelings of the moment, he wanted her to stay with him, to get undressed then and there and sleep beside him: and he wept over her— "He literally soaked the bed with his tears," recalled Joséphine.

But the most extraordinary thing about him was the almost com-

² See above, p. 101 n. 5.

plete control which his calculating, lucid mind usually exercised over his actions. His will-power was even greater than his intelligence, and to get an idea of its strength it is not enough simply to note the fascination it aroused: one also needs to try and imagine the force and fury of the feelings which this will-power kept in check, which it handled as a coachman handles a team of rearing horses. Picture his will as a coachman who, with arms braced, manages his almost ungovernable steeds as the coach rushes, thundering, close to the edges of chasms and precipices. The force behind his will-power is the tremendous energy inside him, an energy which has its roots deep in his feelings and temperament. Through these roots flows a vigorous sap, an instinct dating from the origins of man, stronger than his intelligence, stronger even than his will itself, man's natural instinct to want to be the centre of all things, to want to make everything relate to himself, in other words man's instinctive *egoism*.

His egoism was active and all-embracing, not passive and inert, and was closely related to his vigorous mental activity. It was developed in the course of his upbringing and by experience of the world, success and absolute power exaggerating it to such a degree that, monster-like, his ego eventually stood as the Colossus once did, towering over human society. This monstrous ego was always reaching out rapaciously to encircle its prey and was goaded into anger by any show of resistance or independence: it could tolerate no other living creature unless the latter were in its power.

His domineering character was already apparent in the period of his adolescence and even during his childhood. Recalling his early years in his father's house on Corsica, Bonaparte depicts himself as a mischievous little devil, rebelling against every form of restraint and without any conscience at all. "Nothing overawed me and I was afraid of no one. Instead I made everyone afraid of me. I used to bite and hit my brother Joseph, and would put the blame on him before he had time to realise what I was up to." He never tired of repeating this excellent stratagem later in his life. He made his talent for lying the measure of his political superiority and used to like recalling how, when he was still only a child, one of his uncles predicted that one day he would rule the world because he was always lying.

Remember this uncle's remark, for it summarizes the whole outlook of his time and country and reflects the particular spirit of life in Corsica. There the police were powerless, justice was non-existent, public affairs were in the hands of whoever could grab control of them, personal vendettas broke out unchecked and were waged without mercy, everyone went about armed. Deceit, fraud and double-dealing were weapons as common as guns and daggers. Such was life in Corsica in the eighteenth century, and it had been like this in Italy

in the fifteenth. Bonaparte's first impressions were thus like those of
the Borgias and Machiavelli, and his early experience forms the basis
of his whole future personal outlook and his subsequent ideas on human society. . . .

Laws in his view were mere phrases in a statute book and justice a
poetic abstraction. What really mattered was actual strength. The
sight of anarchy in France further marked the character and outlook
of the young man already influenced in his childhood by the lawless
conditions of life in Corsica. The influence was similar because the
lessons to be drawn from a disintegrating society are the same as
those to be drawn from a society which is still fragmentary and un-
formed. He very quickly saw through the façade of theories and
words surrounding the Revolution and spotted its real foundations,
namely the primacy of passion [as against reason] and the conquest
of the majority by the minority. He realised that the only choice lay
between conquering and being conquered. The veils were torn aside
from politics after the fall of Robespierre and the real character of
political life was laid bare. It was a life filled with corruption, strug-
gles for power and selfish greed: there was no concern at all for the
public good and for the rights of the people. The men in command
seemed just like gangsters, treating France as loot—and clearly they
intended to use every means at their disposal to keep that loot in their
hands.

In various divisions of the army, especially in Italy, republican
faith and patriotic sacrifice gave way to a life of pleasure. Bare-foot,
in rags and tatters, with a daily ration of four ounces of bread, the
officers' and soldiers' main wish was to forget their recent hardships.
They had gone through so much and had waited so long. Now that
they had reached the promised land they wanted to enjoy it. From
the very first there was an understanding between the general and
his army, and after a year's experience the understanding was perfect.
Bonaparte could see clearly what they could only glimpse, so that
when he urged them on it was in a direction they already wanted to
take. He was simply quicker than they were in realizing that the
world is like a great banquet to which everyone is invited, but where,
to feed really well, one needs to have long arms in order to help one-
self first and leave only the scraps for the other people. . . .

In Bonaparte's view man was born to obey. This is the only right
he has and he is not fit for anything better. As Consul, then as Emperor, he put this theory into practice and found that the results
further justified his convictions. As soon as he made his first gesture
the French prostrated themselves before him, right from the peasants
and soldiers with their dog-like devotion to the great dignitaries who
bowed down to him with Byzantine servility. The Republicans for

their part offered no resistance. Indeed it was among them that he found his best tools—senators, deputies, counsellors of state, judges and administrators of every grade. He immediately saw through their high-flown talk about liberty and equality and spotted their authoritarian tendencies, their need to be in positions of authority, to be able to give orders to others, no matter how lowly their own position. In most of them he also found signs of a natural acquisitiveness and of a liking for good living. There was little real difference between a delegate of the Committee of Public Safety and an Imperial minister, prefect or sub-prefect. The man was the same, only the garb was different. As for the intelligent and cultured liberals of 1789, he dismissed them in a word as "ideologists," men whose ostensible enlightenment was a combination of drawing-room clichés and the musings of people who had never come out of their studies. "Lafayette is a political ninny, always being taken in"—so Bonaparte remarked to Las Cases. But there was one snag about the people like Lafayette, one awkward fact, namely their proven selflessness, the unfailing concern they showed for the welfare of the people, their respect for others, their moral stature, their loyalty and their good faith. In short their motives were pure and noble. Napoleon refused to accept this, for it contradicted his theory, and in conversation with one of these men he challenged him on his integrity. "General Dumas," he said abruptly, "you were one of those fools who believed in liberty, no?" "Yes, Sire, I was and I still am." "And you took part in the Revolution like the others because of ambition, didn't you?" "No, Sire, and I would have made a bad calculation if that had been my motive, for I am still in exactly the same position as I was in 1790." To this Napoleon replied "You are obviously not fully conscious of your motives. You could not have been different from the others. Self-interest is always involved."

This belief was absolutely fundamental to him. His view was that you could manipulate and control men by taking advantage of their egoism, their fear, greed, sensuality, pride and envy. These were men's feelings when they were in a calm and reasonable mood: and it was not difficult to change that mood, to unbalance a man's character by fostering his pride and vanity, giving him a wildly false notion of himself and of other people. Then you could make him do whatever you wanted. . . . Creatures like that are the right sort of material for an absolute government to mould and shape: if there are lumps in the clay all the potter has to do is knead and press and squeeze a bit harder. That was the conclusion Napoleon came to, and he clung to it more and more obstinately despite all the evidence against it. Nothing could make him abandon it, neither the stubborn vigour of the English, nor the gentle inflexibility of the Pope, neither the open insurrection in Spain nor the undercover resistance in Germany, neither the moral opposition of the Catholics, nor even the gradual defection of the French themselves. His view of mankind had its roots so deep in his character that he saw people as it suited him to see them.

Now at last we come to his ambition. This was the dominant force in his character and the product of his temperament and up-bringing and of his own conscious reflection and theory of human nature. And this was what finally brought about his downfall. Ambition was his motivating force and was what lay behind his will-power. It is so integral to his character that he was sometimes totally unaware of it. "I am without ambition," he said to Roederer, and then, reflecting, added with his customary lucidity "or if I do have any it is so innate and integral a part of my nature, so closely bound up with all I do, that it resembles the blood in my veins or the air I breathe. . . ." And on another occasion he remarked "Power is my mistress. I have struggled too hard to get her to allow anyone to take her from me, or even to allow anyone to run a lustful eye over her." His ambition was as insatiable as it was jealous, the mere thought of a rival making him angry, the mere idea of any check to his power making him feel frustrated, penned in. No matter how much power he had his ambition always wanted more. He never felt full even after the most lavish banquet. On the day after his coronation he said to Decrès "I have arrived on the scene too late, there is nothing great left for me to do. . . . Now in ancient times it would have been different. Look at Alexander! First he conquered Asia and then he declared himself Jupiter's son—and everyone save Aristotle and a few pedantic academics, everyone believed him!"

Napoleon's devouring ambition explains why anyone who came near him had to renounce his own will and become a mere tool in his hands. Any sign of independence annoyed him. If there were people of intellectual or moral stature near him he gradually edged them out of the way. Towards the end the only people he tolerated near him were people who were virtually his slaves. His principal servants were either robots or fanatics, men like his devoted admirer Maret or his gendarme and factotum Savary.[3] Right from the beginning he reduced his ministers to the level of clerks: for he was as much an administrator as he was a ruler, and in each department he busied himself with details as well as the overall picture. Therefore his departmental heads needed just to be busy secretaries, dumb executors, rather than advisors with frank and independent views of their own. "I would not know what to do with them if they were not to a certain extent mediocre in intelligence and character," he said. As for his generals,

---

[3] For Savary and Maret, see above, p. 65 n. 18 and p. 102 n. 6.

he was determined to be solely responsible for making or marring their reputations. This was because a soldier with too brilliant a reputation might have become too conspicuous and important. Furthermore, subordinates must never be tempted to become less subservient. The Bulletins rendered good service here, by deliberately omitting names and altering and recasting events, so that on occasion a general could read there an account of a speech he had never made or of deeds in a battle he had never fought. Then if he objected he was advised to keep quiet or, in compensation, allowed to pillage and make himself rich. On becoming a duke or a prince with a massive income from his estates, he remained as much Napoleon's vassal as he had been before, for the ruler who had made him what he now became was careful to keep him dependent; his reward for services rendered was made to consist of estates scattered about in the conquered territories, and this very effectively linked his interests to the Emperor's own. Moreover he deliberately encouraged these men to spend extravagantly; the less secure they were financially, the more dependent on him they would be. Furthermore, he liked to keep a personal grip on everyone as an extra precaution. Consequently he carefully cultivated everyone's baser instincts and enjoyed spotting and taking advantage of people's weaknesses—Savary's avarice, Maret's sycophancy, Cambacérès' vanity, Talleyrand's cynicism and lack of moral backbone, Fouché's Jacobinism, Berthier's foolishness.[4] He brought out their weaknesses, and used them for his own purposes. . . .

There have been other heads of state who have spent their lives doing violence to other men but they did it with a view to achieving something of lasting value and for some national interest. What they called "the public interest" was not some phantom, some fantasy springing from some combination of their imagination, personal obsessions, ambition and pride. They saw that there existed an outer reality, independent of their own personalities and dreams, a reality more definite and important than themselves, in other words the state and society, the vast social organism that lasts forever as it passes from one generation to the next. If they shed the blood of one generation it was to benefit future generations, to save them from civil war or from foreign domination. More often than not they acted

---

[4] See above, p. 48 n. 12 and 14 and p. 63 n. 14. C. M. de Talleyrand-Périgord, Prince of Benevento, was one of the seven bishops who were "constitutionnels" (see above p. 14 n. 4). A shrewd and unprincipled politician, he was soon involved in diplomacy and, after exile in the United States 1793–96, returned to become Minister of Foreign Affairs—a post which he retained after helping Bonaparte in Brumaire. Pushed out by Napoleon in 1807, he returned to the ministry in 1814 under Louis XVIII. His extraordinary life ended in 1838.

like able surgeons, if not for disinterested reasons of morality, at least for reasons of dynastic sentiment and family tradition. Their first and last consideration was the safety and health of their patient, which is why they rarely operated in cases where the risk of bleeding and of complications was very great. They saw beyond their own lives, looked ahead as far as they could, so that their plans for the state took into account its future after they died, so that it could do without them, survive intact and independent, strong and respected. This is what the term "raison d'état" meant, and this was the principle which for eight hundred years prevailed in the consideration of princes. Undoubtedly "raison d'état" authorized and excused many breaches of faith, many outrages, crimes. On the political level however, especially in foreign affairs, it was a guiding principle which had a beneficial effect. And France had been solidly constructed, province by province, by thirty sovereigns steadily working in accordance with this principle.

Napoleon never took this principle into account. He was always a soldier of fortune, out for his own advantage, whether on his throne or in the camp, whether general, Consul or Emperor. Because of something lacking in his education, because of a defect of character and temperament, he subordinated the state to his own interests instead of the other way round. He did not see beyond his own brief existence to the nation which would remain after he died. He sacrificed the future of his country to the present. Little did he care that people predicted and feared that disaster would follow in the wake of his death. On the contrary, he wanted people to feel just that sort of anxiety. "My brother," said Joseph in 1803, "wants everyone to feel that his existence confers such great benefit on them that they will not be able to look ahead to the future after his death without trembling. He knows and senses that it is this rather than his power or the people's recognition of what he has done that maintains him in office. If the day were to come when you could say, 'Now things are settled and quiet, the succession to the throne is established, Napoleon can die and there will be no upheaval or change,' my brother would no longer feel safe. This is what makes him behave as he does." As the years passed Napoleon never stopped to think of making France ready to go on without him. Indeed he did the reverse, for he jeopardized solid territorial gains by making exaggeratedly large annexations. Right from the start it was clear that the end of the Emperor would mean the end of the Empire. . . .

Because of him more than 1,700,000 Frenchmen perished [5]: two million foreigners also died, killed either fighting for him as allies or

[5] The correct figure is more probably about 900,000.

fighting against him as enemies. And all that the enthusiastic and gullible French gained by entrusting him twice with their government was a double invasion. All that he left them as a reward for their devotion, for all the blood they and others had shed, was a France stripped of the fifteen departments added to her territories by the Republic, and lacking thus the left bank of the Rhine, lacking Belgium, and thus that north-eastern corner needed to complete her boundaries and defend her most vulnerable point. Worse, France was forced back inside the frontiers she had had in 1789, whereas all her neighbours had grown bigger, and at the same time she was regarded with suspicion by the whole of Europe and permanently surrounded by a menacing circle of bitterness and distrust.

Such then is the political achievement of Napoleon, the work of egoism served by genius. His overriding egoism was the flaw in the structure he built in Europe and in France. Right from the start this flaw is evident in the political framework of his European plans, and fifteen years later it caused it suddenly to collapse. The flaw is equally serious, although less obvious, in the structure he gave to France. It will not become apparent for another fifty, or even another hundred years: but its slow and gradual effect will be no less pernicious, and just as certain.

13

Alphonse Aulard (1901)[1]

The conclusion of the Concordat, the Peace of Amiens, brilliant successes in military and diplomatic affairs—a host of events, some fortunate and others presented as being so, and attributed by all to Bonaparte—prepared the public mind for illiberal changes in a constitution already far from liberal,[2] but which at all events limited the power of the First Consul to a period of ten years; and it was already easy for those [about] him to see that if these changes were not granted him he was capable of obtaining them by force.

The Second Consul, Cambacérès, on the occasion of the Peace of Amiens, suggested to the Tribunate that it would be only proper to grant Bonaparte a national reward. The Tribunate expressed the wish that he should indeed be given "an emphatic proof of national gratitude" but . . . informed the First Consul that this was a matter of a purely honorific recompense. But the title of Pacificator or Father of the People did not commend itself to Bonaparte's ambition. He turned to the Senate . . . and the senators were individually solicited to decree a life-Consulship.

They had the courage to refuse. . . . Bonaparte concealed his irritation and wrote to the Senate that he was about to consult the people as to whether he should accept the "sacrifice" which was required of him and prolong his term of office. . . .

Cambacérès [next] convened the Council of State . . . [which] adopted Roederer's project . . . to submit to the people the double question—should the First Consul be named for life and should he have the right to appoint his successor? . . .

Bonaparte feigned vexation, scolded Roederer, . . . spoke of annulling the order and finished by accepting it, erasing, however, the article concerning the right of appointing his successor. And the Consuls on the same day . . . ordered that the French people should be [asked]: Should Napoleon Bonaparte be Consul for life? The plebiscite was thus formulated by a simple Consular order, and as nothing in the constitution authorised such a mode of procedure it

[1] From *The French Revolution, A Political History, 1789–1804,* trans. B. Miall (London, 1910), IV, 228–82.
[2] I.e., that of 1800.

was truly a coup d'état, which was simply notified to the Senate . . .
and the Tribunate, their advice not being solicited. . . .
The Tribunate and the [Senate] bowed to the *fait accompli.*

*In the plebiscite which followed, three and a half million of
those eligible (in a population of some twenty-five million) to
vote, abstained: but a similar number voted in favor of the life-
Consulship, which was proclaimed on August 2, 1802. Only 8,374
had voted "no."*

This plebiscite was indeed the abdication of all France in favour
of one man . . . [and] many of those liberals of 1789 who had approved or even supported the coup of 18 Brumaire, were unable to
stomach the life-Consulate. . . . The plebiscite . . . thus marks the
rupture of Bonaparte with . . . the liberals of 1789. . . . Their eyes
were opened at last: too late. They had been caught in the trap,
these politicians and [intellectuals]. As for Bonaparte, he became *the
enemy,* and [in return] he ridiculed them by calling them *idéologues.*
. . . And they, [for their part, still] did not see that the establishment of individual power was the logical and inevitable outcome of
the coup [of Brumaire]. They blamed Bonaparte, the circumstances
or bad luck, when they should have blamed only themselves. . . .
For it was they who, on 19 Brumaire, had encouraged a soldier to
assault the existing laws in the mad hope of thus obtaining better
ones. And after they themselves had destroyed the law they were
astonished to find that there was no longer any law at all. . . .
From the [very beginning] of the period of the life-Consulate Bonaparte abandoned the [style] of a president after the American fashion.
In the *senatus consultus* which proclaimed him Consul for life he
was no longer "citizen Bonaparte" but "Napoleon Bonaparte." Thus
issued from the shadows this baptismal name of sonorous syllables
which soon was to become the name of an Emperor. Fatuous adulation
[soon followed. One newspaper] declared that Napoleon, according
to its Greek root, meant "Valley of the Lion." . . . The Ministry of
the Interior . . . invited the prefects to celebrate . . . the anniversary
of the birth of the First Consul. Paris was . . . illuminated on that
date: and everywhere the initials N. B. appeared. . . . Shortly afterwards Bonaparte contrived to be given a civil list of six millions
[while his] apartments in the palace of the Tuileries, simple at first,
became luxurious, indeed almost royal. . . . Military and unpolished
at the outset, the Court was now transformed. . . . Silk stockings replaced the boots and the sabre . . . [and though] Bonaparte did not

use powder but wore his hair as before, he encouraged [others] to wear their hair powdered . . . and [encouraged] everything else, too, that might transform his officials and generals into courtiers. . . .

Those who had dreams of overthrowing Bonaparte could realise them only by an insurrection of soldiers and the working class. But police reports show us that in the barracks of Paris Bonaparte was popular. He was popular even in the factories and workshops, and the labouring population . . . admired and loved him far more than they had ever admired Marat and Robespierre. This was not because he had assumed the pose of a kind of democratic Cæsar. On the contrary, he always treated the working classes as inferiors. . . . He placed them under the supervision of the police, obliged them to carry [passes] without which they could be arrested as vagabonds, and prohibited all unions and strikes, confiding to the prefect of police the power of arbitration between workers and employers on the subject of wages. . . . Although the plebiscite was the basis of the new régime, Bonaparte tended, here [in his labour policy] as elsewhere, to destroy equality, to divide French society into a middle class, privileged politically and socially, and a subordinated plebeian class.

Far from complaining, . . . the workers did not even appear to see that [all this] was in contradiction with the principles of 1789. Their love for Bonaparte was inspired and maintained by moral and material advantages.

The material advantages were, especially, that by the vigilance of the First Consul Paris was well provisioned and the necessities of life almost always cheap: industry also revived under the Consulate; work was rarely wanting: wages were higher and later on . . . military conscription had the indirect result of raising them still further.

The moral (or if you will, chimerical) advantages were that Bonaparte won for France a dazzling military glory, and the patriotism of the Parisian working man had become extremely chauvinistic. At the same time the working man was still passionately anti-royalist. He saluted in Bonaparte the leader of the Revolution . . . the protector of the new France against the Bourbons. . . .

This abdication of the Parisian workers—so docile and so complete—in favour of a master, reduced the bourgeois republicans to impotence; henceforth their opposition was merely a futile affair of the *salons*. From this time dates the rupture between the liberals and the people; and for many long years [afterwards] democracy and universal suffrage seemed incompatible with liberty. . . .

The royalist opposition now had no more chance of success than the republican. . . . There was seditious talk in the *salons*, but [even this] became less and less frequent as the power of the First Consul became more monarchical, and as the *émigrés* returned and found their place in the new regime. . . . These converts increased in number every day. But there were still, among those royalists who had not returned to France, a group who, in agreement with the English government, were preparing . . . for the assassination of Bonaparte . . .

The Consular police, however, knew everything [about the plot] and allowed matters to progress [until, in February–March, 1803, they swooped down on the ringleaders]. . . . The discovery of the conspiracy led to a frenzy of adulation with regard to Bonaparte, by which he profited in order at last to crown his dream. A few petitions, more or less spontaneous, demanded that the Consulate should be hereditary in Bonaparte's family, and on 27 March 1804 the Senate prayed the "great man" not to refuse to "complete his work by making it as immortal as his glory." . . . The Council of State, [however] could reach no agreement . . . Cambacérès himself was afraid of the Empire . . . [and] it was only after several weeks of intrigue and hesitation that a member of the Tribunate proposed "that Napoleon Bonaparte . . . should be declared Emperor." . . . The Tribunate, now reduced [in size] to 60 members, feared that it would be suppressed should it exhibit the slightest independence [and voted], by 48 to 9, in favour of the motion. . . . [Next] the Senate . . . was required to look into a projected *senatus consultus* presented [to it by] the Council of State, a [document usually] called the Imperial Constitution.

The people were not allowed to vote upon the [details of the constitution] but only to accept or reject . . . the following proposition: "The people desire the hereditary nature of the Imperial dignity in direct, natural, legitimate and adoptive descent from Napoleon Bonaparte . . . as ordained by the *senatus consultus* of 18 May 1804." . . . There were 3,572,329 *ayes* and 2,569 *noes*. . . .

In 1804, after the Empire had been [thus] established, there was celebrated . . . not only the festival of 14 July [1789] but also that of the establishment of the Republic [in September, 1792]. But in 1805 there was no longer any question of celebrating either. . . . The law of 26 Jan. 1805 erased all republican symbols . . . while in the formula used for promulgating laws the words "Emperor by the Constitutions of the Republic" [were replaced after] 29 April 1809 by . . . "Napoleon by the grace of God and the constitution." But the Emperor did not dare take any direct and final measure against the use of the word "republic." Only . . . in October 1808 . . . did he feel himself, after Erfurt, sufficiently powerful to abolish the last vestige of the Republic by decreeing that "Coin struck from 1 January 1809 onwards will bear the inscription *Empire français* instead of the words *République française*." No one noticed this decree; the word "republic," formerly regarded by the people as the talisman of victory, was forgotten, replaced in the imagination of the French by the name of Napoleon, another talisman of victory. . . .

We are now at the end of this [four-volume] narrative . . . of the political history of the Revolution from the point of view of the origin and development of democracy and the Republic. . . . The Revolution was realised only in part and only for a time. It was even suspended, and appeared to be abolished, during the rule of Napoleon —at least from 1808 to 1814. . . . The French Revolution is, so to speak, a political, social and rational ideal which Frenchmen have attempted partially to realise. . . . The Imperial despotism arrested the Revolution and marked a retrogression towards the principles of the *ancien régime,* provisionally abolishing liberty and partially abolishing equality. But it was the political results of the Revolution, rather than the social results, which were thus suppressed. . . . [For there was, after all, the Civil Code, a] Code less equalitarian than that which the Convention had conceived [in 1793], but infinitely more humane and more reasonable than that of the *ancien régime.* . . . In this manner was the Revolution maintained so far as its social results were concerned; and this explains why . . . that very Napoleon Bonaparte who disorganised the political work of the Revolution as completely as he could, appeared to be, and was able to call himself, "the man of the Revolution."

14

Louis Madelin (1932–33)[1]

Bonaparte was now [in 1799] thirty, but he had really lived twice that length of time, and, tried in the furnace of unique events, his personality, exceptionally strong by nature, had been miraculously matured and strengthened.

Ever since 1792, the aged Paoli, from his native Corsica, had been jealously watching his rise. "Just look at that little man!" he exclaimed. "He has in him the stuff of two Mariuses and a Sulla!" But he was neither a Marius nor a Sulla. He had in him nothing of the brutal soldier or of the bloodthirsty potentate. He towered above Cæsar himself, and had already far surpassed all who had gone before.

His looks were staggeringly strange. . . . Everybody who at that time caught even a glimpse of him referred to his "devouring" gaze. He was still extremely thin; his skin clung to his bones; the bridge of his aquiline nose was painfully sharp, he had a prominent chin, hollow cheeks, dark chestnut hair, which was always untidy, his walk was jerky, his movements sharp and quick. But none of these details were nearly so striking as his eyes, which were deep blue and were not "terrible" to everybody; for though generally piercing, they freuently softened more than the rest of his face and sometimes even smiled. . . .

He talked as though he were making an attack, looking straight at his interlocutor and never allowing him to get on one side of him. "With a foreign accent, disagreeable to the ear (the accent of his native Corsica)," writes d'Andigné, "he said what he had to say briefly and emphatically." His style preserved, even under the Consulate, a touch of revolutionary emphasis and, on rare occasions, was [nevertheless] filled with an astonishing lyric quality. The striking feature about both his conversation and his letters was the close connection between the expression and the idea; it was really his thought that spoke without any beating about the bush. In speaking, he always went straight to the point, and in a few minutes either convinced, seduced or crushed his listener. . . .

"There are two separate men in me," he once observed to Roederer,

[1] From *The Consulate and the Empire, 1789–1815,* trans. E. Buckley (London, 1934–36), I, 26–41. All selections from this volume reprinted by permission of W. Heinemann Ltd. and G. Putnam's Sons.

"the man of brain and the man of heart. Don't imagine I have not a kind heart like other men. I am even a good-natured sort of man. But, from my earliest youth I have done all I can to silence that chord in myself and now it is incapable of giving vent to a sound." He was, as a matter of fact, impressionable to the point of being extremely emotional. One of his enemies felt that "in his heart of hearts he concealed deep sensibilities." He did indeed conceal them as a rule, and, as he said himself, "did all he could to silence them."

Nevertheless, these emotional reserves broke loose when he was in a rage. . . . But, as a rule, his fury soon subsided. "As soon as my rage is over, it is all finished and done with," he wrote to Decrès, who had felt the rough side of his tongue and showed himself aggrieved. "I hope you won't nurse a grudge against me."

The fact was that in his case the brain nearly always retained the upper hand; by the "brain," I mean the will quite as much as the intellect.

"Bonaparte is the finest manifestation of the human will," wrote Schopenhauer, the philosopher, after an interview with the hero. And, indeed, it is doubtful whether any man has ever given such proof of will in every shape and form. He seems to have eliminated . . . the word "impossible" . . . from his vocabulary. . . . This will, by means of which he held both mind and body in subjection, became, in matters of State, an inflexible spirit of authority. . . . But he was far too clever to love authority for its own sake; for him it was merely the necessary prerequisite of order.

And he had order in his very bones. He had long since introduced it into his private life, as he afterwards did into the State over which he ruled. "His is an orderly mind," observed Chaptal, one of his ministers. If before long we find him casting his eye over apparently the most trifling details it was because he could not tolerate a breach of order, however small, remaining unpunished. It was this love of order that was really responsible for his passion for organisation and codification; he wanted every man to be employed in the position for which he was best fitted and to put everybody and everything into their proper places. This concern made him extremely severe. He always believed that prevention was better than repression, and that the only effective method of prevention was to "make examples." "The great secret of an efficient police," he wrote to Fouché, "is to punish severely in order to avoid punishing often." But, with his usual intelligence, he admitted that while severity was indispensable for order, justice was also essential. Reward was all-important as was also punishment; but for no consideration in the world would he remit a punishment any more than he would fail to bestow a reward.

Such strength of will—"a man of bronze," as a certain foreign representative shortly afterwards described him—such energy, such regard for authority and order would, even wielded by a mediocre brain, have been of benefit to the nation, and, in the position in which France then found herself, would indeed have been a great blessing; but for such gifts to be used and illumined by a brain of such outstanding endowments, coordination and power, constituted a boon of surpassing value.

Similar strength of will had possibly existed before, but that it should be supported by such a colossal weight of intellect was, I believe, a phenomenon hitherto unknown.

Endowed by birth in a superlative degree with all the gifts which are supposed to emanate from the brain—imagination, memory, clarity of vision, swift judgment, intellectual curiosity, capacity for work, and an elasticity of thought capable of infinite extension both in depth and in breadth—he had, furthermore, constantly nourished this stupendous brain by a devouring passion for reading. Even among those whose studies had never been interrupted by the call to action few had read more than he had done. . . . And he made notes on all he read and remembered everything, for his extraordinary memory retained the substance of his reading as though it had been engraved on tablets of bronze.

Moreover, he loved work; he had a passion for it. Man of action though ht was, such was the miraculous quality of his brain that he was even more a man of intellectual activity. "I work very hard, and I meditate a great deal," he informed Roederer one day. "If I seem to be always prepared for everything, ready to face everything, it is because before undertaking anything I have always meditated for a long time and foreseen what was likely to happen. . . . I am always working; I work when I am dining, I work at the theatre; in the middle of the night I wake up and work."

This was perfectly true. His brain was constantly at work on the past, the present and the future. It was work that was almost painful. A certain stranger, who saw him at close quarters, bore witness to this: "I know no man who is surer of himself when once he has made up his mind, but I also know of no man who, before doing so, holds longer consultation with himself."

He holds consultation with himself; but he held consultation with others perhaps even more. Never did a man extract so much information from every quarter. "What is it? How much? How? Why?" these four expressions recur probably more often than any other in his correspondence. His intellect was too alert not to recognise his own limitations and the gaps in his knowledge, and when he seized the reins of power in Brumaire he was well aware that he was ignorant of much. . . . He insisted upon being given State papers, historical summaries, statistics, returns and statements; if the returns he was studying were not quite up to date he would write complaining that they were very old and ask for something more recent to be sent him. He asked questions, he listened and he read with such profound attention that, with the help of his unrivalled memory everything, as I have already observed, was engraved on his brain as it were on tablets of bronze. But all these things merely provided him with food for reflection. Whereupon he proceeded to elaborate his plans, and then he was always at his best. Day and night he would be working out his ideas, taking his sleep, as Thibaudeau could bear witness, "when it suited him."

Thus he was prepared for all contingencies. "Luck is not responsible for anything," he observed to Fouché. He would deal with three or four alternatives at the same time and endeavour to conjure up every possible eventuality—preferably the worst. This foresight, the fruit of meditation, generally enabled him to be ready for any [setback]; nothing ever took him by surprise. . . .

His vision, as I have said, was capable of both breadth and depth. And perhaps the most astonishing characteristic of his intellect was the combination of idealism and realism which enabled him to face the most exalted visions at the same time as the most insignificant realities. And, indeed, he was in a sense a visionary, a dreamer of dreams, nay, one would almost be tempted to say that he pursued fantasies, were it not that his dreams—and even his fantasies—were nearly always realised.

It was impossible for him to take a narrow view. In him imagination, the leaven of all genius, had reached the highest possible degree of development. . . . [And yet] none of his dreams, however fantastic they might appear, was really pure fantasy; in the first place because he stood firmly embedded in realities which he had carefully studied, and secondly because his dreams were immediately translated into facts by concrete action and practical measures.

He was indeed extraordinarily realistic. He was constantly rejecting those [of his dreams] which, on reflection, he found held out no hope of being more or less swiftly realised; and if he did not reject them he postponed them. In any case he knew how to modify them to suit the necessities of the moment. In this sense he was a great opportunist, entirely opposed to any idea of abiding by a hidebound system. "[Statesmanship]," he remarked more than once, "is nothing but common sense applied to great matters."

This definition was fully justified in the early days of the Consulate, when the task with which he was faced was precisely that of making good the harm done by the frenzied ideology of the Assemblies and discovering, as opposed to it, methods dictated by common sense—realism in its most agreeable form.

The second characteristic of this realism lies in the fact that a man like Bonaparte adapts himself to circumstances. True, there were instances in which he thought fit to "force the issue," but, more often than not, in politics as well as in strategy, he bowed to circumstances. "I am sometimes a fox and sometimes a lion. . . . The whole secret of government lies in knowing when to be the one or the other."

But this realism shines out even more brilliantly in his concern about details of execution than in his anxiety to seize every opportunity. This is characteristic of all great organisers. Cardinal de Retz accused Richelieu of "being too much concerned about trifles"; but, on the contrary, it is a sign of genius to be able to combine with grandiose designs that "concern about trifles" on which the success of the former so often depends. In this connection, Bonaparte's correspondence is well-nigh staggering. That the same man who had just conceived some colossal plan of campaign in the field of diplomacy or of war, some great scheme of political reconstruction, or of worldwide upheaval, should, in a flash, be able to concentrate his mind on calculating the number of mules necessary for moving an army across the Alps or the number of cartridges required for a particular division, was indeed a miracle. But in his case thousands of such instances could be given.

The way he employed individual men belongs to the same category. Comines says somewhere of Louis XI, that of all the princes of his day he "worked hardest to win over to himself those who had the power to serve him." The same can be said of Bonaparte. In his invincible desire, from the very first days of the Consulate, to call to his side every Frenchman, regardless of party or birth, he was animated, I confess, to some extent by the determination to re-unite at a time when everything was divided; but there was also the longing to make full use of every gift, every activity, every experience. He engaged in this "man-hunt" with an almost passionate ardour, and he nearly always succeeded, knowing in every case how to use the arguments best calculated to attract and to bind [a man to him]. . . . So irresistible was his love of capacity that it occasionally developed into a source of weakness; for he always found it extremely difficult to part from an unreliable man whom he knew to be capable. . . . When he had laid hold of a man, he, so to speak, extracted the last ounce from him. . . . Nobody knew better than he did how to stimulate industry and he urged his men on until they begged for mercy. . . . His methods wore men out and sometimes killed them. "Never to let men grow old," he wrote as early as the year IV to Carnot, "should be the great art of government." Moreover, life was worth living to the full, and then what did death matter! "In every career glory comes only at the end!"

Hard, cruel, barbaric!—so men called him. And he did indeed, to use a harsh expression, run his men to death; but he did so in the public [interest]. We shall have occasion to describe the unrivalled achievements of his government, which were due to the fact that, under the leadership of great public servants, who were themselves unremitting in their labours, the various administrative bodies, the general staffs, the offices, and all the civil and military functionaries, put their backs into their work, and had their heart and soul in it. And the main reason for all this was that at the head of that same government was a man of iron, whose untiring hand guided the machine of state which he himself had restored to working order. With a will and a brain that never for a single moment flagged, the First Consul considered himself in 1800 superior to his day. But he was far too clear-sighted to imagine himself all-sufficient: "A man is only a man," he observed of himself. . . .

It was, indeed, a miracle that at a moment when France was seeking to raise herself from the ruins she found a man in whom all the qualities of a leader were combined, one who in the almost inconceivable richness of his gifts, far surpassed the wildest dreams of ambition.

Moreover, since his character responded to the demands of an extraordinary state of affairs, it also came about that his ideas responded to those born of the country's aspirations.

And what were these ideas?

They were derived from what he found in his own heart, and from his study of history and of the spectacle which, for the last ten years, had been unfolded before his own eyes.

When he was quite young he had welcomed the Revolution, and for some time it even seemed as though he would go to extreme lengths of "Jacobinism." . . . But it is by no means certain that he approved of all the destruction that took place between 1789 and 1792. . . . [Indeed] he told Mollien that "while he wished to preserve all the useful innovations which the Revolution had succeeded in introducing, he had no intention of giving up the good institutions which it had been foolish enough to destroy."

He [held]—quite rightly—that the upheaval of 1789 had been merely a struggle "for equality." "Liberty," he added, "was only the pretext." Before the Council of State, in which so many old members of the Constituent Assembly had seats, he passed severe condemnation on the Assembly of 1789 which "had violated justice," and "in attacking the sovereign had attacked all property." He had a horror of the period between 1789 and 1792, which, he declared, owing to the very existence of the Assembly, was one of complete anarchy. "The Convention [of 1792–95] was less to blame; it was merely consistent *and moreover it saved the country!*"

The last few words reveal his real feelings. He loved the Revolution "in its military and warlike aspect, as victorious and Roman," to use Albert Vandal's apt description. The conquest of the natural frontiers, the apotheosis of French glory, and the preparation for French hegemony were, undoubtedly, together with *"la carrière ouverte aux talents,"* what he most admired in the achievements of the Revolution.

Truth to tell, the Revolution was, in his eyes, *a fact.* . . . In any case France remained irrevocably devoted to it. . . . [And Bonaparte] had no intention of wiping out the principles, the institutions and the conquests of the Revolution; [it was simply a question of getting rid of] parasitical elements [and excrescences]. He agreed that the French Revolution was an egalitarian revolution; equality appealed to him. He agreed that the Revolution had prepared the way for the establishment of that centralised state which the French Kings had never entirely succeeded in realising and which, now that the ground had been cleared, was to be raised by his hands. He agreed that the Revolution had made the conquest of the natural frontiers popular and had sanctified their retention. All this was enough, with the support of the old revolutionary ardour of his early days, to make him, on mature reflection, regard the Revolution as a boon. To be considered "the incarnation of the Revolution," as Metternich called him, was by no means displeasing to him, and he put what he felt into words when he declared that he "respected the results of a Revolution which he wished to end but not to disavow."

It was all these ideas that gave rise to the policy which in any case he regarded as obvious—the reconciliation of past and present, implying the fusion of parties, or rather their extinction.

"To govern in the interests of a party," he declared just after Brumaire, "is sooner or later to become dependent on it. They will never get me to do it. *I am national.*"

He was indeed "national." He loved France. He loved her present, but he also loved her past, and unreservedly identified himself with it. "From Clovis to the Committee of Public Safety, I belong heart and soul to it all." . . . He intended to be a *national leader.*

He was, as I have already observed, temperamentally a man of authority. And to be strong [authority] had to be concentrated in the hands of a single individual. This explains his detestation of Assemblies . . . [and it] also explains his fear of the Press. . . . A Government free of undue control, and meeting with no serious obstacle in the Assemblies—this was the first pre-requisite of authority. [But] this did not mean that he had any intention of ruling without the people. On the contrary, his object was to rely on Democracy against the various oligarchies.

He both feared and loved the people, and the popularity which, from the very beginning, he enjoyed among humble folk, workmen, peasants and soldiers, encouraged him to place his confidence in them. . . . He was also delighted that his power had been thrice based on the "will of the people"—the plebiscite. The advantage of the plebiscite was that it enabled him to escape the dangerous influence of the oligarchies more easily.

Of all these oligarchies the one he hated most was the financial caucus which was supreme under the Directory. . . . He refused to tolerate the rule of the rich; but stranger still, he also refused to tolerate the rule of the soldier, "military rule." He loved the soldier, but he would have been horrified at the idea of generals attempting to lay down the law. . . . In later days he was proud of the fact that in an "entirely military Empire" he had succeeded in keeping soldiers out of the conduct of affairs.

No plutocracy! No military oligarchy! But he also refused to tolerate "the domination of the priests," and set his face quite as resolutely against the rule of "the lawyers." In short, from 1800 onwards, he was determined to protect the government against any influence that might hamper its freedom of action. . . . Only thus could Authority be assured.

And, like the country at large, he had, in 1800, one last reason for desiring the establishment of this authority, which was so vital for the reorganisation of the state and the restoration of order—namely, the necessity of defending France against the coalition of Europe and of securing peace with glory. . . .

This is not the place to discuss whether Napoleon, as has been maintained, desired peace throughout his career. But this much at least is certain, that in 1800 he desired it whole-heartedly, that in 1802 he greeted its conclusion with what might almost be called alacrity, and that in 1802 and 1803 he made great efforts to preserve it.

The formidable task awaiting him at home, and in which he came to take a more passionate interest than in any military campaign, demanded all his attention and necessitated his presence. Peace alone would allow of his carrying through the enterprise with rapidity and vigour. When, in 1802, he publicly proclaimed the conclusion of a general peace, he conveyed the impression that France, now partially restored, was on the point of consecrating to fruitful labours the energy which she had known so well how to devote to the prosecution of a victorious war. . . .

But the day came when, attacked by Austria, Russia and Prussia in turn, he declared, "I can never have a real alliance with any of the Great Powers." And then he made it his object to reduce to impotence those whom he would fain have seen living in peace and amity with him. There were occasions when he seemed to take the offensive, but in this connection he explained his position quite clearly to Talleyrand. "I do not wish for war," he said, "but I prefer to make it too early rather than too late."

Moreover, he regarded as aggression any menace to the frontiers won by the Revolution. The possession of the [left bank of the] Rhine was "the fundamental principle." . . . But he was well aware that Europe accepted this most unwillingly, nay did not accept it at all. . . . True, in 1800 he desired peace, but it was to be a lasting peace, a glorious peace which would consecrate, once and for all, the conquests won by France to the strains of the *Marseillaise*.

We know that, eager though she might be for peace, France did not think very differently, and that while she placed herself unreservedly in the hands of a great master of war, it was because she hoped that by his victories he would secure that glorious and lasting peace for which he himself was longing.

But she also agreed with him that the first prerequisite of this victory was the establishment of a strong government over a nation reconstructed and at one with itself. This, as we know, was the main principle of the great enterprise conceived by the First Consul. And thus not only his gifts but also his ideas tallied with the wishes of the nation. . . .

15

Georges Lefebvre (1953)[1]

ON THE GENERAL

In the closing years of the Old Regime, French writers on military affairs had demonstrated the disadvantages of the classical methods of warfare brought to perfection by Frederick II. An inflexible army, deploying slowly in file along a single road was incapable of encompassing the entire theatre of operations, and so could not compel the foe to fight or force him to abandon a strong defensive position. Nevertheless, it took the French Revolution to bring about a departure from the former practices. With the advent of mass warfare, involving very large numbers of troops, generals were forced to split their armies into divisions in order to render them manageable. Soon, however, these new groupings were found inadequate, for as they grew in number it became more difficult to co-ordinate their movements. Because the cavalry and artillery were attached to the separate divisions, it was impossible to concentrate their force. A higher organization, the army corps, had been haltingly attempted during the Directory, and in 1800 Moreau had commanded three corps of four divisions each, but without reserves. Napoleon derived his ideas of strategy from the teachings of Guibert and Bourcet,[2] as well as from the practical experience of the Revolution; but it was at Marengo that he decided upon his final formula: two or three divisions per corps, with a minimum of cavalry; most of the cavalry organized separately, and a reserve of artillery directly under the commanding general. This organization was applied to the whole army under the Consulate.

The strength of these divisions and corps remained extremely variable. In 1805, the latter consisted of two to four divisions, totalling from 14,000 to 40,000 men. The divisions were made up of six to eleven battalions ranging from 5,600 to 9,000 men; regiments comprised one to three battalions. In the following year, the army achieved a more regular definition—divisions numbered 6,000 to 8,000, and every regiment was composed of two battalions.

[1] From *Napoleon,* trans. H. Stockhold (London, 1969), I, 63–68, 228–31. All selections from this volume reprinted by permission of Columbia University Press and Routledge and Kegan Paul Ltd.

[2] Whose treatises had appeared in the 1770s.

Napoleon's military genius was best revealed in his ability to combine the movements of several army corps. The art lay in deploying and directing them so that the entire area of operations might be encompassed, making it impossible for the enemy to slip away. At the same time, the various army corps had to remain close enough together to be able to mass their forces for battle. The disposition of the corps generally took the shape of a flexible quincunx. Marching upon the enemy, the front progressively tightened as one or another of the corps found itself open to sudden attack. Sometimes, as at Eylau, they massed together on the battlefield itself, the corps having been aimed towards a distant point in such a way as to flank and envelop the enemy by their very advance. The arrangement of a campaign called for two different plans of action, depending upon whether Napoleon intended to fight a single army or occupy a central position in the midst of several adversaries, as in 1796–1797 around Mantua, or as in 1813. In any event, the pattern varied according to circumstances, and was never confined to one formula. Napoleonic strategy was an art which, while possessing certain principles, allowed neither tradition nor calculation ever to impoverish its inventiveness.

Victory was contingent upon the speed and daring of Napoleon's decisions, followed by a precipitate execution of troop movements. Surprise was an important element, and demanded the utmost secrecy. Always covered by cavalry, the army used rivers and mountains as a natural screen for its marches, whenever possible. But while cloaking its own movements, it was quite as essential to discover the enemy's: this was a function of the cavalry, as well as the intelligence service, which made use of diplomats, agents of all types . . . and, above all, spies. . . . Once the army was under way, Napoleon placed no great importance on lines of communication with France, since he invariably expected a short campaign. The lines of operations, on the other hand, were a matter of grave concern, and were to be protected at all costs. These were the roads connecting the army with the fortress where the headquarters was located, and whose location was shifted as the army advanced. Heavily travelled highways, dotted by postal relay stations guarded by a few soldiers, linked the army with France. Hence, fortifications had their place in the Napoleonic system. They served as a base of operations and could, by blocking rivers and passes, serve as a bridgehead and supporting cover for the army. They did not, however, play as important a role as in pre-revolutionary strategy. In campaigns aimed solely at forcing a decisive encounter and destroying the enemy, fortified places were never in themselves military objectives.

On the battlefield, Napoleon sought to compel the foe to exhaust his reserves by engaging him along the entire front. This was to be accomplished with a minimum of strength, so as to keep intact a concentrated striking force. Next, he would break the enemy's spirit with infantry and artillery fire, sustained by threats along his flank and line of retreat. Finally, when Napoleon felt that the enemy was sufficiently weakened, he would hurl forward his fresh troops, break all resistance, and pursue the beaten foe without mercy. This pursuit, which Frederick II with his small army never dared to order, was the most original feature of Napoleonic warfare. The battle plan, carried out with unparalleled precision, did not alter tactics at the unit level, a subject which Napoleon rarely touched upon. As a rule, the units adhered to the drill manual of 1791: the division was drawn up into brigades on two lines, one regiment deployed to the front, the other massed in columns. But, in fact, the methods of the revolutionary armies persisted: the infantry sent ahead a swarm of skirmishers, all picked men, who advanced under cover of the terrain. The first line of infantry gradually followed, often deployed in the same way. It was this kind of mobile shooting at will which so unsettled the enemy, who was accustomed to facing linear formations where soldiers, ranged elbow to elbow in three rows (the last two rows standing), offered perfect targets. At the signal to attack, the second line of infantry advanced in deep columns. They rarely had to use the bayonet; by this time the adversary was usually in flight.

Still, tactics underwent certain changes. Brimming with confidence, the French tended to replace much of the preliminary skirmishing by massed charges with naked weapons; officers became more partial to the use of columns as the number of untried recruits increased. But once the English, and even the Germans, adjusted to these new methods, the results were disastrous. Perhaps one of the weaknesses of Napoleonic warfare was the lack of attention to unit-level tactics and the failure to revise them in view of the improvements and advantages of the Coalition armies.

Owing to financial limitations, Napoleonic wars tended to be brief. This ensured the Emperor enormous prestige. The overpowering vigour of the campaigns, and the faultless dexterity with which they were brought to a swift finish, evoke our romantic admiration to this day. Their speed and daring bore the unmistakable imprint of Napoleon's fiery temperament. As in the case of provisioning the army, his ideas about the conduct of war were conceived in terms of the arena where he fought his first campaigns. The valley of the Po, hemmed in by a ring of mountains, allowed the enemy no chance of escape. It was small enough in area to be easily controlled by the army, cleverly deployed so that it might overrun the territory without taxing its strength. It was fertile enough to provide ample means of recovery. Already in South Germany the distances became greater and the army suffered accordingly. Yet this land, parcelled as it was, could still fit the original strategy. But once the army broached the limit-less plains of North Germany, Poland, and Russia, things went differently. The enemy could now make his escape, vast distances required exhausting marches, and victualling became an insoluble problem. Soldiers were dropped off to act as occupation forces all along the way, and the army dissolved before it had even begun to fight. The economy failed to provide the required means of transport, and the organization of the military being what it was, reserves were lacking. Napoleon's strategy, which by its origin was totally Mediterranean, did not anticipate these new geographic conditions, and so never fully succeeded in adapting itself to them.

ON THE MAN

What sort of a man was he? His personality evolved in so singular a manner that it defies portrayal. He appeared first as a studious officer full of dreams, garrisoned at Valence and Auxonne. As a youthful general, on the eve of the battle of Castiglione, he could still hold a council of war. But in the final years as Emperor, he was stupefied with his own omnipotence and was infatuated with his own omniscience. And yet distinctive traits appear throughout his entire career: power could do no more than accentuate some and attenuate others.

Short-legged and small in stature, muscular, ruddy, and still gaunt at the age of thirty, he was physically hardy and fit. His sensitivity and steadiness were admirable, his reflexes quick as lightning, and his capacity for work unlimited. He could fall asleep at will. But we also find the reverse: cold humid weather brought on . . . coughing spells, dysuria; when crossed he unleashed frightful outbursts of temper; over-exertion, despite prolonged hot baths, despite extreme sobriety, despite the moderate yet constant use of coffee and tobacco, occasionally produced brief collapses, even tears. His mind was one of the most perfect that has ever been: his unflagging attention tirelessly swept in facts and ideas which his memory registered and classified; his imagination played with them freely, and being in a permanent state of concealed tension, it never wearied of inventing political and strategic motifs which manifested themselves in unexpected flashes of intuition like those experienced by poets and mathematicians. This would happen especially at night during a sudden awakening, and he himself referred to it as "the moral spark" and "the after midnight presence of the spirit." This spiritual fervour shone through his glittering eyes and illuminated the face, still "sulphuric" at his rise, of the "sleek-haired Corsican." This is what made him unsociable, and not, as Taine would have us think, some kind of brutality, the consequence of a slightly tarnished *condottiere* being let loose upon the world in all his savagery. He rendered a fair account of himself when he said, "I consider myself a good man at heart," and indeed he showed generosity, and even kindness to those who were close to him. But between ordinary mortals, who hurried through their tasks in order to abandon themselves to leisure or diversion, and Napoleon Bonaparte, who was the soul of effort and concentration, there could exist no common ground nor true community. Ambition—that irresistible impulse to act and to dominate—sprang from his physical and mental state of being. He knew himself well: "It is said that I am an ambitious man but that is not so; or at least my ambition is so closely bound to my being that they are both one and the same." How very true! Napoleon was more than anything else a temperament.

Ever since his military school days at Brienne, when he was still a poor and taunted foreigner, timid yet bursting with passion, Napoleon drew strength from pride in himself and contempt for others. Destined to become an officer, his instinct to command without having to discuss could not have been better served. Although he might on occasion have sought information or opinion, he alone was master and judge. Bonaparte's natural propensity for dictatorship suited the normal practice of his profession. In Italy and in Egypt he introduced dictatorship into the government. In France he wanted to put himself forward as a civilian, but the military stamp was indelibly there. He consulted often, but he could never tolerate free opposition. More precisely, when faced with a group of men accustomed to discussion, he would lose his composure. This explains his intense hatred of the *idéologues*. The confused and undisciplined, yet formidable masses inspired in him as much fear as contempt. Regardless of costumes and titles, Bonaparte took power as a general, and as such he exercised it.

Beneath the soldier's uniform, however, there dwelled in him several personalities, and it is this diversity, as much as the variety and brilliance of his gifts, which makes him so fascinating. Wandering about penniless in the midst of the Thermidorian festival, brushing past rich men and beautiful women, the Bonaparte of 1795 burned with the same desires as others. Something of that time never did leave him: a certain pleasure in stepping on those who had once snubbed him; a taste for ostentatious splendour; an over-tender care for his family—the "clan"—which had suffered much the same miseries as himself; and a few memorable remarks of the citizen-turned-gentleman, as on the day of his coronation when he exclaimed, "Joseph, if only father could see us [now]!" But even much earlier there lived in him a nobler trait, a passionate desire to know and understand everything. It served him, no doubt, yet it was a need which he fulfilled for its own sake, without any ulterior motive.

As a young officer he was a tireless reader. . . . He also wrote, and it is obvious that had he not entered the royal military academy at Brienne, he could have become a man of letters. Having entered into a life of action, he still remained a thinker. This warrior was never happier than in the silence of his own study, surrounded by papers and documents. In time he became more practical, and he would boast that he had repudiated "ideology." Nevertheless, he was still a typical man of the eighteenth century, a rationalist, a philosopher. Far from relying on intuition, he placed his trust in reason, in knowledge, and in methodical effort. "I generally look ahead three or four months in advance to what I must do, and then I count on the worst"; "all work must be done systematically because left to chance, nothing can succeed." He believed that his insights were the natural fruit of his patience. His conception of a unitary state, made of one piece according to a simple and symmetrical plan, was entirely classical. At rare moments his intellectualism revealed itself by his most striking characteristic: the ability to stand off from himself and take a detached look at his own life, and to reflect wistfully on his fate. From Cairo he wrote to Joseph after having learned of Joséphine's infidelity, "I need solitude and isolation. I find grandeur tiring, my feelings drained, and glory dull. At twenty-nine I am completely played out." Walking with Girardin at Ermenonville, he would exclaim shortly thereafter, "The future will tell if it would not have been better for the sake of world peace had Rousseau and I never been born." When the state counsellor Roederer remarked, while visiting the abandoned Tuileries Palace with Napoleon, "General, this is all so sad," Bonaparte, already First Consul for two months, replied, "Yes, and so is grandeur." Thus this firm and severe intellect could [suddenly] give [way] to the romantic melancholia characteristic of Chateaubriand and de Vigny. But these were never more than flashes, and he would pull himself together at once.

He seemed to be dedicated to a policy of realism in every way, and he was, in fact, a realist in execution down to the slightest detail. During the course of his rise, he made the rounds of human emotions, and well did he learn to play upon them. He knew how to exploit self-interest, vanity, jealousy, even dishonesty. He knew what could be obtained from men by arousing their sense of honour and by inflaming their imagination; nor did he for a moment forget that they could be subdued by terror. He discerned ever so clearly what in the work of the Revolution had captured the heart of the nation and what fitted in with his despotism. To win the French people, he declared himself both a man of peace and a god of war. That is why he must be ranked among the great realists in history.

And yet he was a realist in execution only. There lived in him an alter-ego which contained certain features of the hero. It seems to have been born during his days at the military academy out of a need to dominate a world in which he felt himself despised. Above all he longed to equal the semi-legendary heroes of Plutarch and Corneille. His greatest ambition was glory. "I live only for posterity," he exclaimed, "death is nothing, but to live defeated and without glory is to die every day." His eyes were fixed on the world's great leaders: Alexander, who conquered the East and dreamed of conquering the world; Cæsar, Augustus, Charlemagne—the creators and the restorer of the Roman Empire whose very names were synonymous with the idea of a universal civilization. From these he did not deduce a precise formulation to be used as a rule, a measure, or a condition of political conduct. They were for him examples, which stimulated his imagination and lent an unutterable charm to action. He was stirred less by the accomplishment of his heroes than by the consuming spiritual zeal which had engendered their work. He was an artist, a poet of action, for whom France and mankind were but instruments. How well he expressed his sense of grandeur when, in St. Helena, he evoked memories of the victory at Lodi and the awakening in his consciousness of the will to power! "I saw the world flee beneath me, as if I were transported in the air."

That is why it is idle to seek for limits to Napoleon's policy, or for a final goal at which he would have stopped: there simply was none. As for his followers who worried about it, he once remarked, "I always told them that I just didn't know," or again, more significantly, despite the triteness of his expression, "To be in God's place? Ah! I would not want it; that would be a cul-de-sac!" Here, then, we see that dynamic temperament which struck us at first glance in its psychological manifestation. It is the romantic Napoleon, a force seeking to expand and for which the world was no more than an occasion for acting dangerously. But knowing the disposition of one's means alone is not the mark of a realist. On the contrary, the realist also fixes his goal in terms of the possible, and although his imagination and his flair for grandeur push him on, still he knows where to stop.

That a mind so capable of grasping reality in certain respects should escape it in others, as Molé so accurately observed, can only be due to Napoleon's origins as much as to his nature. When he first came to France, he considered himself a foreigner. Until the time when he was expelled from Corsica by his compatriots [in 1793], his attitude had been one of hostility to the French people. Assuredly he became sufficiently imbued with their culture and spirit to adopt their nationality; otherwise he could never have become their leader. But he lacked the time to identify himself with the French nation and to adopt its national tradition to the point where he would consider its interests as a limitation upon his own actions. Something of the uprooted person remained in him; something of the *déclassé* as well. He was neither entirely a gentleman nor entirely common. He served both the king and the Revolution without attaching himself to either. This was one of the reasons for his success, since he could so easily place himself above parties and announce himself as the restorer of national unity. Yet neither in the Old Regime nor in the new did he find principles which might have served as a norm or a limit. Unlike Richelieu, he was not restrained by dynastic loyalty, which would have subordinated his will to the interest of his master. Nor was he motivated by civic virtue, which could have made him a servant of the nation.

A successful soldier, a pupil of the philosophes, he detested feudalism, civil inequality, and religious intolerance. Seeing in enlightened despotism a reconciliation of authority with political and social reform, he became its last and most illustrious representative. In this sense he was the man of the Revolution. His frenzied individuality never did accept democracy, however, and he rejected the great hope of the eighteenth century which inspired revolutionary idealism—the hope that someday men would be civilized enough to rule themselves. He did not become cautious through a concern for his personal safety, as were other men, because he was indifferent to it. He dreamed only of greatness through heroism and danger.

What about moral limits? In spiritual life he had nothing in common with other men. Even though he knew their passions well and deftly turned them to his own ends, he cared only for those that would reduce men to dependence. He belittled every feeling that elevated men to acts of sacrifice—religious faith, patriotism, love of freedom—because he saw in them obstacles to his own schemes. Not that he was impervious to these sentiments, at least not in his youth, for they readily led to heroic deeds; but fate led him in a different direction and walled him up within himself. In the splendid and terrible isolation of the will to power, measure carries no meaning.

Unaware of Bonaparte's romantic impulse, the *idéologues* believed him to be one of their own. Perhaps they could have succeeded in restraining this elemental urge by keeping him in a subordinate position under a strong government. But by pushing him to supreme power, the Brumairians renounced any such precaution.

16

Albert Soboul: The Hero and History[1]

Napoleon is a genuine hero, the Great Man *par excellence*, "one of the most astonishing phenomena in history," in the words of Tarlé. For the Romantics he was "the Man of Destiny," "the Man of the Century," and Georges Lefebvre adopts this expression in his now classic work. For Driault, the founder in 1912 of the *Revue des Études Napoléoniennes*, he was the "Emperor of the West," while for many historians associated with the [French] Academy he remains "Napoleon the Great." In the more limited perspective of military affairs, vitally important however since it was one of his stepping-stones to success, he is "the God of War." Without admiring him as much as this, the average Frenchman nevertheless felt a simple pride when he thought of Napoleon:

> Ah! qu'on est fier d'être Français
> Quand on regarde la Colonne! . . .[2]

But what an outcry, what loathing and denigration from the other side! Bonaparte "the Bandit," "the Corsican ogre" . . . the black legend depicts the Emperor as a despot destroying freedom, a cynic governed by ambition, his conduct shaped by his scornful contempt for mankind. Certainly he was neurotic, perhaps an epileptic; Taine even talked of incest. Intelligent?—no question, but in an uneven way: in Fourier's view he was "hopeless, except on the battlefield" (but then, the Emperor had left his petitions unanswered).

But defending or denigrating Napoleon means, in either case, bowing down to the cult of personality. This is the wrong way of approaching the problem, forcing the great man (for unquestionably

---

[1] A paper read to the colloquium organized by the Société d'histoire moderne on October 25–26, 1969, and printed in the *Revue d'histoire moderne et contemporaine*, XVII (1970), pp. 333–8 and also in the *Annales historiques de la Révolution française* (1970), 1–7. Translated by K. Gladstone. Reprinted by kind permission of the author.

[2] From an ode (1818), by Debraux, to the column commemorating Napoleon's victories (see below p. 172, n. 15).

he was great) to step outside history instead of integrating him into it so as to understand him better.

A question mark stands after Napoleon's name in history. After the failure of the great Napoleonic ambition—the building of a great European empire and the founding of a new dynasty—poets saw the Emperor as a modern Prometheus chained to the rock of Saint Helena as punishment for his audacity—a symbol of Genius battling against Fate. Historians try to find a more rational interpretation than this and look for a line of argument in the labyrinth of actual facts. For Albert Sorel and his successor Albert Vandal, and for what one must call the official Napoleonic historiography (which does not emerge from university circles), the Revolution inevitably led to dictatorship, while the acquisition of natural frontiers condemned France to a state of everlasting war. According to this interpretation the logic of historical determinism governed Napoleonic politics. In reply to this, Georges Lefebvre readily agreed that an authoritarian government was necessary for the safety of the Revolution so long as the aristocracy were plotting with foreign governments and so long, too, as the annexation of Belgium and of the left bank of the Rhine was not recognised by the other powers. However the military dictatorship did not in itself imply the restoration of hereditary monarchy, still less that of an aristocracy. Nor did it necessarily imply additional conquests. These were Napoleon's own undertakings which, although favoured by circumstances, nevertheless had their origin in his own will to power.

When he became master of France Napoleon stepped into the centre of history. He, indeed, so filled the stage that his accession to power for a long time obscured the fact that there was a unity underlying his reign and the ten years of Revolution.

On 18 Brumaire when Napoleon assumed power in France, the Revolution and the Ancien Régime had for more than seven years been engaged in a war which was to continue for another fifteen, apart from the brief interval of the Peace of Amiens. Seen in this perspective the *coup d'état* does not mark the beginning of a new era. Considered in relation to the earlier history of France, the *coup* certainly did restore the tradition of personal power: and in this respect there is a definite disjunction between the Revolutionary period and the Napoleonic era—although even so Brumaire fits perfectly well into the pattern, the series of coups during the Directory.

But the break marked by Brumaire, magnified by the enduring legend which surrounds the Consulate, must not be allowed to mask the essential unity which underlies the Napoleonic era and the Revolutionary period. Bonaparte owed his own extraordinary success to the Revolution, for it opened up a career to him. If, moreover, he managed to come to power in Republican France, it is primarily because the country was condemned by internal necessity to an authoritarian régime for as long as the supporters of the Ancien Régime went on trying to reestablish the old order. In this they were backed by foreign monarchs who were frightened that the contagion of Revolution might spread and destroy their own thrones. Another reason why Bonaparte was able to take over as leader of the French was that he respected the social achievements of the Constituent Assembly of '89. His victories gave permanence to these achievements, enabling them to become firmly established.

According to Guizot, comparing Charlemagne and Napoleon in his *Civilization in France,* "the great man . . . understands better than anyone else the needs of his time, the real needs of the moment, what his society requires if it is to prosper and steadily develop. But he not only understands his time better than anyone else, he also knows better than anyone else how to mobilise the various forces in society and direct them towards this goal. This is how he achieves power and glory, and this explains why from the moment he appears on the scene he is understood, welcomed and followed. It also explains why everyone participates in the work which he directs for the common good."

In 1802, on the morrow of the Treaty of Amiens, Bonaparte had satisfied the French by giving them the peace they so desperately wanted, by safeguarding those social consequences of the Revolution to which the people were deeply committed—just as they were committed to keeping the newly acquired natural frontiers which flattered their national pride. Because the aspirations of the nation as a whole seemed to coincide with the political objectives of Bonaparte, he seemed a national hero at the very moment when his secret ambitions were making him cease to be one. . . .

Even if he did not achieve his personal ambitions, Bonaparte's actions, coming in the wake of the Revolution, nevertheless profoundly marked the age. The new state, after ten years of upheaval, had no proper foundation until he provided it with an administrative framework. The Revolution of 1789 had brought the bourgeoisie into power, but in the year II their authority was challenged by democracy. Under Napoleon's protection the "notables," the well-to-do, reassumed their dominant position in society. The growth of capitalism, and therefore of the bourgeoisie, had been tending for the past two or three centuries towards the same result; the Revolution, and after it Napoleon, gave considerable impetus to this process by destroying the Ancien Régime and introducing the principles of the modern state and society, not only in France but also in all the countries of Europe occupied by the French army. The historian therefore must not underestimate the result of those "extra" conquests, namely those which did not correspond with the needs of the nation. The victories of Napoleon guaranteed the spreading throughout Europe of the principles of the Revolution with a speed and effectiveness which ordinary influences and propaganda could never have equalled. The spreading of "enlightenment" and of the ideas of the Revolution, and the proclamation of the principles of popular sovereignty foreshadowed later national awakenings; and indeed by his redrawing of boundaries and his reforms Napoleon encouraged this process.

But to return to Guizot: "After he has dealt with nearly all the urgent general problems of his time, the great man's ambition makes him look further afield. He launches out beyond immediate matters and begins to adopt a personal perspective, taking pleasure in imagining schemes on a more or less gargantuan scale and more or less specious in character. Unlike his earlier plans, these schemes bear no relation to the actual needs of society and are remote from the general aspirations and wants of the population."

Napoleon's influence was considerable so long as it flowed in the same direction as the currents which had been shaping France and Europe since '89. But he was led beyond the historical necessities of the moment by his ambition—and in this he was encouraged by the coterie round him and also by the passive complaisance of the majority of Frenchmen. By reaching out beyond the natural frontiers of his country, thus making war inevitable, and by breaking with the Republic and with Equality, Bonaparte was setting himself objectives which were no longer those of the nation. . . .

But no matter how, increasingly, he tended towards despotic rule, Napoleon could not erase the indelible mark of the origin of his power. . . . Speaking of his coronation . . . he said "I took this crown from the gutter and the people placed it on my head; let their decision be respected!" This expresses perfectly the affinity of imperial regime with the Revolution. In the eyes of the Europe of the Old Régime, Napoleon remained the soldier of the Revolution of '89, the Revolution of the "Notables"; it is as such that he left his mark on the century and it is how he appears in the long perspective of history.

It was in vain that the Emperor tried to form a new legitimacy and a new aristocracy, and in vain too that he wished to dominate the future as he had the present. "This is where egoism and fantasy begin," continues Guizot: "for a while, because of what he has already done, people follow the great man in his new career, believing in him and obeying him. People enjoy his fantasies vicariously, as it were, while sycophants and dupes admire and praise them to him as being sublime. Previously the great man had placed his powerful brain and ambition in the service of the people and their common good. Now however he wants to subordinate the people to his own personal ends, his own desires. At first the people feel uneasy, then their interest flags. For a time they follow the man feebly and reluctantly, next they protest and complain, then in the end they part company with him and the great man stands alone, and falls. And all the dreams that he alone had dreamed, and all the purely personal and arbitrary part of his achievement falls with him." These are the broad outlines within which to consider the relationship between the great man and history.

The history of the Napoleonic era has for too long been the history of the Hero separated from the history of other men . . . history in the style of Carlyle, history centred upon the hero, history seen from above. The programme of this colloquium represents an attempt to change this perspective by returning to the level of men, to history seen from below . . . and in all the complexity of its multiple elements—some of which the great man did not grasp, others which in the circumstances of the time increased his chances. The deeper movements which bore Napoleon along were favourable to him, for example the demographic or the economic tides of the period. At the beginning of the nineteenth century France was still "The Great Nation," strong in manpower. Incomes, rents from the land and wages were rising, and people have been able to speak of "wartime growth." Whatever fluctuations and crises there were, it remains true that Napoleon's actions coincided with a long and favourable combination of circumstances. And so it is all the more important to calculate just what were the chances offered to Napoleon's genius, where by "chances" I mean phenomena like a well-populated and prosperous nation, not "chance" in the sense of events like his frigate, the *Muiron,* escaping Nelson's patrols on his return from Egypt, or Desaix arriving in the nick of time at the battle of Marengo. In this way the relationship between the great man and history will become clearer.

In the current of historiography, which is itself a reflection of the movement of history, various aspects of the totality are revealed in turn to successive generations of historians who bring to light things hitherto hidden by the very complexity of the facts. The same thing happens with the actors of history and Napoleon will always remain the subject of inquiry. The writing of his history will never be finally completed. From generation to generation, as the history which he made possible unfolds, he will continue to be the subject of impassioned likes and dislikes—but also, let us hope, the subject of erudite research and critical reflection.

Afterword

"The Legend of Napoleon" is not made up of distinct components, each quite separate. Rather, it is the result of elements interacting with one another, each influenced by events and moods and each, therefore, constantly changing shape as the years went by. These elements may be termed "the Cult" and "the Explanation."

The Cult of Napoleon was born when his exploits in Italy gripped the French imagination. And when he had gone his mighty achievements still remained—whereas time eroded memories of the grimmer features of his reign. Thousands of men all over Europe had their careers cut short when the kings climbed back on their thrones, when reaction set in under the Bourbons and under the Holy Alliance of Austria, Russia, and Prussia. The aristocrats were back in France—and so the disaffected young sported shaggy moustaches, and veterans' tales found audiences as eager as Goguelat's in *The Country Doctor*.[1] Béranger's adulatory songs sold thousands of copies,[2] while to Julien Sorel "the best loved of all his books" was Las Cases' *Mémorial*.[3] Naturally: for, to this ambitious youth, the Empire meant opportunity, the Emperor action and energy—traits with a seductive appeal to those captured by the romantic mood then flowing at springtide force in Europe. And the Emperor also meant victory; so that, like that of Mao,[4] his story became so entwined with patriotic sentiment that, at Waterloo, even Chateaubriand felt obliged to "pray . . . for the oppressor of France that he might save our honour and rescue us from the dominion of foreigners." [5] Especially when regimes lacked glory, the memory of those invincible years rekindled in the minds of Frenchmen—conscription, oppression, taxation forgotten. That was when "The Man" got things done, unlike the talking shops called

---

[1] See Chapter 15 of Balzac's novel, published in 1833. Drooping moustaches had been worn by the Napoleonic Guard and the *sans-culottes* before them.

[2] 11,000 copies of an 1821 collection of his songs—like 'Waterloo', 'Les deux Grenadiers', 'Les Souvenirs du Peuple' ("Parlez-nous de Lui, grandmère")—were sold in one week (J. Lucas-Dubreton, *Le culte de Napoléon, 1815–48* [Paris, 1960], p. 239).

[3] Julien, the hero of *Le Rouge et le Noir* (see above, p. 100, n. 4). For the *Mémorial de Sainte-Hélène* see above p. 20, n. 14.

[4] "The symbol of China's unity" (J. Ch'en, *Mao* (Great Lives Observed), (Englewood Cliffs, N.J.: Prentice-Hall, Inc., 1969), p. 43.

[5] Quoted from his *Mémoires d'Outre-Tombe* by H. A. L. Fisher, *Bonapartism*, (London, 1961), p. 113. "Even," because if Napoleon won, the author of *De Buonaparte et des Bourbons* (1814) would have to go back into exile: as it was he became a minister of State—though briefly—under Louis XVIII.

parliaments. How attractive the strong man seems in times of crisis!—and how appealing the strong man martyred, chained like Prometheus to a rock—chained there by kings and aristocrats, chained there by foreigners.

In "the Cult" (the popular sentiment clustering around him and around his memory) "He" appears human, a man much like us (only larger in scale), a man whose experience meshes with ours. But "He" also appears a touch other-than-human—whether "angelic" or "diabolic." [6]

The "Cult of Napoleon" meant that there was an audience ready for "the Explanation"—as one may call the official version of Napoleon's life and work. The Explanation was a blend of history and surmise, a version of the events of his reign combined with "if-onlies" and with "might-have-beens." Already during his reign propaganda had been quite consciously employed to shape the way men looked at what was happening. On St. Helena that work continued.

In exile Napoleon *did* "replace sword(s) by pen(s)" [7]—his own and those of the devoted Evangelists in his household.[8] He and they were not the sole creators of "the friendly version"—poets, historians, novelists, playwrights, and writers of memoirs all contributed. But the books from St. Helena combined with the earlier propaganda to give this version direct authority, content, a shape; and they defined certain themes with which different groups, at different times, could identify (and identify still). Some began with the Cult, and therefore went on to accept part or all of the Explanation. But others in the course of time came to find bits of the Explanation appealing to them, and were to greater or lesser degrees touched in consequence by the Cult. "Cult" and "Explanation" together make up the Legend.

One crucial element in the Legend regards Napoleon as the man of '89, the defender of, above all else, equality ("[which] is the passion of the age"),[9] the democrat who governed for the whole community,[10] and who founded his rule on consent. He was also the man good Catholics knew, "[to whom], after God," as the Pope himself said,

---

[6] "Tu domines notre âge; ange ou démon, qu'importe?"—from Hugo's poem 'Lui' (written in 1827).

[7] See above p. 67.

[8] Pre-eminently Las Cases (see above p. 20, n. 14); O'Meara, whose *Voice* . . . (see above p. 31, n. 19) was crucial to the "martyrdom" element in the Legend; and Montholon, who, apart from his *History* . . . (see above p. 37, n. 1) edited, with Gourgaud (see p. 28, n. 12), the incomplete (and primarily concerned with military matters) *Memoirs of the History of France During the Reign of Napoleon, Dictated by the Emperor at St. Helena to the Generals who Shared His Captivity* (first published in 8 vols. in 1822–25).

[9] See above, p. 33.

[10] See above, p. 75.

"[was] chiefly due the re-establishment of religion in . . . France. . . .
The Concordat [had been] a healing act." [11] And he had not only
brought peace to France but also tried to bring it to Europe. Yet
for all his efforts he never could. The kings, the oligarchs, kept attacking him, kept on forcing him into war. If only he had won in
1812 however, "the foundation of [a new] European system would
have been laid." [12] This would have been a confederacy of nations,
and as "national aspirations" [13] were widespread and powerful in
the nineteenth century, this aspect of the Legend attracted Poles,
Italians, Greeks, and all those nationalists whose oppressors were so
often the same powers that had broken "the Liberator."

Outside France the Legend, partly founded on fact, but more on
intentions, fostered a sentiment and reinforced attitudes. For about
a generation that was all that happened in France. But then, with
the sentiment persisting among the masses (the peasants especially),
there emerged amid certain secetions of the politically active, something more like a stance—and in due course something like a program.

Romantics disappointed with the Bourbons were, by the late 1820s,
joined in the praise of Napoleon by many liberals who (unlike
Lamartine) forgot the warnings of Mme. de Stael [14]—so that we have
Victor Hugo swinging to write his ode *To the Vendôme Column*[15]
and Lafayette calling for the dead Emperor to be brought home.[16]
After the Bourbons had been swept away in the revolution of 1830,
the new Orléans regime tried hard to turn this swelling mood to its
own advantage. In 1836 the Arc de Triomphe was at last completed,
and in 1840—as the Prime Minister, Thiers, wanted—the Emperor's
body came back to the Invalides.[17] But in 1836 and 1840 two other
incidents occurred to remind the French of a living Napoleon.

[11] Pius VII to Consalvi, Oct. 1817—quoted by E. E. Y. Hales, *Napoleon and the
Pope* (London, 1962), p. 207.

[12] Napoleon to Las Cases, August 24, 1816 (*Mémorial* . . .).

[13] See above, p. 77.

[14] See above, p. 106. Lamartine (1790–1869), poet and historian, opposed the
Orléans regime in the Assembly and became minister of foreign affairs in the
second Republic, 1848. Under the second Empire he returned to private life.

[15] Five years earlier, in his "Buonaparte" (1822), Hugo the royalist had written
of the "despot." The column in the Place Vendôme (1810), made of bronze from
cannon captured in the campaign of 1805, was topped by a statue of Napoleon. This
was removed in 1814—and restored in 1833. The column was pulled down in
1871—and replaced in 1873.

[16] "To rest on the banks of the Seine, in the midst of the people of France
whom I have loved so dearly"—to quote perhaps the most effective phrase in Napoleon's will. Drafted April 15–26, 1821, this brilliant contribution to "the Legend"
reached a very wide audience (see P. Gonnard, *Les origines de la Légende Napoléonienne* [Paris, 1907], p. 285 n. 2).

[17] And his son's remains were returned there, from Austria, by Hitler in 1940.

On the death of Napoleon's son in 1832, Louis-Napoleon Bonaparte became the head of the family—and an ambitious, determined one.[18] In 1830 there had been no leader, no party to seize the chance which revolution had opened: these defects now had to be remedied. His methods were action, propaganda—and waiting for the next opportunity.

The coups he attempted in '36 and '40 were flops. Nevertheless, they did generate publicity, they did mean a chance to proclaim at his trial that he "represent[ed] . . . a principle, a cause, a defeat: the principle is the sovereignty of the people, the cause is the cause of the Empire; the defeat, Waterloo" [19]—a defeat good patriots wanted avenged, in the same way that democrats wanted a franchise wider than Orléans would allow them. In his *Napoleonic Ideas* (1839), Louis-Napoleon had propounded the Legend version of the first Empire—an example, he argued, neither irrelevant nor out of date. Next, in 1844, his *Extinction of Pauperism* showed that he was indeed "a man" in sympathy with "new ideas": "Ce n'est pas un prince qui revient, c'est une idée," exulted Hugo.[20] That was when Louis-Napoleon took his seat in the Assembly of the recently formed Second Republic. Three months later, in December 1848, five million votes made him President; three years later he kept himself in power by a coup;[21] and one year after that the Second Empire was proclaimed.[21]

He *had* proved a prince after all—and so Hugo went into exile. But not every Bonapartist shared his scruples, while millions of others saw the new Emperor as a savior. He broke a republic which was detested by supporters of Orléans and of Bourbon, a red republic which scandalized Catholics and frightened the masses of peasant farmers. Here was the man who, as he claimed, stood "for order and authority, religion, the welfare of the people and . . . for national dignity." [22] Here was the man whom anyone gripped by the Legend must feel was the right man for France.

He was not—or, at any rate, his regime collapsed.[23] But that only meant that *he* was inadequate, not that his uncle had been inglorious.

[18] Born in 1808 to Hortense and Louis (see above, p. 16, n. 8).

[19] And he continued, addressing the judges, "That principle *you* have recognised, that cause *you* have served, that defeat *you* would revenge. No, there is no disagreement between you and me." Quoted by F. A. Simpson, *The Rise of Louis Napoleon* (London, 1909), p. 191.

[20] Quoted by M. Descotes, *La légende de Napoléon et les écrivains français du 19ème siècle* (Paris, 1967), p. 221. About "new ideas"—in this case about the social question (one barely touching the attention of the first Napoleon)—see above, p. 76.

[21] On December 2—the anniversary of Austerlitz.

[22] Quoted by Fisher, *Bonapartism,* p. 143.

[23] In 1870—see above, p. 122.

It only meant the collapse of his party, not the demise of a sentiment nor the discrediting of the Explanation. The real Napoleon, safely dead, was in no danger of having his Legend destroyed by the unpleasant realities of a later fiasco. For a time, the Legend of which Louis-Napoleon had made use did, in fact, suffer a certain eclipse. But the dull days of the Third Republic soon stirred fresh interest in the Great Man, while bitter political disputes, stemming from a revolution-torn history, prompted Frenchmen in search of examples (either to follow or to avoid) to study the Legend and the Emperor. And no matter how much more detached and more scientific historians became about him, the Legend persisted—and persists. And it is likely to do so even if ever "good history" [24] drives out bad. This is partly because the history in the "Explanation" is not wholly true or wholly false, and so is not accessible to demolition or substantiation. It is partly because the might-have-been element in it cannot be dealt with by any research, however conceived or conducted. But it is also because the "Cult" strand in the Legend connects with impulses deep in men: and while they need heroes, examples and myths, they will find all three provided for them—in the Napoleonic Legend.

[24] In the sense used above, p. 123.

Bibliographical Note

The *Correspondance de Napoléon Ier*, ed. Prince J. Napoléon, 32 vols. (Paris, 1858–69) contains some 22,000 items; but these are only a portion of his correspondence (he probably wrote fifty or sixty thousand letters), and furthermore they were, particularly from vol. XVI on, items selected, and sometimes amended, in accordance with the criterion, "what the Emperor [himself] would have published" (to quote the editors of vols. XVI–XXXII: see J. Tulard, "La Correspondance de Napoléon," *Journal des Savants*, 1966–67, pp. 48–56). J. M. Thompson's *Napoleon's Letters* (London, 1964) prints about 300 of these items in translation and others appear in the fuller collection edited by J. E. Howard, *Letters and Documents of Napoleon* (New York, 1961–) vol. I, *1784–1802*. Of the several anthologies of Napoleon's writings and speeches, perhaps the most fascinating is that by J. C. Herold, *The Mind of Napoleon* (New York, 1961).

There was an extensive market for memoirs in the nineteenth century; and besides, the traumatic events of 1799–1830 in France encouraged many to justify, or simply explain, their lives to themselves, their families, and posterity. Some of these memoirs have been translated (these are marked with an asterisk), though some have been abridged; several have appeared in more than one edition—the dates given are those of good French editions (all published in Paris). For Napoleon's private life (and F. Masson used many contemporaries' accounts for his *Napoleon at Home*, 2 vols. [Philadelphia, 1894]) see the memoirs of the Comtesse de Rémusat* (1905–6) and those of Marshal Junot's wife, the Duchesse d' Abrantès* (1893); but like the ghost-written memoirs of L. Bourrienne* (1899–1900) and of Constant (1894; his real name was L. C. Wairy), they are not always reliable. For Napoleon's public life see the memoirs/souvenirs/journals (their titles vary) of F. Fain (1908), P. Roederer (1909). F. Mollien (1898), L. Molé* (1922–30), and C. Méneval * (1894); those of C. M. de Talleyrand * (1891–2) should be viewed very cautiously, while those of J. Chaptal (1893) and of A. Caulaincourt* (1933) are more reliable. J. Savant used these and many other sources to make his interesting selection, *Napoleon in his Time*, trans. K. John (New York, 1958).

For the years on St. Helena—about which see R. Korngold, *The Last Years of Napoleon* (New York, 1959—the memoirs of G. Gourgaud * (1944) and H. Bertrand * (1949–59) are less tendentious than those of M. J. Las Cases, *Mémorial de Sainte Hélène* (1961), C. Montholon, *Récits de la Captivité de l'Empereur à Ste. Hélène* (1847) and B. O'Meara, *Napoleon in Exile, or a Voice from St. Helena* (New York, 1853). These last three works were prime sources for the "Legend" summed up and developed in Louis-Napoleon Bonaparte's *Napoleonic Ideas*, edited by B. D. Gooch (New York, 1967). This topic is also treated in A. L. Guérard, *Reflections on the Napoleonic Legend* (New York, 1924)—but omit Book One.

On Napoleon and his work the books and articles are legion. Specialists will find guides to these in the *Revue des Études Napoléoniennes* and *Revue de l'Institut Napoléon*; the *Bibliographie Annuelle de l'Histoire de France*; the "biography" section of the entry "Napoleon" in the *British Museum General Catalogue of Printed Books*; and the reports in each issue of *French Historical Studies* and certain issues of the *Revue Historique*—see vols. 196 (1946), 205 (1951), 213 (1955), 221 (1959), 227–8 (1962), 236 (1966), and 238 (1967). All students will find valuable the guides to further reading in Lefebvre (see below) and in J. Godechot, *L'Europe et l'Amérique à l'Époque Napoléonienne, 1800–1815* (Paris, 1967).

Two brief studies place the Napoleonic achievement admirably: G. Rudé, *Revolutionary Europe, 1783–1815* (New York, 1966) and N. Hampson, *The First European Revolution, 1776–1815* (New York, 1969), while R. Holtman analyzes *The Napoleonic Revolution* (New York, 1967), one important aspect of which is the subject of Godechot's article, "Sens et importance de la transformation des institutions révolutionnaires à l'époque napoléonienne," *Revue d'Histoire Moderne et Contemporaine*, XVII (1970), 795–813.

Biographies: very brief—M. Hutt, *Napoleon* (London, 1965); brief —H. A. L. Fisher, *Napoleon* (1912; see the London, 1967 edition) and F. Markham, *Napoleon and the Awakening of Europe* (London, 1954); full length studies—F. Markham, *Napoleon* (New York, 1963), J. H. Rose, *The Life of Napoleon I*, still useful although published (in London) back in 1901 (use the two-volume 1934 edition) and, preeminent, G. Lefebvre's superb work, *Napoléon* (Paris, 1953), translated in two volumes from the 1965 edition by H. Stockhold (New York, 1969).

Lefebvre's is the last work to be considered in P. Geyl's interesting study of the different ways in which Napoleon has been represented in historical literature since 1814—*Napoleon, For and Against* (New Haven, 1963). He has, of course, had a varied "press." *Napoleonic Propaganda* (the title of a book by R. Holtman—Baton Rouge, 1950) did not convince everyone—see L. de Villefosse and J. Bouissounouse, *L'opposition à Napoléon* (Paris, 1969). D. Chandler, *The Campaigns of Napoleon* (New York, 1966), is a comprehensive survey of Napoleon's activities in the field, and R. S. Quimby, *The Background of Napoleonic Warfare: the Theory of Military Tactics in 18th Century France*

(New York, 1957), is an analysis of the debate which Napoleon studied and transmuted into brilliant practice. The strategist, the map-redrawing statesman, is considered in H. A. L. Fisher, *Studies in Napoleonic Statesmanship; Germany* (Oxford, 1903); H. Deutsch, *The Genesis of Napoleonic Imperialism* (Cambridge, Mass., 1938); and by H. Kohn, "Napoleon and the Age of Nationalism," *Journal of Modern History,* XXII (1950), 21–37.

Index

A

Alexander I, 6, 7n, 55, 56, 112
Amiens, peace of, 3, 6, 128, 143, 166, 167
Austerlitz, battle of, 6, 47, 55, 56, 61–62, 69
Austria, 6, 129, 156

B

Beauharnais, Eugéne, 16n
Beauharnais, Hortense, 16n
Beauharnais, Joséphine, 16, 50, 51, 67, 68, 135, 162
Berthier, L. A., 48, 57–58, 60, 61, 87, 93
Bertrand, H. G., 23, 28, 33, 36, 58, 78
Beyle, H. (see Stendhal)
Bonaparte, Jérôme, 34, 122n
Bonaparte, Joseph, 6, 14, 15, 47, 66–67, 136, 161, 162
Bonaparte, Letizia, 13
Bonaparte, Louis, 6
Bonaparte, Louis-Napoleon, 173
Bonaparte, Lucien, 14, 39–40
Bourbons, 1, 3, 4, 7, 66, 170, 172
Brumaire, coup of 18me, 1, 21, 99, 132, 144, 166

C

Cambacérès, J. J. R., 60n, 143, 146
Caulaincourt, L., 15, 24, 25, 38, 44, 53–54, 85–87

Chaptal

Chaptal, J. A., 36, 58, 63–64, 71, 84, 90, 149
Codes, 1, 8, 125, 127
Concordat of 1801, 4, 7, 128, 143, 172
Confederation of the Rhine, 130
Constant (see Wairy, L. C.)
Continental System, 6, 52n
Corsica, 12, 13, 148

D

Dresden, 6, 56
Duroc, G. C., 60, 93

E

Education, 4, 49
Egypt, 27
Elba, 7
Émigrés, 1, 25, 26, 127, 145–46
England, 5, 6, 129
Erfurt, conference, 6
Eylau, battle of, 69

F

Fain, F., 65n, 82–83
Fesch, J., 14, 29–30
Fouché, J., 26, 48, 149, 151
Friedland, battle of, 6

G

Germany, 6, 34, 129
Gourgaud, G., 28, 50, 171n